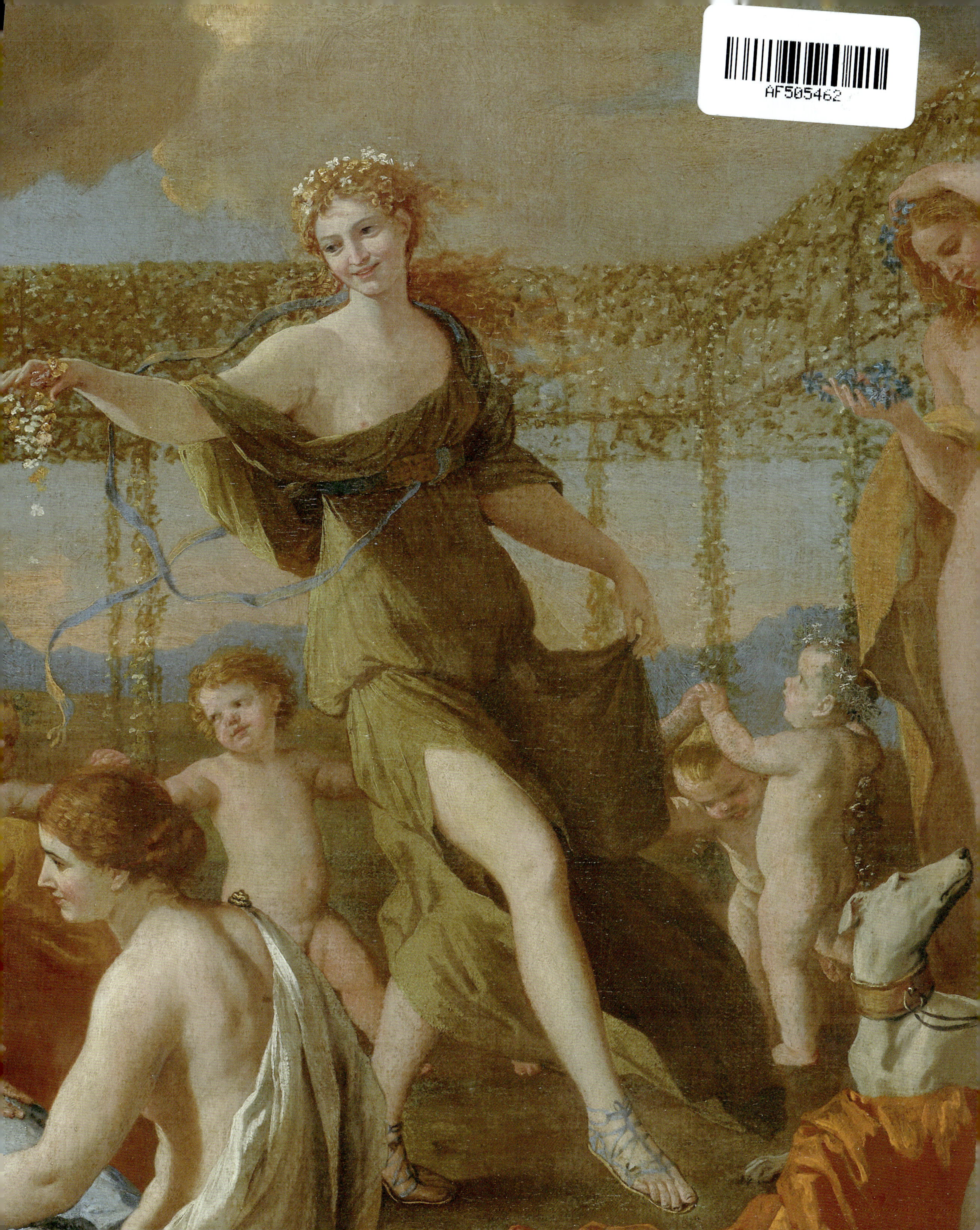

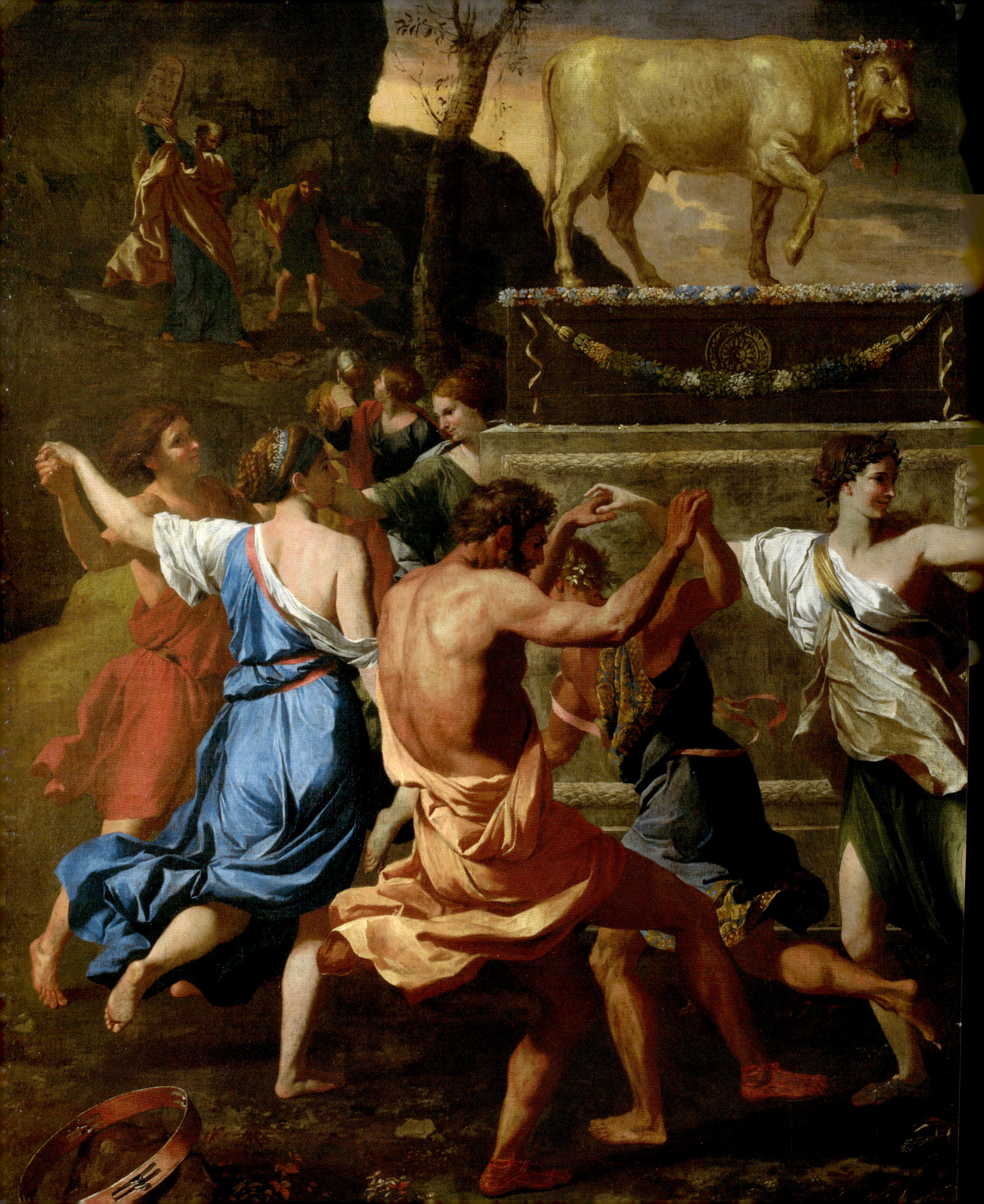

POUSSIN
AND THE DANCE

EMILY A. BEENY

FRANCESCA WHITLUM-COOPER

WITH CONTRIBUTIONS BY
PIERRE ROSENBERG
JONATHAN UNGLAUB

J. PAUL GETTY MUSEUM, LOS ANGELES
NATIONAL GALLERY COMPANY, LONDON

This publication is issued on the occasion of the exhibition *Poussin and the Dance*, on view at the National Gallery, London, from October 9, 2021, to January 2, 2022, and at the J. Paul Getty Museum at the Getty Center, Los Angeles, from February 15 to May 8, 2022.

This exhibition was organized by the National Gallery, London, and the J. Paul Getty Museum.

The presentation in London is in collaboration with The Wallace Collection, London, and is made possible through support from Gregory Annenberg Weingarten, GRoW @ Annenberg, Graham and Joanna Barker, Mr. and Mrs. Shigeru Myojin, Mr. and Mrs. Sherif Nadar, Marco Voena, and other donors.

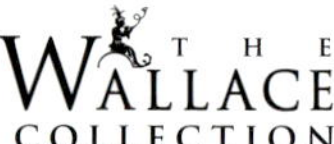 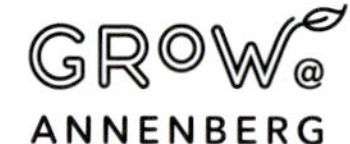

The presentation in Los Angeles is generously supported by the Leonetti/O'Connell Family Foundation.

It is sponsored by City National Bank.

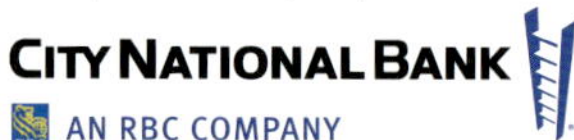

The exhibition is supported by an indemnity from the Federal Council on the Arts and the Humanities.

Published in the United States of America by the J. Paul Getty Museum, Los Angeles

Getty Publications
1200 Getty Center Drive, Suite 500
Los Angeles, California 90049-1682
getty.edu/publications

Published in the United Kingdom by National Gallery Company Limited
St. Vincent House
30 Orange Street
London WC2H 7HH
nationalgallery.co.uk

Nola Butler and Laura diZerega, *Project Editors*
Johanna Halford-MacLeod, *Manuscript Editor*
Catherine Lorenz, *Designer*
Michelle Woo Deemer, *Production*
Kelly Peyton, *Image and Rights Acquisition*

Distributed in the United States and Canada by the University of Chicago Press
Distributed outside the United States and Canada by Yale University Press, London

Separations by iocolor, LLC, Seattle
Printed in China by Artron Art Group

Library of Congress Cataloging-in-Publication Data
Names: Beeny, Emily A., contributor. | Whitlum-Cooper, Francesca, contributor. | Rosenberg, Pierre, writer of foreword. | Unglaub, Jonathan, contributor. | Poussin, Nicolas, 1594?–1665. Works. Selections (2021) | J. Paul Getty Museum, host institution, issuing body. | National Gallery (Great Britain), host institution.
Title: Poussin and the dance / Emily A. Beeny, Francesca Whitlum-Cooper ; with contributions by Pierre Rosenberg, Jonathan Unglaub.
Description: Los Angeles : J. Paul Getty Museum, [2021] | Includes bibliographical references and index. | Summary: "This publication was prepared to accompany the exhibition Poussin and the Dance, scheduled to open at the National Gallery, London, in 2021, and at the J. Paul Getty Museum at the Getty Center, Los Angeles, in 2022. The catalogue examines how Nicolas Poussin brought dance to bear on every aspect of his artistic production"—Provided by publisher.
Identifiers: LCCN 2020045448 | ISBN 9781606066836 (paperback)
Subjects: LCSH: Poussin, Nicolas, 1594?–1665—Exhibitions. | Poussin, Nicolas, 1594?–1665—Criticism and interpretation. | Dance in art—Exhibitions. | LCGFT: Exhibition catalogs.
Classification: LCC ND553.P8 A4 2021 | DDC 759.5—dc23
LC record available at https://lccn.loc.gov/2020045448

A catalogue record for the National Gallery Company edition of this book is available from the British Library.
ISBN 978-1-85709-672-9

Page i: detail, plate 9; pages ii–iii: detail, plate 15; pages xiv–1: detail, plate 1; page 4: detail, plate 3; pages 16–17: detail, plate 2; pages 28–29: detail, plate 11; page 34: detail, plate 13; pages 42–43: detail, plate 12; pages 50–51: detail, plate 17; page 58: detail, plate 18; pages 66–67: detail, plate 22; pages 78–79: detail, plate 30; pages 92–93: detail, plate 28; pages 102–3: detail, plate 33; pages 112–13: detail, plate 34

CONTENTS

DIRECTORS' FOREWORD

Nicolas Poussin was and is an artist's artist. The careful structure of his compositions, the precise contours of his draftsmanship, and the chromatic clarity of his palette have attracted generations of admirers, including Paul Cézanne, Edgar Degas, Pablo Picasso, and Francis Bacon. But Poussin's reputation in the wider art world and among museum audiences has proved more complicated. Often seen as cold, classicizing, and erudite, Poussin's reputation as an artist of the very first rank has been somewhat overshadowed by more forward-looking artists and tastes. Even in his own day, Poussin's almost Cartesian intellectualism set his work apart from the dramatic and emotive naturalism of the *caravaggisti* who surrounded him in Rome and dominated the Baroque movement in southern Europe. This exhibition seeks to inflect that familiar narrative by focusing on an aspect of Poussin's work that, while still reflecting his trademark seriousness of mind, is also full of delight and revelry.

Centering on Poussin's early career in Rome, *Poussin and the Dance* explores his influences, ambitions, and, above all, his artistic process in creating some of his most joyful and appealing imagery: bacchanals, dancing rings, and parades of festive movement. These depictions of dance and dancers, captured in oil paint or ink and wash, helped make Poussin's name and fortune in the decade following his arrival in the Eternal City in 1624. They are presented in the exhibition alongside ancient sculptures—neo-Attic kraters, a Roman relief—that were among the vast array of ancient art that inspired Poussin's interest in dancing subjects. By examining his work through the lens of dance, a universal human impulse, the exhibition offers visitors a novel and uniquely engaging point of access to Poussin's achievement: through their own lived experience. Organized in tandem with contemporary dance programming in both London and Los Angeles, the exhibition promises to breathe new life into an old master, "animating the frieze," as the curators have put it.

The National Gallery in London is home to one of the world's finest collections of Poussin's paintings, and yet this is the first exhibition devoted to the artist to be held at Trafalgar Square, and the first in London in more than a generation.

Somewhat less surprisingly, *Poussin and the Dance* is also the first major exhibition of the artist's work ever presented on the West Coast of the United States. There can be no doubt, therefore, that Poussin is ripe for rediscovery by a new generation of visitors, nor can it be disputed that this aspect of his work is the ideal one to add surprise to familiarity for connoisseurs and new audiences alike. Co-organized by Emily Beeny, associate curator of drawings at the J. Paul Getty Museum, and Francesca Whitlum-Cooper, the Myojin-Nadar Associate Curator of Paintings 1600–1800 at the National Gallery, the exhibition and its accompanying catalogue draw on new research into Poussin's methods and his early collectors—among them dancers and patrons of ballet, whose involvement with dance surely informed their reception of these works.

We congratulate the curators of the exhibition and the many other colleagues at both institutions who brought this project to fruition. Special thanks are due to the lenders, without whose willingness to share some of their most prized possessions this project would not have been possible. The National Gallery is particularly grateful to The Wallace Collection for the exceptional loan of Poussin's most celebrated dance picture, his *Dance to the Music of Time*, which is the subject of one of the essays in this catalogue. We wish to thank our generous donors, including the Leonetti/O'Connell Family Foundation and City National Bank, who supported the presentation at Getty, and Gregory Annenberg Weingarten, GRoW @ Annenberg, Graham and Joanna Barker, Mr. and Mrs. Shigeru Myojin, Mr. and Mrs. Sherif Nadar, Marco Voena, and other donors, who supported the presentation at the National Gallery.

Timothy Potts
Maria Hummer-Tuttle and Robert Tuttle Director
J. Paul Getty Museum, Los Angeles

Gabriele Finaldi
Director
The National Gallery, London

FOREWORD

Things that are perfect in some way should not be looked at hastily, but over time, with judgment and intelligence. One must use the same means to judge them as to make them. No doubt the sight of the beautiful girls in Nîmes will have delighted your mind no less than the beautiful columns of the Maison Carrée, the latter being but old copies of the former.
—Nicolas Poussin to Paul Fréart de Chantelou, March 20, 1642

This wonderful declaration requires no further explanation. Here the "beautiful girls" of Nîmes are transformed into so many Terpsichores. The columns of the Maison Carrée are, in reality, none other than the joyful dancers that Emily Beeny and Francesca Whitlum-Cooper have set out to celebrate. It was in Rome rather than Nîmes that Poussin would have admired the sight of dancers: dancers at the many public festivals in Roman neighborhoods, or dancers in the musical ballets enjoyed by Urban VIII and the court of the Barberini. But did Poussin, a man of secluded habits, take pleasure in attending public festivals? Was he invited to the sumptuous entertainments of the papal court? We do not know. Or did Poussin content himself, in painting these dancers, with the inspiration of antiquity, to which the exhibition in London and Los Angeles rightly accords a great importance?

Of all the muses, Terpsichore (dance) occupies the most important place in Poussin's oeuvre, along with Polyhymnia (poetry and pantomime) and Calliope (music), but only for a brief span of time. It was during the fifteen years that separated his arrival in Rome and his departure for Paris in 1640 that Poussin devoted himself to dancers. They are full of vitality; they smile; they bare their legs and present their breasts, unashamed. They are joyful. Pan often joins them: a Pan of stone who, watching them dance, comes vividly to life. For they know the pleasures of life, an ephemeral life, given its rhythm by the inexorable march of time. The joy of his dancers is contagious. Here the austere, severe Poussin smiles at us . . .

Pierre Rosenberg
Member of the Académie Française

NOTES
Epigraph: See Jouanny 1911, 121–22, no. 56. Poussin here refers to the ancient Roman temple at Nîmes renowned for its Ionic columns, whose proportions, according to Vitruvius, were modeled on those of an ancient Greek girl.

Translated from the French by Emily A. Beeny.

ACKNOWLEDGMENTS

We owe a debt of gratitude to the many colleagues on both sides of the Atlantic who have contributed expertise, time, and—above all—precious loans to this exhibition. We wish to thank the following directors, trustees, curators, conservators, collection managers, registrars, librarians, and others who supported our loan requests, granted access to works of art not on view, and shared research and insight: at the British Museum, Hugo Chapman and Sarah Vowles; at Chatsworth House, Kate Brindley and Charles Noble; at the Dulwich Picture Gallery, Peter Björn Kerber and Helen Hillyard; at the Fondation Jan Krugier, Tzila Krugier, Nader Tewelde, and Marianne Casimo; at the Gallerie degli Uffizi and Gabinetto dei Disegni e delle Stampe, Eike Schmidt, Maria Elena De Luca, Massimo Pivetti, Maurizio Bacci, and Laura Donati; at the Harvard University Art Museums, Édouard Kopp and Mary Lister; at the Metropolitan Museum of Art, Max Hollein, Keith Christiansen, Stephan Wolohojian, David Pullins, Perrin Stein, and Allison Rudnick; at the Musée Bonnat-Helleu, Cécile Bignon and Maïtena Horiot-Ortega; at the Musée Condé, Nicole Garnier; at the Musée du Louvre, Jean-Luc Martinez, Sébastien Allard, Nicolas Milovanovic, Françoise Gaultier, Cécile Giroire, Xavier Salmon, Victor Hundsbuckler, and Juliette Trey; at the Museo Archeologico Nazionale di Napoli, Marialucia Giacco, Paolo Giulierini, Riccardo Berriola, and Paola Rubino De Rittis; at the Museo Nacional del Prado, Miguel Falomir, Miguel Zugaza, Andrés Úbeda de los Cobos, Alejandro de Vergara Sharp, Inma Echevarria, and Elena Cenalmor Bruquetas; at the Museu de Arte de São Paulo Assis Chateaubriand, Adriano Pedrosa, Sofia Hennen, Mariana Leme, Ana Luiza Maccari, Paula Coelho Magalhaes de Lima, Marina Moura, and Cecilia Winter; at the National Galleries of Scotland, Sir John Leighton, Aidan Weston-Lewis, Francis Fowle, and Graeme Gollan; at the Nelson-Atkins Museum of Art, Julián Zugazagoitia, Aimee Marcereau DeGalan, Mary Schafer, John Twilley, Rachel Freeman, Meghan Gray, and Tiffany Hamblin; at the Norton Simon Museum, Walter W. Timoshuk and Emily Talbot; at the Philadelphia Museum of Art, Timothy Rub and Jennifer Thompson; at the Royal Collection, Martin Clayton and Rosie Razzall; at the Staatliche Kunstsammlungen Dresden, Gemäldegalerie Alte Meister, Stephan Koja, Roland Enke, Andreas Henning, Larissa Mohr, and Yvonne Wagner; and at The Wallace Collection, special thanks to Xavier Bray, Yuriko Jackall, Clare Simpson, and Félix Zorzo.

In the course of developing this exhibition we have also relied on the aid and advice of many other colleagues on matters large and small. We offer thanks to Stijn Alsteens, Ronni Baer, Gabriel Batalla-Lagleyre, Hugh Brigstocke, Alvin L. Clark Jr., Marie-Anne Dupuy-Vachey, David Freedberg, Angélique Franck, Bénédicte Gady, Gloria Groom, Guillaume Kientz, Frederick Ilchman, Laure de Margerie, Olivier Meslay, Mary Morton, Sir Nicholas Penny, Louis-Antoine Prat, Lionel Sauvage, George Shackelford, Julia Siemon, Timothy Standring, Nathalie Strasser, Mickaël Szanto, Hope Stockton, Daniel Thierry, Carol Togneri, Paul Spencer-Longhurst, and Richard Verdi. The J. Paul Getty Museum presentation of the exhibition is made possible by the National Endowment for the Arts and by the US Department of State through grants of federal indemnity and immunity from seizure. We are most grateful for this support and indebted to the colleagues who lent their expertise during the preparation of our applications, namely Scott Schaefer, Stephen Ongpin, and Michael Ward.

At Getty, Emily Beeny would like to thank the following for their crucial support: James Cuno, president and CEO of the J. Paul Getty Trust; Timothy Potts, Getty Museum director; Carolyn Marsden-Smith, associate director for exhibitions; Richard Rand, associate director for collections; Julian Brooks, senior curator of drawings; Davide Gasparotto, senior curator of paintings and chair, curatorial affairs; Jeffrey Spier, senior curator of antiquities; Marc Harnly, senior paper conservator; Ulrich Birkmaier, senior paintings conservator; Susanne Gänsicke, senior conservator of antiquities; Jessica Harden, head of design, and her predecessor Merritt Price; and Betsy Severance, chief registrar. For their collaboration and guidance throughout the development of this project, Emily Beeny likewise thanks Amber Keller, principal project specialist in Exhibitions, without whose superb diplomatic and organizational skills none of this would have been possible; Sandy Choi

Beacom, associate exhibitions registrar, who faced the challenges of contract negotiation during a pandemic with good cheer; Amanda Ramirez and Matthew Kelm, exhibition designers, whose ingenuity and enthusiasm have made installation planning a joy; Michelle Sullivan, associate paper conservator, and Laura Rivers, associate paintings conservator, whose technical insights are always illuminating; and Maite Álvarez, associate interpretive content specialist, and Sheila Flaherty-Jones, labels editor, whose attentiveness to visitor experience is inspiring. Special thanks for their collaboration and advice are also due to Stephanie Schrader, curator of drawings; Anne Woollett, curator of paintings, and Scott Allan, associate curator of paintings; Kenneth Lapatin, curator of antiquities; and Anne-Lise Desmas, senior curator of sculpture and decorative arts.

The contemporary dance dimension of this exhibition at Getty has taken on increasing importance over the last year. Emily Beeny offers profound thanks to the Los Angeles choreographers who have taken part—Ana Maria Alvarez, Chris Emile Bordenave, and Micaela Taylor—and to Sarah Cooper, project specialist for performing arts, who co-curated the resulting series of contemporary dance films. Thanks for this aspect of the project are likewise due to Laurel Kishi, head of public programs; Erik Bertellotti, head of interpretive content; Mustafa Eck, video producer; Anne Martens, content producer; and Ava Robles, Marrow undergraduate intern.

Emily Beeny gratefully acknowledges the following Getty departments for additional contributions: Exhibitions, especially Marisa Weintraub; Registration, especially Cherie Chen, Jennifer Garpner, and Debby Lepp; Paper Conservation, especially Ron Stroud; Paintings Conservation, especially Gene Karraker and Devi Ormond; Antiquities Conservation, especially Erik Risser; Sculpture and Decorative Arts Conservation; Exhibition Design; the Office of the Director; the Office of the Associate Director for Collections; Museum Administration; Public Programs; Interpretive Content; Education; Museum Public Affairs; Trust Public Affairs; the Office of the General Counsel; and Janet McKillop and her lovely staff in Development. Additional thanks go to Kevin Marshall and his expert preparators,

and most especially to Drawings Department colleagues past and present: Edina Adam, Breanne Bradley, Reyna Colt-Lacayo, Sara Frier, Lee Hendrix, Sharon Kendall, Jamie Kwan, Casey Lee, Talitha Schepers, and Robin Trento. For inspiration and support, Emily offers thanks, always, to Abraham Frank.

At the National Gallery, Francesca Whitlum-Cooper would like to thank the following colleagues for their enthusiasm and support for the project throughout its many phases of development: Gabriele Finaldi, director; Caroline Campbell, director of collections and research; Susan Foister, director of public programmes and partnerships (deputy director); Jane Knowles, head of exhibitions; Sunnifa Hope, senior exhibitions programme manager; Samantha Cox and Robyn Earl, senior exhibition managers; Liam Jackson, exhibitions assistant; Christine Riding, the Jacob Rothschild Head of the Curatorial Department; Letizia Treves, the James and Sarah Sassoon Curator of Later Italian, Spanish and 17th-Century French Paintings; Lucy Chiswell, the Dorset Curatorial Fellow; Daniel Herrmann, curator of modern and contemporary projects; and Priyesh Mistry, associate curator of modern and contemporary projects. Particular thanks for their generosity in sharing expertise during conservation treatments and scientific investigations are due to Larry Keith, head of conservation and keeper; Hayley Tomlinson, conservator; Rachel Billinge, research associate; Marika Spring, head of science; Catherine Higgitt, principal scientist; and David Peggie, senior scientist.

In addition, Francesca Whitlum-Cooper would like to thank the following National Gallery staff and departments: Eleanor Richards; Belinda Phillpot and her team in Creative; Development; Learning and National Programmes; Photography and Imaging; as well as the wonderful team at the National Gallery Company, especially Laura Lappin, publisher; Sarah Derry, commissioning manager; and Jan Green. Cécile Sureau's meticulous help in assembling research files has been invaluable. On a personal note, Francesca also wishes to thank Alex Manthei.

Both curators wish to express their gratitude to Getty Publications, particularly Kara Kirk, publisher, and Karen Levine, editor in chief, as well as Clare Davis, design and production manager; Michelle Woo Deemer, senior production coordinator; and Kelly Peyton, image rights coordinator. We are most grateful to Nola Butler, managing editor, and Laura diZerega, editor, who have piloted this project across the last year's stormy sea with grace and aplomb, and to Catherine Lorenz, senior designer, who created a beautiful book. Kurt Hauser, senior designer, and Victoria Gallina, senior production coordinator, also provided invaluable support. Several freelancers made crucial contributions: the proofreader Dianne Woo, the indexer Theresa Duran, and, most of all, the extraordinarily adept and tactful manuscript editor Johanna Halford-MacLeod. We thank them all. Finishing a book during a global pandemic presents special challenges. We could not have met these without the dedication and generosity of our colleagues—in Circulation, Reference, Acquisitions, and Interlibrary Loans—at the Getty Research Institute and the National Gallery Library.

Finally, we are grateful to the other contributing authors: Jonathan Unglaub for lending us his expertise in an engrossing essay that places the most important of Poussin's dancing pictures in a rich cultural context, and Pierre Rosenberg, to whom this project owes more than we can adequately express. His initial enthusiasm for the exhibition confirmed that we were on the right track, and the extraordinary generosity that he and his collaborator Christel Dupuy showed by sharing their research with us has enriched the book beyond measure. M. Rosenberg's forthcoming catalogue raisonné of Poussin's paintings will mark the culmination of a half century spent studying, collecting, and exhibiting the work of this greatest of French painters on behalf of the French people. All *poussinistes* are in his debt.

Emily A. Beeny
Associate Curator of Drawings
J. Paul Getty Museum, Los Angeles

Francesca Whitlum-Cooper
The Myojin-Nadar Associate Curator of Paintings 1600–1800
The National Gallery, London

LENDERS TO THE EXHIBITION

Fondation Jan Krugier, Switzerland

Le Gallerie degli Uffizi, Florence

Gemäldegalerie Alte Meister, Staatliche
     Kunstsammlungen Dresden

The J. Paul Getty Museum, Los Angeles

The Metropolitan Museum of Art, New York

Musée du Louvre, Paris

Museo Archeologico Nazionale di Napoli

Museo Nacional del Prado, Madrid

Museu de Arte de São Paulo Assis Chateaubriand

National Galleries of Scotland, Edinburgh

The National Gallery, London

The Nelson-Atkins Museum of Art, Kansas City

The Norton Simon Foundation, Pasadena

Philadelphia Museum of Art

Royal Collection/Her Majesty Queen Elizabeth II, Windsor

The Wallace Collection, London

CHRONOLOGY
POUSSIN'S DANCING PICTURES IN THE CONTEXT OF HIS LIFE

Nicolas Poussin was born at Les Andelys, Normandy, in 1594. His father belonged to a ruined noble family, and his mother was the daughter of a local magistrate. They probably sent their son to the Jesuit College at Rouen, where he would have received a liberal education unusual for a painter. He embarked on artistic training late, likely in his mid-teens, and ran away to Paris, where he studied under the Mannerist Georges Lallemant (ca. 1580–1636) and the portrait painter Ferdinand Elle (ca. 1580–1649). Poussin seems to have set out for Italy around 1617, making it as far as Florence, but by the following summer he was back in Paris. A second attempt to reach Italy in 1622 seems to have taken him only as far as Lyon, where he ran out of money and painted his earliest surviving canvas. Returning to Paris that summer, he settled in the neighborhood now called the Latin Quarter and took part in the decoration of the Palais du Luxembourg. In a single week, he painted six pictures (now lost) for festivities at the Jesuit College. These attracted the attention of his first important patron, the court poet Giambattista Marino (1569–1625). Marino left for Rome the next spring, and Poussin followed that winter. Here our story begins.

1624 Poussin arrives in Rome by April. Marino, in failing health, leaves for Naples a month later. Within about a year, Poussin has likely met the antiquarian Cassiano dal Pozzo (1588–1657), who will become his greatest Roman patron.

1625 Marino dies in Naples, and Cassiano leaves for France with a papal delegation; Poussin is poor and friendless. He sells two large paintings for a few *scudi* apiece and lives alone in rented rooms. In this period, he probably manifests the first symptoms of syphilis.

1626 Poussin lives with three roommates, including the Flemish sculptor François Duquesnoy (1597–1643), with whom he studies antiquities and apparently visits the Villa Ludovisi to copy Titian's paintings.

Poussin has begun to sell his own pictures, often painted in the manner of Titian. In the fall, he serves on a committee of the Roman artists' society, the Accademia di San Luca. Cassiano returns to Rome. Things are looking up.

1627 Lodging with a stonemason, Poussin paints *The Death of Germanicus* (Minneapolis Institute of Art) for Cardinal Francesco Barberini (1597–1679), Cassiano's employer. Poussin opens a bank account; for the first time since arriving in Rome, he has enough money to need one.

1628 In January, Poussin delivers *The Death of Germanicus*; it is well received.

In February, he receives a papal commission for an altarpiece at Saint Peter's Basilica. He will paint the *Martyrdom of Saint Erasmus* (Musei Vaticani) over the next year.

1629 Poussin can now afford to keep a servant.

In February, Cassiano seeks guidance from a Bolognese physician on remedies for venereal disease, possibly for Poussin, whose illness seems to have reached a crisis point. He is nursed back to health by his neighbor, a French cook named Jacques Dughet.

Poussin manages to complete his altarpiece by the summer, but the response is mixed. He will receive no further papal commissions.

1630   On September 19, Poussin marries Anne-Marie Dughet (1613–1665), daughter of the French cook. She is seventeen; he is thirty-six. They will have no children.

1631   In July, Poussin is a witness at the trial of Fabrizio Valguarnera (d. 1632), a jewel thief and art collector who owns Poussin's *Realm of Flora* (plate 9) and *Plague at Ashdod* (Musée du Louvre, Paris).

1632   Poussin and Anne-Marie have moved into a modest house on the via Paolina: it will be their home for the rest of their lives. Anne-Marie's brother Gaspard (1615–1675) lives with them and studies with Poussin. Gaspard is Poussin's only known pupil.

Poussin is commissioned to paint *The Adoration of the Golden Calf* (plate 15) and *The Crossing of the Red Sea* (National Gallery of Victoria, Melbourne) by Cassiano's cousin Amedeo dal Pozzo (1579–1674).

1633   Exceptionally, Poussin signs and dates a painting (*The Adoration of the Magi*, Gemäldegalerie Alte Meister, Dresden), identifying himself as a member of the Accademia di San Luca.

1633–34   From June 1633 to July 1634, Charles I de Créquy (1578–1638) serves as French ambassador to Rome. He acquires Poussin's *The Abduction of the Sabine Women* (plate 30).

In about the same period, Poussin paints *A Dance to the Music of Time* (plate 33) for Giulio Rospigliosi (1600–1669), later Pope Clement IX, who apparently supplies the painter with subjects for two other allegorical pictures: *Et in Arcadia Ego*, also known as *The Arcadian Shepherds* (Musée du Louvre, Paris), and *Time Saving Truth from Discord and Envy* (lost).

ca. 1634–38   Poussin paints a group of pictures for Philip IV's Buen Retiro palace in Madrid: *Hymenaeus Disguised as a Woman during an Offering to Priapus* (plate 16), *The Hunt of Meleager* (fig. 14), and *Landscape with Saint Paul the Hermit* (Museo Nacional del Prado, Madrid). Poussin's inclusion in the project confirms his growing celebrity.

1635   Gaspard Dughet leaves the Poussin household and is replaced by his younger brother, Jean (1614–after 1679), who will serve as secretary and assistant to Poussin for the rest of the artist's life.

1635–36   Poussin undertakes a series of bacchanalian subjects for Cardinal Richelieu (1585–1642): *The Triumph of Bacchus* (plate 18), *The Triumph of Pan* (plate 17), and *The Triumph of Silenus* (plate 24). The first two canvases are shipped from Rome to France in May 1636.

1637   Poussin begins a series of paintings depicting The Seven Sacraments for Cassiano (Washington, DC, National Gallery of Art; Fort Worth, Kimbell Art Museum; Cambridge, UK, Fitzwilliam Museum; and Grantham, UK, collection of the Duke of Rutland). With this project, he turns the page on his dancing subjects.

At the end of the 1630s, Poussin was recalled to Paris to serve as Louis XIII's First Painter; he left Rome in October 1640 and spent less than two years at the French court. In September 1642, he quit Paris, promising to return with his wife. He never did. Remaining in Rome for the rest of his days, he created increasingly profound pictures for a clientele of mostly French connoisseurs: a second set of The Seven Sacraments, and scenes from Roman history and the Bible, a series of gravely beautiful landscapes. His last works were painted with a trembling hand. In a letter of 1663, he declared, "I have given up my brushes forever." His wife died in October of the following year, and Poussin himself on November 19, 1665.

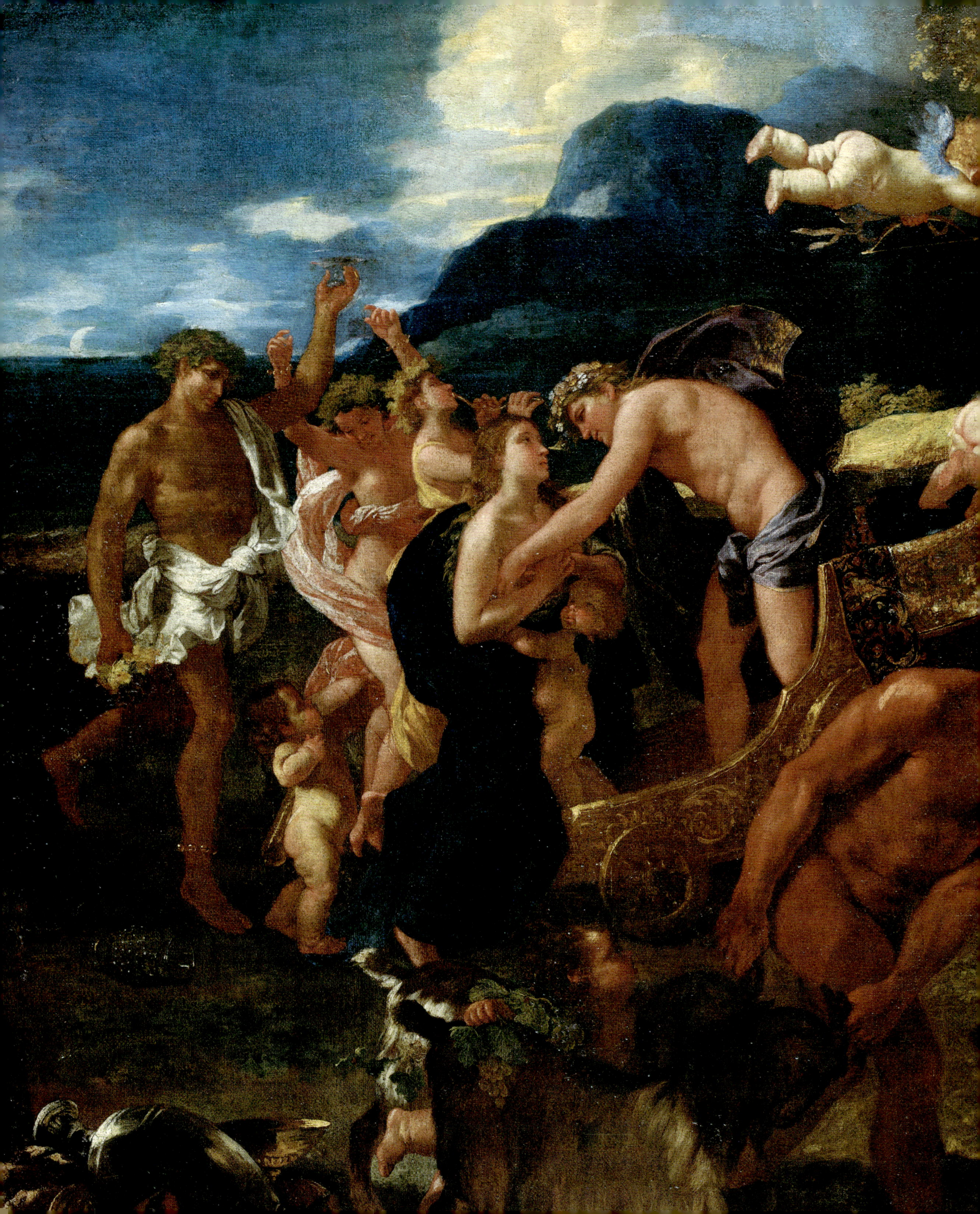

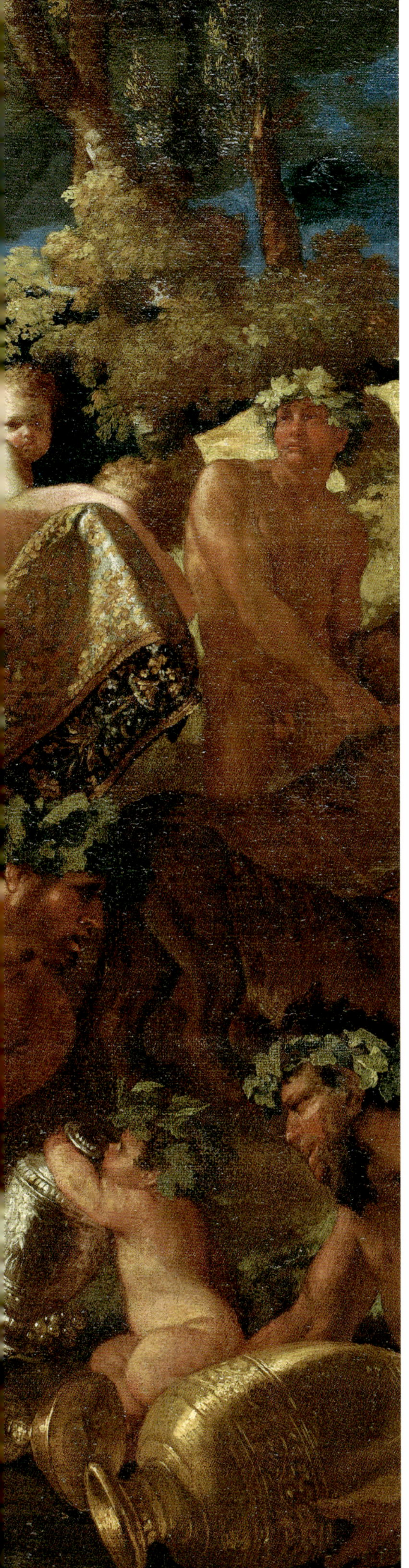

INVITATION TO THE DANCE
POUSSIN IN ROME

EMILY A. BEENY

Nicolas Poussin is remembered today as the father of French classicism, a *serious* painter—more revered, perhaps, than loved—whose learning and stoic self-restraint furnished a model for generations of artists from Charles Le Brun to Paul Cézanne. The pictures Poussin painted in his later years (the mid-1640s to 1660s) can seem stern and remote: all frozen gesture and philosophy lessons. But the works he produced during his early Roman career—in the 1620s and 1630s—are full of "wine and blood": the impulses and appetites of a man still in the process of becoming.[1] Here amid drunken revelry, sexual abandon, violence, and passion of every kind, we find scenes of dancing. For in this period, Poussin made a name for himself as a painter of dances, furnishing examples to the king of Spain (plate 16), the first minister of France (plates 17, 18, and 24), and a future pope (plate 33). With these dancing pictures he charted a new course for his art.[2]

Living and working in Rome, Poussin drew inspiration from antique bas-reliefs, where maenads frolicked in frozen rites (plates 3, 23) and maidens skipped with measured steps (plate 11). Portraying dancers allowed him to work through the problem of arresting motion, to explore the expressive potential of the body, and to devise new methods of composing his pictures. He brought lessons learned from dance to bear on every aspect of his work, famously using wax figurines to stage the scenes he drew and painted. It is no accident that the words "dance" and "ballet" are commonly used to describe Poussin's *battle* paintings: he approached dramatic action with a choreographer's eye.[3] Nor should it surprise us to learn that several of his earliest collectors back in France were themselves dancers or patrons of the ballet.[4]

From the standpoint of style, Poussin's dancing pictures employ an increasingly cool, abstract formal language to describe the heated movements they represent. If we compare his earliest dancing picture, *Bacchus and Ariadne* (plate 1), painted around 1626, to one of his last, *The Triumph of Bacchus* (plate 18), painted a decade later, we observe that his dancers look less and less like flesh and blood, more and more like stone. Visible brushstrokes give way to crisp contour as rowdy figures snap

1

into an orderly frieze. Despite the similarity of their subjects, these two pictures look so different that they could almost have been painted by two different artists. This sea change in style matters for our understanding not only of Poussin but also of the whole classical tradition to which he gave rise. Addressing the painter's early exploration of dancing themes, this essay will also consider the origins of his stylistic transformation. For in the dancing pictures, we watch a new style take shape.

Cassiano dal Pozzo and antiquity

On a wooded shore, beneath a cloudy sky, revelers make their way, dancing: painted within a year or two of Poussin's arrival in Rome, *Bacchus and Ariadne* (plate 1) portrays the god of wine surrounded by his retinue as he bends to scoop the abandoned princess Ariadne into his chariot.[5] Cymbals clash, bells ring, a drum is beaten, and a trumpet blown. Bringing up the rear of the procession, two dancers, merry with wine, throw their arms in the air and kick up their heels. In substance and style, this picture betrays a profound debt to Titian, the sixteenth-century Venetian painter whose bacchanals captured Poussin's imagination upon his arrival in Italy. But in its horizontal presentation of the parade and its reliance on antique sources, the composition already anticipates Poussin's classical turn. His colors have shifted in the nearly four centuries since he made this painting, but it remains an ambitious work, conceived on a grand scale, with a profusion of figures. It is in any case a picture much too ambitious to have been painted on spec by an artist struggling to find his way in a new city.[6]

Poussin was thirty years old when he arrived in Rome in early 1624. He had pursued an artistic career in Paris for a decade but remained stylistically somewhat unformed.[7] He had attempted the journey twice before and must have been dazzled, upon his arrival, by the treasures of the Eternal City: great chunks of ancient sculpture that stood in the gardens and courtyards of its villas, frescoes by Raphael, murals by Polidoro, and oil paintings by Titian, not to mention the contributions of more recent artists, from the Carracci (whom Poussin revered) to Caravaggio (1571–1610) (whom he despised) to Pietro da Cortona (1597–1669) (who would become a kind of rival and foil). Poussin had followed his first true patron, the poet Giambattista Marino (1569–1625), from Paris to Italy.[8] Failing health compelled the poet to abandon Rome for Naples shortly after Poussin's arrival, but before his departure, Marino introduced his protégé into the elite circles, where he would meet Cassiano dal Pozzo (1588–1657). Whoever the patron of *Bacchus and Ariadne* may have been, this painting seems indelibly stamped with Cassiano's influence.[9]

Secretary to the powerful Cardinal Francesco Barberini (1597–1679), Cassiano was an antiquarian and natural scientist. He collected paintings and maintained a learned correspondence with the likes of Galileo, but he is today best remembered for his so-called Museo Cartaceo (Paper Museum). This vast collection of over ten thousand drawings, watercolors, and prints served as an encyclopedia of ancient sculpture, architecture, and visual culture (as well as botany, zoology, and geology).[10] Poussin became a close friend and a collaborator in the enterprise; he both contributed to and consulted the Paper Museum, deriving from it an unusual intimacy with the ancient world. Cassiano may have commissioned Poussin to make his first drawings after the

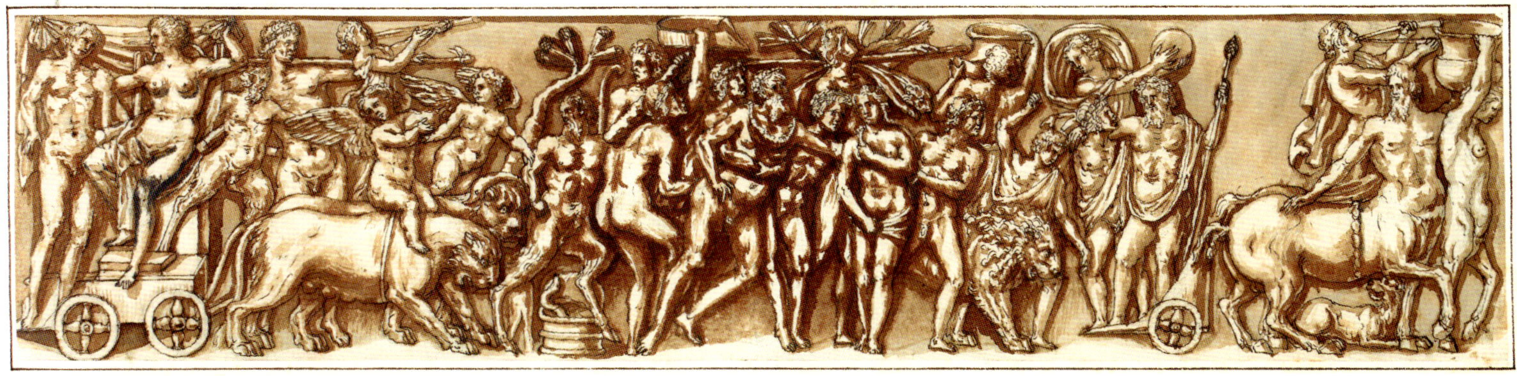

antique in early 1625,[11] and likely began buying his pictures a year or so later, possibly in response to the impoverished artist's pleas for financial support.[12]

Eager to demonstrate his growing knowledge of antiquities, Poussin crowded the cortege of *Bacchus and Ariadne* with maenads and satyrs inspired by Roman sarcophagi. These commonly took the triumph of Bacchus as a theme and were richly represented in the Paper Museum (fig. 1).[13] Indeed, in a drawing of roughly even date (plate 2), we sense not only Poussin's close study of such works but also his use of this study as a jumping-off point to generate compositions of his own. Here again the subjects are Bacchus and Ariadne, now riding side by side in triumph. Their chariot is drawn by centaurs and surrounded by putti, with dancers and musicians bringing up the rear. Delicately applied gray washes and paper trimmed to a horizontal format simulate the appearance of a sarcophagus relief. The composition is, however, Poussin's own.

Those who knew Poussin associated his reverence for ancient sculpture with his interest in dancing themes. His French biographer André Félibien (1619–1695), for example, remarked, "he often imitated with skill and delight what is most pleasant in bas-reliefs of dancers," citing the specific examples of the Borghese Vase (plate 23) and the Salpion Vase (plate 3), two neo-Attic kraters made in the first century BCE, which the painter held in "particular esteem."[14] The Paper Museum contained drawings after the dancing figures on both of these objects,[15] but Poussin would have had ample opportunity to study them in life as well. By the time he arrived in Rome, the first may have been installed at the Villa Borghese and was in any case among the city's most celebrated antiquities.[16] The second had recently been repurposed as a baptismal font in the cathedral at Gaeta, where Poussin might reasonably have stopped on a journey south to visit Marino and his friends in Naples.[17] Motifs borrowed from the Borghese Vase echo throughout Poussin's dancing pictures, and he seems to have adapted the figure with a panther skin on the Salpion Vase for the dancer with a glass of wine at far left in his painting of *Bacchus and Ariadne*.

Such figures have many analogues in neo-Attic sculpture. That of the dancing satyr, springing forward onto one foot with the opposite arm extended, was an especially popular motif, and Poussin may have encountered it not only on the Salpion Vase but also on an ancient *oscillum* (a kind of hanging ornament) or gem (fig. 2).[18] In the

FIGURE 1
Dionysiac Procession, after a sarcophagus formerly at the Villa Ludovisi (now in the Villa Savoia), early seventeenth century. Pen and brown ink and brush and brown wash on paper, 9.2 × 42.2 cm (3⅝ × 16⅝ in.). London, British Museum, Department of Prints and Drawings, inv. 2005,0928.14, fol. 14

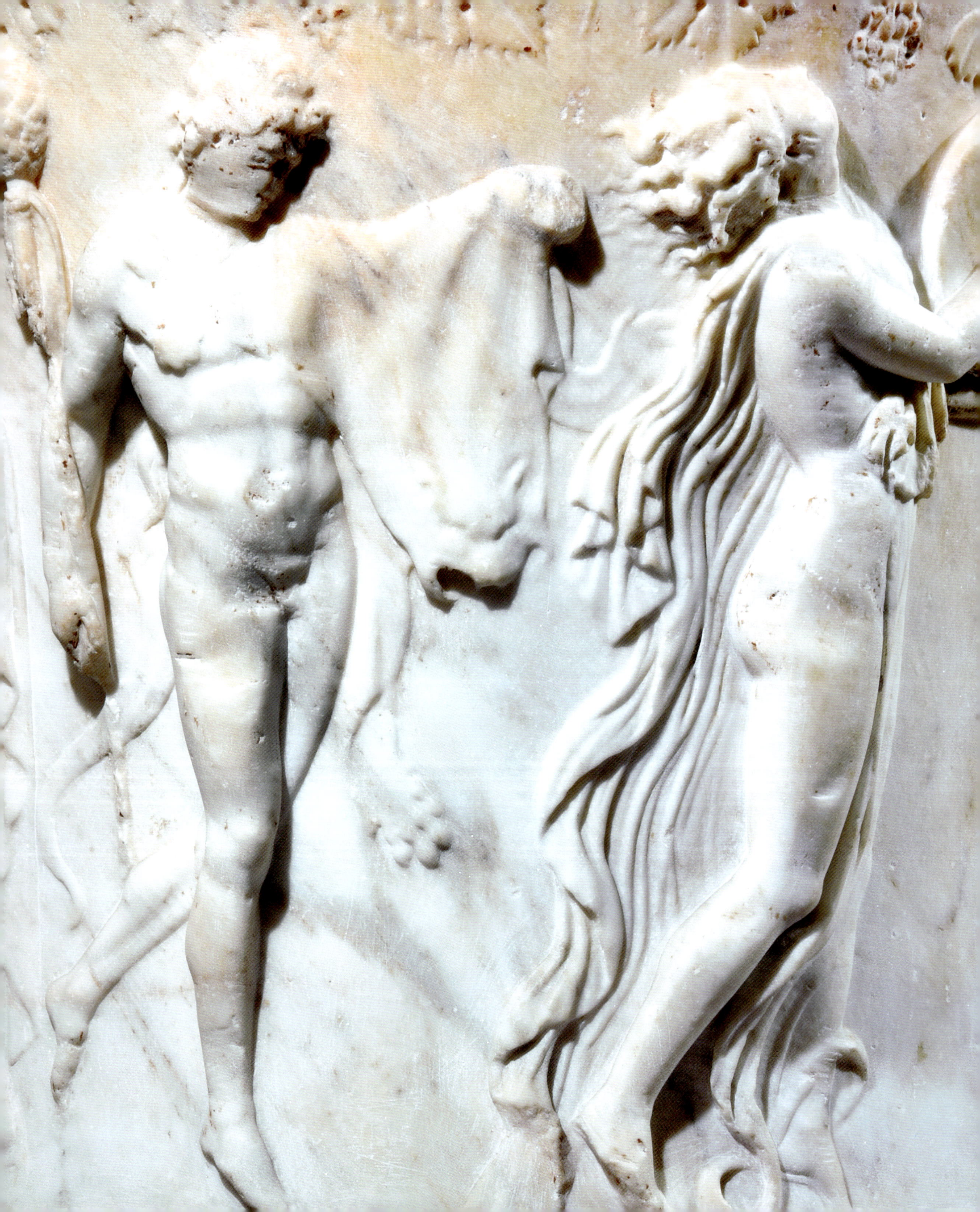

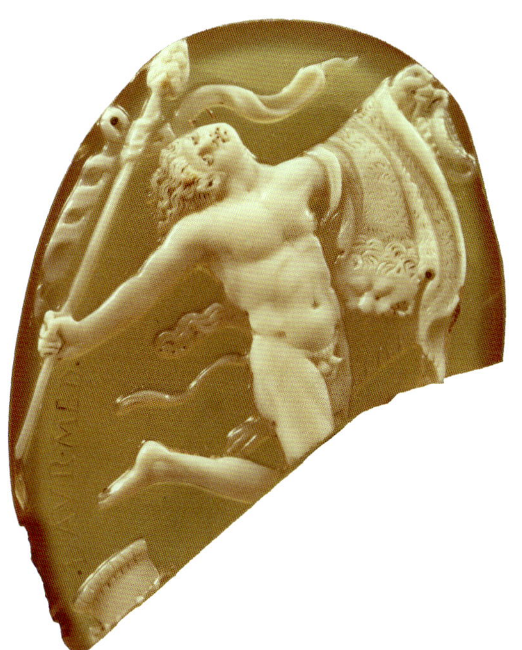

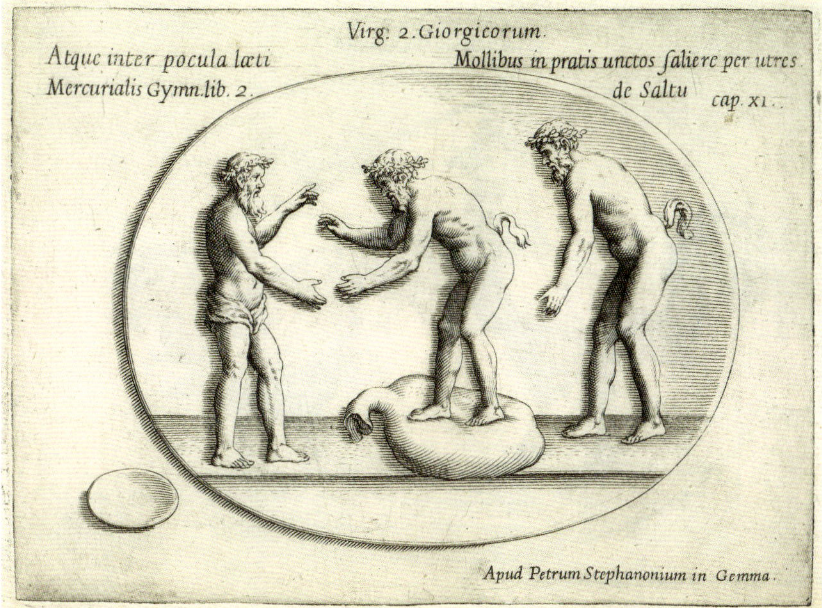

mid-1630s he produced two drawings that depict a closely related figure (plates 4 and 5); in each the motif is enclosed in a rondel, with careful washes and neat pen lines used to mimic the appearance of shallow relief and incised detail.[19] Both dancers wear panther skins and ivy wreaths, but the implements in their hands are different: one holds a ewer (plate 4), while the other carries a pair of lit torches (plate 5). The source for these drawings may have been a damaged cameo imaginatively "restored" by the artist in two different ways.[20]

Whatever their point of reference, these sheets indicate that drawing after the antique was, for Poussin, not merely a mechanical exercise or even an aesthetic one but an intellectual undertaking, a means of imagining his way into the past. An exquisitely finished sheet made for Cassiano's museum in the 1630s offers another case in point (plate 6). Beneath a vine, two satyrs egg on a third, who dances upon a wineskin. Here the cameo effect is more pronounced: an even application of wash in the background allows the design to stand out from the page as if in relief. Poussin's source was a print (fig. 3) after an ancient gem in the collection of Pietro Stefanoni (ca. 1557–ca. 1642).[21] Stefanoni belonged to Cassiano's circle, and the Paper Museum would surely have contained an impression of the print, which includes an inscription identifying the subject with a passage from Virgil's *Georgics*.[22]

Unlike most contemporary painters, who were apprenticed in childhood, Poussin had received a basic liberal education.[23] He knew the writings of Virgil, Ovid, and other ancient authors well,[24] and his alteration of the Stefanoni gem motif suggests that he consulted Virgil's poem. There the satyrs' dance is described within a broader context: angry with goats for grazing on his sacred vines, Bacchus "bleeds the goat at every altar" and causes satyrs to dance on its skin, fashioned into a vessel for wine and made slick with oil: a mythological drinking game. Poussin's imaginary cameo is subtler in every respect than the Stefanoni engraving, but his most important addition is

FIGURE 2
Cameo of a Dancing Satyr, Roman, first century BCE. Agate and onyx. Museo Archeologico Nazionale di Napoli, inv. 25873

FIGURE 3
Three Satyrs Dancing on a Wineskin. Engraving from Pietro Stefanoni, *Gemmae antiquitus sculptae*, 1627. Windsor, Royal Collection/ HM Queen Elizabeth II, inv. RCIN 809028

the grapevine borrowed from Virgil as a background, both literal and figurative, for the satyr's dance. Here again an intimate knowledge of the ancient world helped Poussin invest a dancing subject with poetry and imagination.

François Duquesnoy and Titian

Of course, ancient gems and sarcophagi were not the only sources available for imagery of bacchanalian dancing; nor was Poussin the first early modern artist to turn to them for inspiration. Annibale Carracci's magisterial fresco of Bacchus triumphant (fig. 4), for example, had graced the ceiling of the Galleria Farnese since the turn of the century, and a series of early sixteenth-century cabinet pictures by Titian treating the wine god and his retinue hung at the Villa Ludovisi and the Palazzo Aldobrandini in the 1620s (figs. 5, 10).[25] Poussin would later express profound admiration for the Farnese ceiling,[26] and his *Triumph of Bacchus and Ariadne* drawing seems to confirm his acquaintance with Annibale's composition in the mid-1620s, but at this early stage his heart belonged to Titian, and it was from the Venetian master that his first paintings of dance took their stylistic cues.

The early biographers Giovanni Battista Passeri (1610–1679) and Giovanni Pietro Bellori (1613–1696) inform us that Poussin made a regular study of Titian's bacchanals, and his production from 1625 through about 1627 fairly overflows with Titian's influence: recumbent nudes and chubby putti, saturated colors and lowering clouds.[27] To this group belong both the *Bacchus and Ariadne* (plate 1) and *Bacchanal with a Guitar Player* (plate 8), another of his earliest dancing pictures. Each of these works is explicitly indebted to Titian: in the flourish of the wine god's cloak, the stamp of drunken revelers' feet, the sparkle of glassware against sky. With crowded compositions and

FIGURE 4
Annibale Carracci (Italian, 1560–1609), *The Triumph of Bacchus*, 1597. Fresco. Rome, Palazzo Farnese

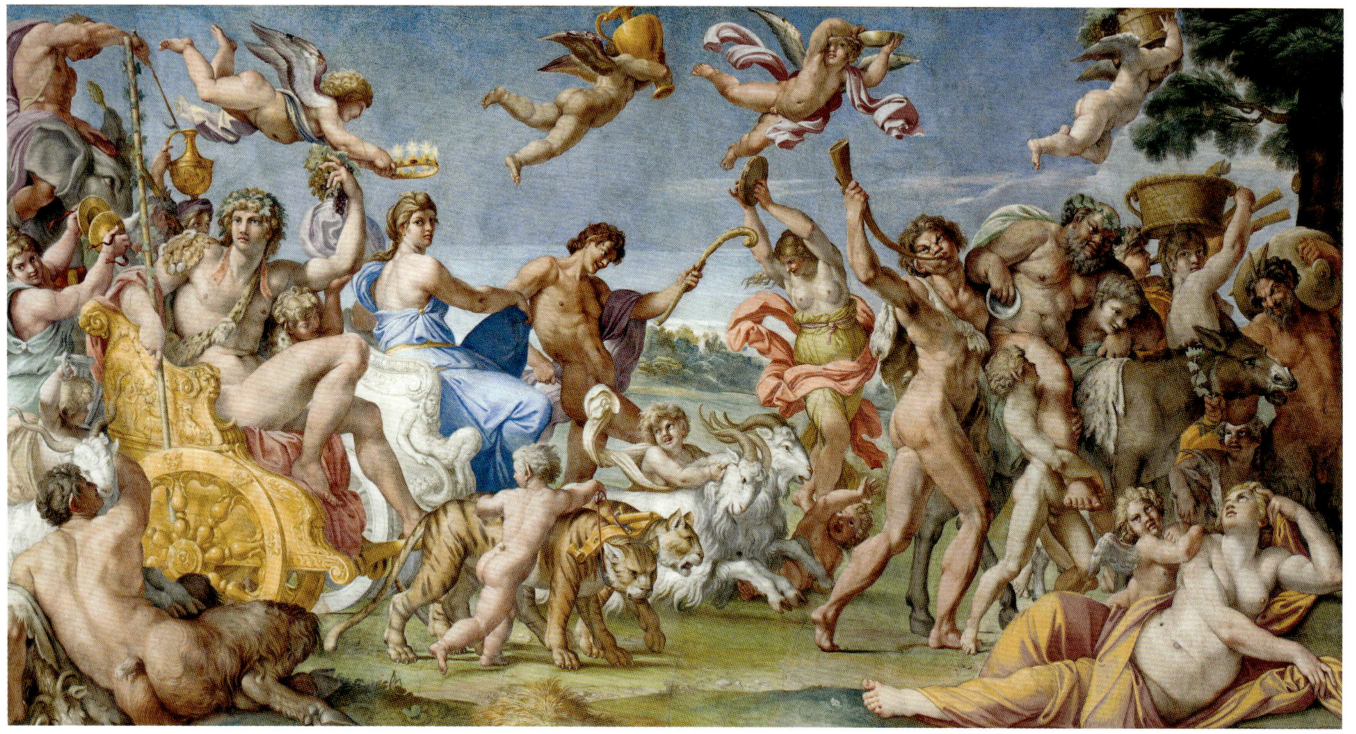

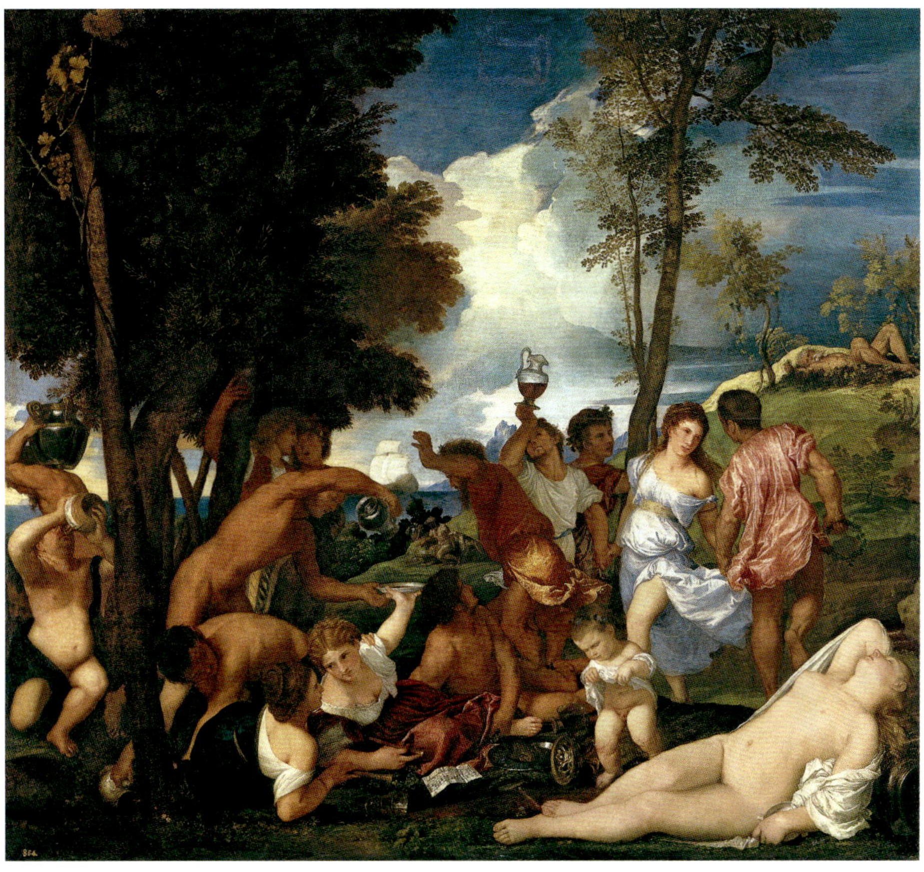

FIGURE 5
Titian (Tiziano Vecellio) (Italian, ca. 1489/90–1576), *The Andrians*, 1523–26. Oil on canvas, 175 × 193 cm (68⅞ × 76 in.). Madrid, Museo Nacional del Prado, inv. P00418

a rich, saturated palette, Poussin mimicked Titian's manner and even borrowed the subject for *Bacchanal with a Guitar Player* from Titian's *The Andrians* (see fig. 5).[28] The inhabitants of Andros make merry in both pictures, for Bacchus has caused their river to run with wine. Tellingly, both painters figured this merrymaking as a dance: in Titian's case, a tipsy ring at right; in Poussin's, a solo performance by the central reveler.

That Poussin's earliest explorations of dance were entwined with his study of Titian's bacchanals is of interest here not least because the means by which he undertook this study had a determining effect on his subsequent working methods. Poussin shared his admiration for Titian with his closest friend (and roommate) during these first years in Rome: the Flemish sculptor François Duquesnoy (1597–1643). Duquesnoy would go on to pioneer a classical style in sculpture analogous to Poussin's in painting. At this early stage the two roamed the city together, studying sculptures and copying the Titians at the Villa Ludovisi.[29] Indeed, Bellori tells us that they made copies after the Venetian master's chubby putti not only in paint but also in "bas-reliefs": sculptures that reimagined the Renaissance painter's two-dimensional compositions in three and that taught Poussin to model figures from clay.[30]

Poussin was by no means a natural draftsman in the way we might use that phrase to describe Leonardo, say, or indeed Poussin's own contemporary Guercino (1591–1666). He produced many accomplished collector's drawings—copies after the antique or *ricordi* of his own painted compositions—and he habitually jotted down observations in a sketchbook.[31] But he seldom used his chalk or pen truly to *invent*, that is, to generate and explore new concepts or forms on the page.[32] Nor do his surviving drawings follow the progression we see in the graphic production of his contemporaries: rough compositional sketches followed by life studies of individual figures, heads, and hands, and finally full-scale paper cartoons.[33] What we have instead are schematic (and not a little odd) compositional studies of faceless figures carefully arranged and lit (plates 14, 19b, 26–29).

We know from contemporary accounts that Poussin generally worked out the postures and arrangement of his figures using little wax models, formed with his own hands and arranged in a kind of toy-theater tableau.[34] Exactly when he began this practice is unclear, though it seems to have evolved from his study after Titian with Duquesnoy. The German painter Joachim von Sandrart (1606–1688) witnessed it at work during his stay in Rome between 1629 and 1635, and the bordelais painter Antoine Le Blond de La Tour (1630–1706) offered a detailed description of the process some years later:

> He dressed them in clothes suited to the figures he wished to paint, forming the draperies with the tip of a little stick . . . making their heads, feet, hands, and nude bodies, as one makes those of Angels, and the high points of Landscapes, the bits of Architecture, & the other ornaments with soft wax, which he handled with a singular swiftness and ease: And having expressed his ideas in this fashion, he erected a box . . . following the shape of his board, which served as the base for his Picture, enclosing all sides snugly, except for that occupied by the board supporting his Figures, thus surrounding and embracing, so to speak, the whole contraption . . . And at last he made a little opening at the front of his box to see the whole face of his Picture from a distance; & he created this opening so carefully as to prevent any stray light from getting in, for he closed [the opening] with his eye, looking through to draw his Picture.[35]

Poussin did not invent such tools. Since the early Renaissance artists had used figurines of wax and clay to work out figures and poses.[36] But whereas the idea that Tintoretto or El Greco relied on wax maquettes can be difficult to square with the dynamic appearance of their finished paintings, it is easier to imagine that the careful arrangements of frozen, faceless bodies we find in Poussin's drawings began as arrays of wax figurines, observed through the little hole in his purpose-built box.

Flora and the transformation of style

Surely one such drawing is the *Study for the Realm of Flora* (plate 7), datable, by its somewhat congested arrangement of figures and by the combined use of red chalk and a stiff pen, to about 1627. Though Poussin's precise literary source for this composition has been much debated,[37] the subject is reasonably clear: Flora, Roman goddess of flowers and spring, dances with a ring of putti amid a kind of human garden. Here are the mortals transformed into flowers in Ovid's great mythological poem, the *Metamorphoses*: Ajax, Clytie, Narcissus, Hyacinth, Adonis, Smilax, and Crocus.[38]

A sculpted herm looks on at left, while the sun god Apollo rides his chariot overhead. A trellis encloses the composition rather like a scenery flat.

Here Ovid's characters are rendered with striking concision—their ovoid heads barely marked with facial features, their bodies outlined with a few pen strokes—but Poussin took some pains in the application of wash. We are struck at once by the precision and consistency with which the light seems to fall on these figures, articulating the muscled torso of the warrior Ajax, the *rondeurs* of Flora's navel and breasts, the slender, sinewy forms of Adonis's hunting dogs. The play of light and shadow here seems not invented but observed. And so it surely was—from the little bodies that Poussin had fashioned in wax and arranged with care.[39]

The immediate purpose of this drawing remains somewhat mysterious, for Poussin did not turn it into a painting at once,[40] but he seems to have been quite attached to the vignette of Flora dancing with a ring of putti.[41] He reused this motif in reverse for a picture of about the same date: *The Triumph of Venus* (fig. 6), where the goddess of flowers, a barefoot girl in green, dances at the head of a procession.[42] Titianesque in conception and execution (note the wet landscape, the rich palette, and the joyous, crowded composition), this painting portrays Venus, goddess of love, riding in triumph, surrounded by the lovers turned to flowers from the *Metamorphoses*. Here Flora plays a supporting role. For her star turn in a painting, she would have to wait until the end of 1630 or the very beginning of 1631, when Poussin returned to the schematic drawing, which he had evidently set aside for later use.

The Realm of Flora (plate 9) marks an abrupt stylistic shift, "Poussin's entrance," as Pierre Rosenberg once remarked, "into a new world."[43] With it begin the so-called blonde pictures,[44] characterized by shallow, relief-like compositions, golden light, and clean contours, in a change so abrupt that scholars once dated this painting to the late 1630s, unable to reconcile its serenity and restraint with the crowded, sensuous appearance of pictures such as *The Triumph of Venus*, painted just a few years earlier.[45] Indeed, it is only thanks to the checkered career of its first owner that we can date *The Realm of Flora*—and hence pinpoint Poussin's stylistic shift—to a precise moment in time.

Poussin seldom signed or dated his pictures, and few from his early career can be dated on the basis of documents.[46] But *The Realm of Flora* served as evidence in the criminal trial of its patron. Fabrizio Valguarnera (d. 1632), a Sicilian gentleman-crook, was arrested in July 1631 for laundering stolen diamonds through the Roman art market.[47] His possessions, seized and inventoried, included five pictures by or after Poussin, among them *The Realm of Flora*, delivered earlier that year.[48] Valguarnera visited painters' studios, buying completed works or commissioning new ones on the basis of drawings or other preparatory materials.[49] *The Realm of Flora* seems to have fallen into the latter category: a picture painted in Poussin's new manner on the basis of a drawing executed in his old one.

Where the composition of the drawing is rather crowded, that of the painting forms a well-ordered frieze. Here, in the golden light of Flora's garden, each mythological vignette becomes clearly legible. At left, the mad warrior Ajax falls on his sword, a carnation springing from the wound. Beside him Clytie reclines with her

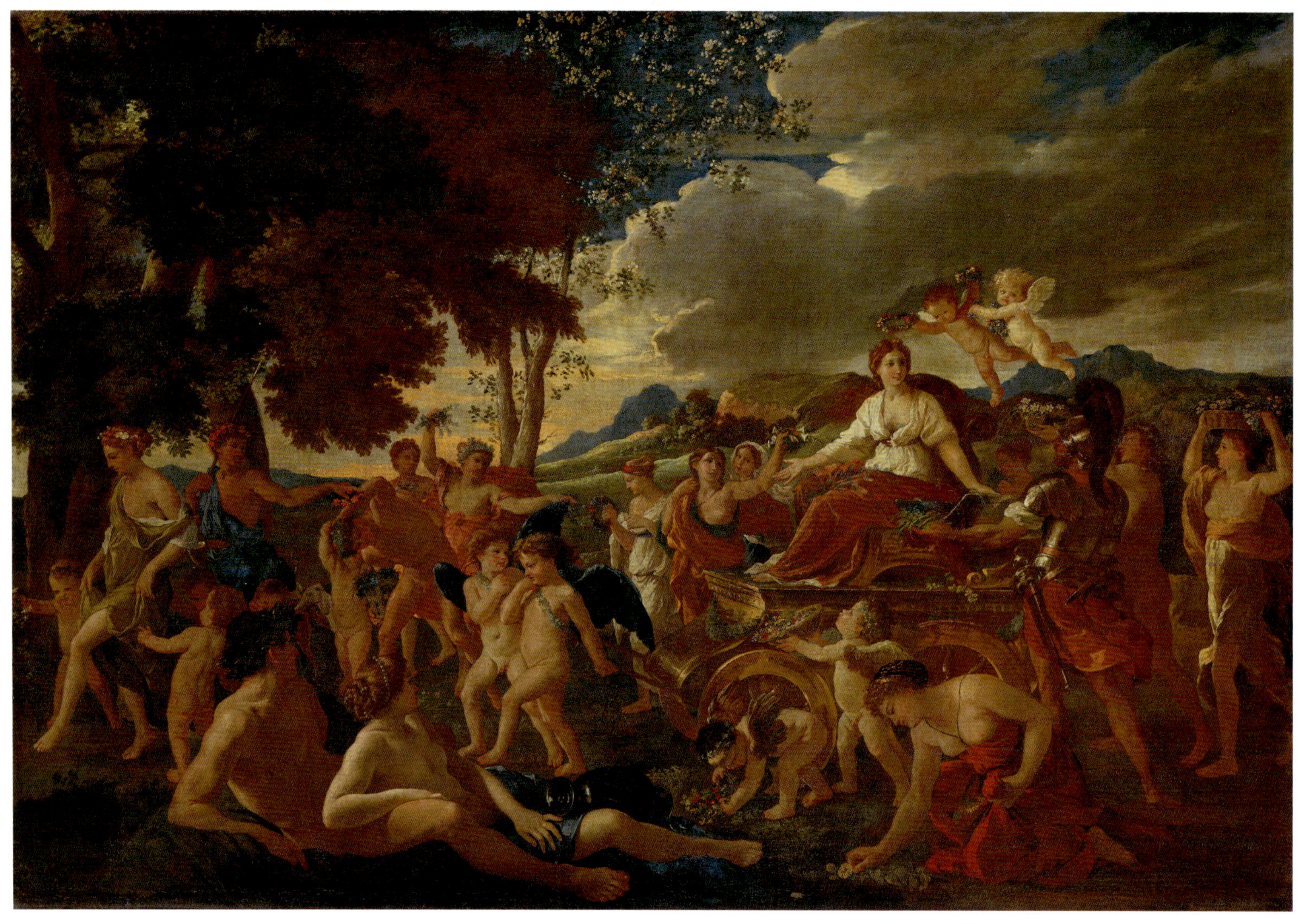

basket of sunflowers, shielding her eyes from Apollo's chariot. In the foreground, Narcissus gazes at his own reflection in a vase held by Echo, as white narcissi bloom by his knee. Right of center, Hyacinth catches petals streaming from his injured head, while Adonis the hunter, with spear and hounds, studies a wound in his thigh that "bleeds" anemone blossom. Finally, at right, Smilax embraces her lover with a garland of bindweed; a crown of white and purple flowers identifies him as Crocus.

Surrounded by these dying mortals, Flora dances with her chorus of putti. Poussin picked out her wreath, ribbons, and fluttering curls with bright licks of color and girded her gown below the waist in an explicit reference to the Farnese Flora, a colossal first-century sculpture that was among the antiquities most revered by Poussin and his friends.[50] Her choreography remains much the same as in his earlier depictions: she kicks one leg before her, balancing on the ball of her supporting foot. But while in both the compositional drawing and the painted *Triumph of Venus*, Flora looks down at her feet, here she turns to the dying Narcissus with a smile, sprinkling petals as if to effect his transformation from man to flower.

By all rights the picture should be disturbing, filled as it is with allusions to violent passion and painful death: the suicide of Ajax, the drowning of Narcissus, the goring of Adonis by a wild boar. And yet the mood is oddly tranquil, particularly when we compare this work with the stormy landscapes, the riotous color and movement of neo-Venetian pictures painted just a few years before. Specialists have accounted for this sudden shift in various ways, but it is worth mentioning that 1630 also marked a turning point in the artist's life. Poussin suffered from a chronic illness. This, according to Passeri, was the "male di Francia" (French disease): syphilis.[51] He may have experienced symptoms as early as 1625,[52] and letters exchanged four years later by Cassiano and a Bolognese physician seem to contain prescriptions for Poussin's treatment.[53] Tortured by symptoms and remedies alike, he survived thanks to the care he received from his neighbor, a French cook named Jacques Dughet.[54] On October 18, 1629, Poussin was engaged to Dughet's daughter, Anne-Marie (1613–1665), and on September 19, 1630, they were married.[55]

The disease would cause Poussin intermittent discomfort for at least a decade and apparently left him sterile, but his recovery and marriage had a transformative effect on his life. The dowry he received from Dughet allowed him to purchase a lifetime lease on a modest house in the via Paolina, putting an end to the precariousness of his early years in Rome and granting him the peace, in Passeri's words, "to attend in earnest to his studies."[56] The close coincidence of his painting of *The Realm of Flora* with his physical recovery and marriage adds a personal dimension to our understanding of Poussin's stylistic turn at this moment.[57] Just as Flora's dance transforms mortals into flowers, the painting transforms suffering into cosmic order: mortality itself into beauty.[58] In this sense, *The Realm of Flora* anticipates the dancing pictures that would follow; there we watch Poussin transform movement into stillness, passion into serene delight.

The end of the dancing pictures

Poussin would paint many other subjects in the 1630s, but as the essays that follow explain, dancing pictures emerged in this period as a signature genre, admired and sought after by collectors across Europe. His last effort in this vein seems to have been a lost painting known as the *Bacchanal before a Temple*, whose composition survives in an engraving and a handful of copies (fig. 7).[59] In it, surrounded by drinkers and putti, two figures danced in time to a flute, kicking up their heels and playing cymbals and castanets. "It is one of the pictures with which he took the greatest pains," Félibien explained, following "proportions derived from statues and the most beautiful antique bas-reliefs."[60]

Given the painting's disappearance, its date may be impossible to ascertain,[61] but a pair of surviving preparatory drawings was surely made in the late 1630s (plate 10; fig. 8).[62] The first is highly finished: dark washes here create a rhythmic play of light and shadow frankly reminiscent of a bas-relief. This version of the revel is somewhat wilder than the painting was; tumbling dancers enclose the scene at left, while a visibly excited celebrant offers wine to a bacchante at right. Poussin was evidently dissatisfied with this treatment. He rearranged his wax figurines and sketched them swiftly again in the second drawing (see fig. 8), whose configuration is much closer

FIGURE 7

After Nicolas Poussin, *Bacchanal before a Temple*, seventeenth century. Oil on canvas, 74.9 × 101.3 cm (29½ × 39⅞ in.). San Francisco, Legion of Honor Museum, Roscoe and Margaret Oakes Collection, inv. 1952-12-0

FIGURE 8

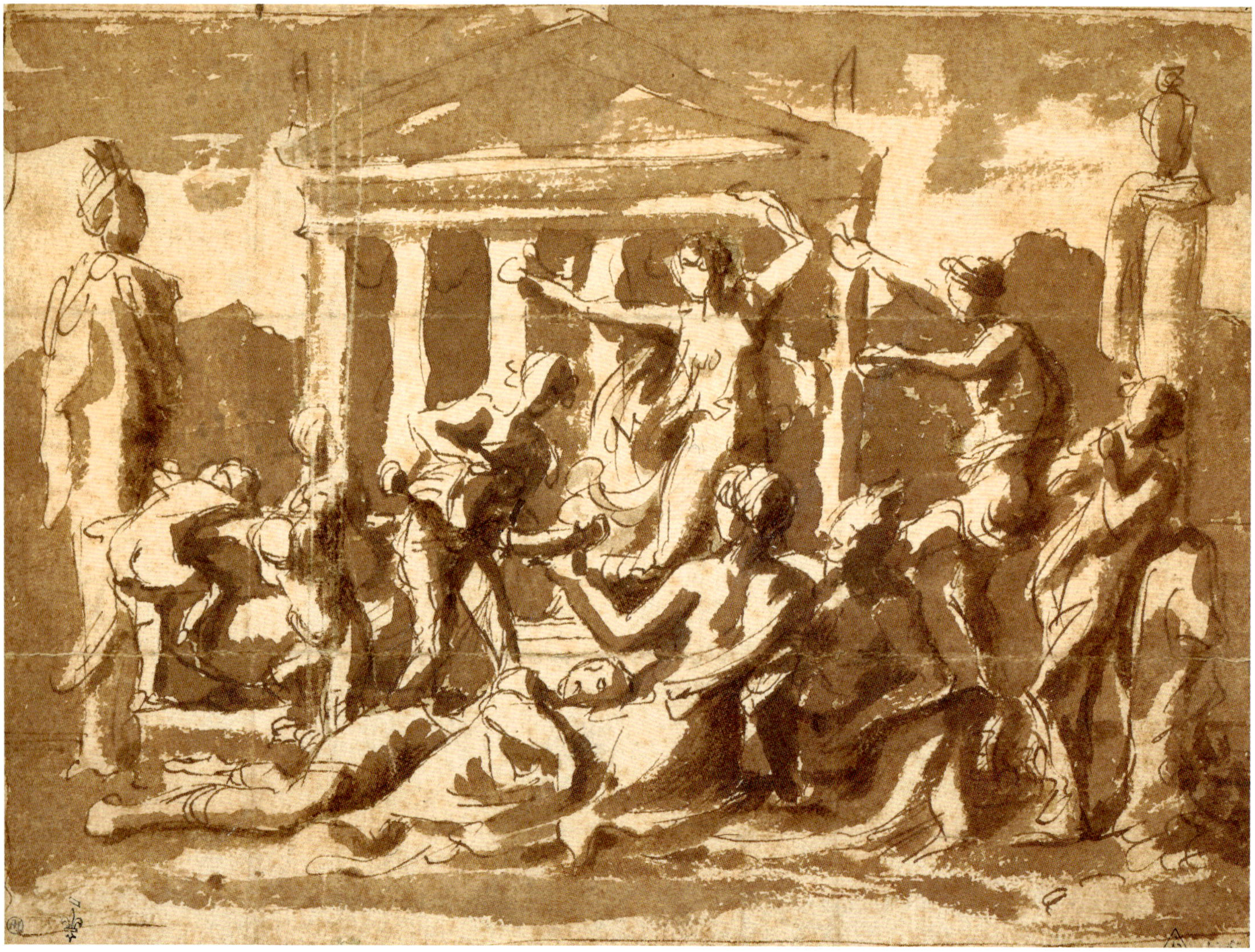

Nicolas Poussin, *Study for Bacchanal before a Temple*, ca. 1635–40. Pen and brown ink and brush and brown wash on paper, 16.4 × 21 cm (6½ × 8¼ in.). Chantilly, Musée Condé, inv. DE 213

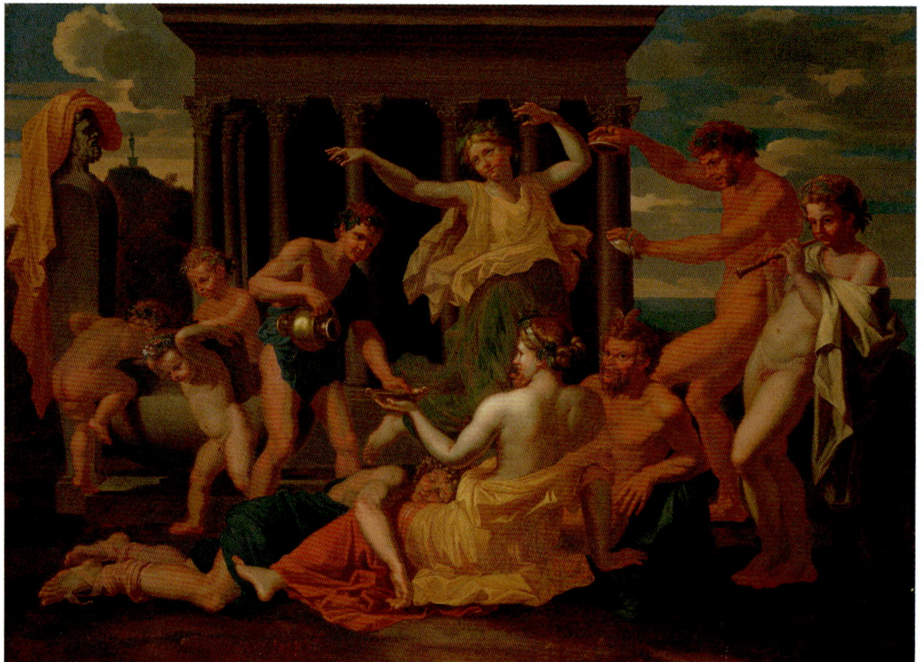

to the final composition. Curiously, he also seems to have torn up his first attempt. Rescued from the studio floor and lovingly pasted back together, this sheet still bears the scars of its maker's frustration.[63]

Was Poussin already growing tired of dances? The dancing pictures had helped make his name, but his turn to weighty, severe subjects around 1640 seems to have signaled a dwindling interest in "wine and blood" and dancing.[64] Dance may disappear from pictures painted in Poussin's maturity, but what lingers is an almost magical ability to render stilled motion, a system of orchestrated movements that even today exerts a powerful tug on our bodies and imaginations: the elusive "balletic" quality of his work.

NOTES

I am most grateful to David Freedberg for all his guidance. I also wish to thank Julian Brooks, Stephanie Schrader, Julia Siemon, Francesca Whitlum-Cooper, and Abraham Frank for their close reading and thoughtful feedback on both of my essays. Unless otherwise noted, translations are my own.

1   Thuillier 1994a, 66.

2   Few scholars have treated the dancing pictures as a group. See the lively (if fanciful) accounts in Pilon 1911 and Magne 1914, 23.

3   On the painter as choreographer, see Powell 2012. On balletic metaphors in Poussin scholarship, see my essay "Choreographing Violence: The Abduction of the Sabine Women," in this volume, especially note 5.

4   Charles I de Créquy, Maréchal de France, who brought the first examples of Poussin's new classical manner back from Rome to Paris in 1634, was an amateur ballet dancer. Cardinal Richelieu, the most prolific collector of Poussin's work at the French court in the 1630s and early 1640s, was also the most important patron of court ballets in this period. Louis XIII, whom Poussin served as First Painter from 1640 to 1641, was both a dancer in and a patron of annual ballet performances. The generation that made Paris the epicenter for the collecting of Poussin's work in the 1660s–1680s included Charles III de Blanchefort, duc de Créquy (grandson of Charles I), who built his own collection of Poussins, danced at court, and mounted private ballet performances at his home; Armand-Jean de Vignerot du Plessis, duc de Richelieu (grandnephew of the cardinal), who amassed an enormous collection of Poussin's work and danced in ballets at court; Pierre Beauchamps, the owner of three Poussins, who was not only a professional dancer and choreographer but also a dancing master to Louis XIV; and that king himself, the most powerful collector of Poussin and the most celebrated ballet dancer of the seventeenth century. See Beeny 2016, especially 40–52, 66–70, and 165–67.

5   Ovid, *Metamorphoses* 8.174–78. Or conceivably Ovid, *Fasti* 3.459–516.

6   As Denis Mahon observed (Rome 1998–99, 82). This canvas is half again as large as the largest that Poussin painted for the picture dealer Giovanni Stefano Roccatagliata (see Cavazzini 2013 and Pierguidi 2012). On Poussin's early production for the Roman art market, see Standring 2009 and Cavazzini 2008.

7   For an overview of these years, see Thuillier 1995.

8   On Poussin's drawings for Marino, see Prat 2013, 18–22; London et al. 1995–96, no. 1–15; and Rosenberg and Prat 1994, no. 2–17.

9   According to Poussin's early biographers Bellori (1672, 411) and Passeri (1772, 249), Marino introduced him to the Sacchetti family, bankers to the Barberini pope. As discussed below, Cassiano was secretary to the pope's nephew, and Mahon (Rome 1998–99, 22–25, and 82) proposed that he was the first owner of *Bacchus and Ariadne*, identifying this canvas with a "Bacchanal" listed in the dal Pozzo family inventories (on these see also Standring 1988 and 2000, and Sparti 1992). Rosenberg has ruled out this possibility, identifying the dal Pozzo "Bacchanal" with another work; see Rosenberg 2022.

10 The Paper Museum's contents are today dispersed. The largest groups are in the British Museum and the Royal Collection; see Claridge and Clayton 1996–. On the drawings after the antique, see Vermeule 1960. On Cassiano as a collector, see also Freedberg 2002, 15–64; Rome 2000b; Sparti 1992; Solinas 1989; Standring 1988; and Haskell's classic study (Haskell, 1963, 98–114).

11 Before he left for Paris with a papal legation; he was absent from March to December 1625. Mahon (Rome 1998–99, 21–23) argued for the dating of Poussin's first letter to Cassiano (Poussin 2014, 35–36; Jouanny 1911, no. 1) to late 1625 or early 1626; in it the painter writes, "As for your drawings, I think of them every day, and soon I will finish something." For an alternative hypothesis regarding the drawings mentioned here, see London et al. 1995–96, 58.

12 On Poussin's desperation in this period, see Passeri 1772, 349–50; and Bellori 1672, 411. His finances appear to have been more stable by 1627, when he opened a bank account (Sparti 1993–94).

13 On the early modern reception of Dionysian sarcophagi, see Bober and Rubenstein 1986, 105–25.

14 Félibien 1725, 4:147. Félibien also lists the Medici Vase (Musée du Louvre, Paris), which portrays no dancers, though Poussin made a drawing of it (British Museum, London); see Rosenberg and Prat 1994, no. 159.

15 Both in an album at the British Museum (inv. 2005.0927 / vol. II); that from the Borghese Vase is fol. 123, no. 512; that from the Salpion Vase, fol. 56, no. 378. Neither is by Poussin.

16 Unearthed on the Roman estate of Carlo Muti by September 18, 1569, the vase's presence at the Villa Borghese is first documented in 1645 (Perrier 1645, nos. 10 and 11). Haskell, Penny et al. 2021, no. 81; see also Francesca Whitlum-Cooper's essay "Dances for Richelieu" in this volume.

17 As Anthony Blunt first surmised (Blunt 1967, 56 and 138), the vase was installed by Pedro de Oña, who served as bishop of Gaeta from 1605 to 1625 (Ferraro 1903, 144).

18 On the oscillum suggestion, see Goldner and Hendrix 1992, no. 71. Compare to Naples, Museo Archeologico Nazionale, inv. 6636 (Carrella et al. 2008, 105–7).

19 No other two drawings so similar in design are both accepted by Rosenberg and Prat (1994, nos. 163 and 164). The sheets bear nonconsecutive numbers in the same hand and belonged to a collector with the initials "GFM." See Blunt 1979b, 139–40.

20 On the damaged-cameo hypothesis, see Blunt 1979b, 139–40. Rosenberg and Prat (1994, no. 163) suggest the cameo might be one in Maffei 1707–9 (pl. 55). Fig. 2 (an ex-Farnese cameo) seems closer to Poussin's designs, though its damage does not correspond to Poussin's "repairs."

21 Stefanoni 1627, n.p.

22 Virgil, *Georgics* 2.380–84. See the classic translation by James Rhoades (1881).

23 Poussin had likely studied at the Jesuit College in Rouen. See Thuillier 1995, 18.

24 Though Poussin could read Latin, he also relied on modern translations, notably Giovanni Andrea dell'Anguillara's 1561 Italian translation of Ovid's *Metamorphoses* and Blaise de Vigenère's 1578 French translation of Philostratus's *Imagines* (see Anguillara 1584 and Vigenère 1614). See Panofsky 1950, Worthen 1979, and Bull 1998.

25 *The Feast of the Gods* (painted with Giovanni Bellini; National Gallery of Art, Washington, DC); *Bacchus and Ariadne* (National Gallery, London); *The Andrians* (Museo Nacional del Prado, Madrid); and *The Worship of Venus* (Museo Nacional del Prado, Madrid). Painted for Alfonso d'Este, the pictures were removed from Ferrara in 1598 by Cardinal Pietro Aldobrandini. Upon his death in 1621, *The Andrians* and *The Worship of Venus* were given by Aldobrandini's heirs to Cardinal Ludovico Ludovisi, whose heirs, in turn, sold them to the Spanish crown in 1638. On the seventeenth-century Roman reception of Titian's bacchanals, see Loh 2007, especially 64–71; and Colantuono 1989. Poussin may have passed through Venice en route to Rome, there seeing Titian's work for the first time. The stop is mentioned only in Giulio Mancini's ca. 1627 biographical notes; see Marucchi 1956–57, 1:261.

26 Bellori 1672, 80.

27 See Passeri 1772, 351; and Bellori 1672, 412. On his emulation of Titian's technique, see also Sandrart 1675, bk. 3, chap. 26, 368. For a more precise analysis of Poussin's technique in these early years, see Standring 2017, especially 72–73.

28 Probably taken from Philostratus, *Imagines* 1.25, though the subject of Poussin's picture has been debated; see Rosenberg 2015, no. 4, and Dempsey 2010.

29 See further discussion in Francesca Whitlum-Cooper's essay "Animating the Frieze" in this volume. Poussin has sometimes been identified as the author of a copy after Titian and Bellini's *Feast of the Gods* (National Galleries of Scotland, Edinburgh).

30 Bellori 1672, 412. On Poussin as a sculptor, see Kerspern 1996 and Coural 1960.

31 Félibien 1725, 14.

32 On Poussin's peculiarities as a draftsman, see London et al. 1995–96, especially 8. See also Prat 2013, especially 35–36; and Brigstocke 1996, especially 205–6.

33 One surviving cartoon fragment (Musée Condé, Chantilly) is directly linked to *The Triumph of David* (Dulwich Picture Gallery, London), though some (principally Louis-Antoine Prat) do not accept either picture or drawing as by Poussin. See Chantilly 2017–18, no. 11 (Rosenberg), London et al. 1995–96, 66; Chantilly 1994–95, no. 119 (with Prat's argument); and Rosenberg and Prat 1994, no. R253.

34 See Bellori 1672, 437; Sandrart 1675, bk. 3, chap. 26, 368; and Le Blond de Latour 1669, 38–41. See also Bätschmann 1990, 27–29; Arikha 1994–95; DeGrazia and Steele 1999; and Cambridge and Paris 2014–15, 17–19.

35 Le Blond de Latour 1669, 38–41.

36 See, for example, Venice and Washington 2018–19, 67–68.

37 Some maintain that Poussin's sole source was Ovid; others have suggested poems by Marino or Antonio Bruni (1593–1635). For a summary and complete bibliography, see Beeny 2019a, especially 42n5.

38 Ovid, *Metamorphoses* 13.394–98 (Ajax); 4.266–70 (Clytie); 3.508–10 (Narcissus); 10.203–19 (Hyacinth); 10.725–39 (Adonis); 4.283–84 (Crocus and Smilax); several of these characters are also mentioned in Flora's boast of her transformative powers in Ovid's calendar poem, the *Fasti* (5).

39 A faint red chalk design on the verso shows much the same composition. A notable difference is in the placement of Crocus and Smilax, who there appear configured in the same way but at the center of the scene (London et al. 1995–96, no. 20). Might this figural unit correspond to a pair of wax figurines that Poussin shifted before embarking on the recto drawing?

40 Martin Clayton (London et al., 1995–96, no. 20) offers the enticing hypothesis that this drawing, another in the Royal Collection (*Study for Perseus and Andromeda: The Origin of Coral*, RCIN 911984), and presumably a third, now lost (portraying Venus and Adonis: *The Tinting of the Rose*), were preparatory to a series of highly finished *drawings* (now lost) for Cassiano depicting "mythological natural history." Three sophisticated copies, likewise in the Royal Collection (RCIN 911877–RCIN 911879), may convey the appearance of the finished drawings, which Clayton suggests might correspond to the drawings mentioned in Poussin's early letter to Cassiano (see note 10, above).

41 A concept probably inspired by Anguillara's translation of the *Metamorphoses*, which describes Flora as a girl in green, laughing and dancing (Anguillara 1584, 31). See Worthen 1979, 579–80. On Flora's choreography here see also Keazor 1995, 351–52.

42 The picture is generally known as *The Triumph of Flora* but more likely represents the triumph of Venus; see Beeny 2019a and Rosenberg 2022.

43 See Rosenberg and Prat 1994, no. 44.

44 See Mahon 1960.

45 For example, Blunt 1953, 187.

46 *The Death of Germanicus* (Minneapolis Institute of Art) was delivered to Cardinal Barberini in January 1628. The *Martyrdom of Saint Erasmus* (Musei Vaticani) was ordered for Saint Peter's Basilica in February 1628 and paid for from June to November 1629.

47 See Costello 1950. See also Fumagalli 1994–95, 52–53.

48 The others were *The Plague at Ashdod* (Musée du Louvre, Paris), a copy of same, and two paintings of Midas. On *The Plague at Ashdod* and *The Realm of Flora* as pendants, see S. Barker 2004.

49 See Costello 1950, 261.

50 Sandrart drew it (Kupferstich-Kabinett, Dresden, inv. C1963–1974); Duquesnoy viewed it as a model for sculpted draperies (see Lingo 2007, 21–22); and Poussin himself may have owned a reduced copy (see Delisle 1858, 253; and Beeny 2019a, 38 and 43n45).

51 Passeri 1772, 350.

52 According to a letter to Cassiano (Poussin 2014, 35–36; Jouanny 1911, no. 1); on the contested dating of this letter, see notes 11 and 40, above.

53 See Wilberding 2000.

54 Passeri, 1772, 350.

55 See Passeri 1772, 350. On this sequence of events, see also Unglaub 2004; Thuillier 1994a, 112 and 118; and Fort Worth 1988, 233–38.

56 Passeri 1772, 351.

57 See Unglaub 2004, especially 520–21 for the tempting suggestion that the Dresden *Flora* might offer a likeness of Poussin's bride. See also related discussion of Poussin's art and illness in Cropper and Dempsey 1996, especially 228–37.

58 See Panofsky 1936, 240.

59 On the lost painting, see Rosenberg 2022; and Blunt 1966, no. 140. On the engraving, by Jean Mariette, see Wildenstein 1958, no. 131.

60 Félibien 1725, 4:80–81.

61 Félibien described the lost picture as "made for M. du Fresne" (1725, 4:146), likely Raphael Trichet du Fresne, director of the royal printing press, who was in Rome in 1649 (see Thuillier 1994a, no. 260). Blunt suggested that Poussin could also have intended it for Paul Scarron (1610–1660) (Poussin 2014, 147n9), dusting off an old bacchanalian subject for this burlesque poet; see also Poussin to Paul Fréart de Chantelou (1609–1694), February 7, 1649 (Poussin 2014, 147; Jouanny 1911, no. 169).

62 See London et al. 1995–96, no. 38; and Rosenberg and Prat 1994, no. 97.

63 Clayton has convincingly argued that it was likely the future Cardinal Camillo Massimi (1620–1677), an amateur draftsman who studied with Poussin, who collected the scraps of this drawing and pasted them back together (London et al. 1995–96, 112–13).

64 On the shift from bacchanals to Sacraments at the end of the 1630s, see Edinburgh 1981.

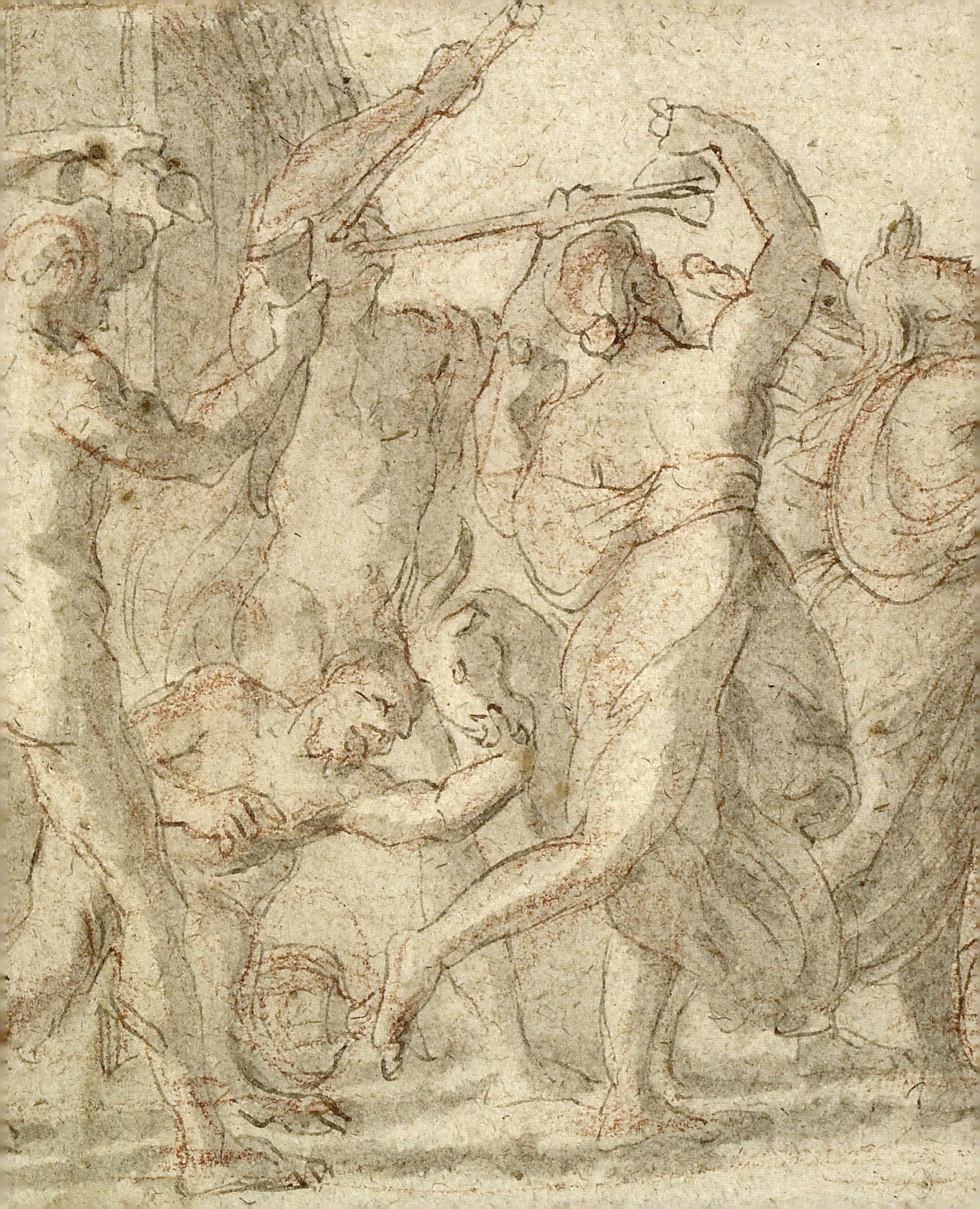

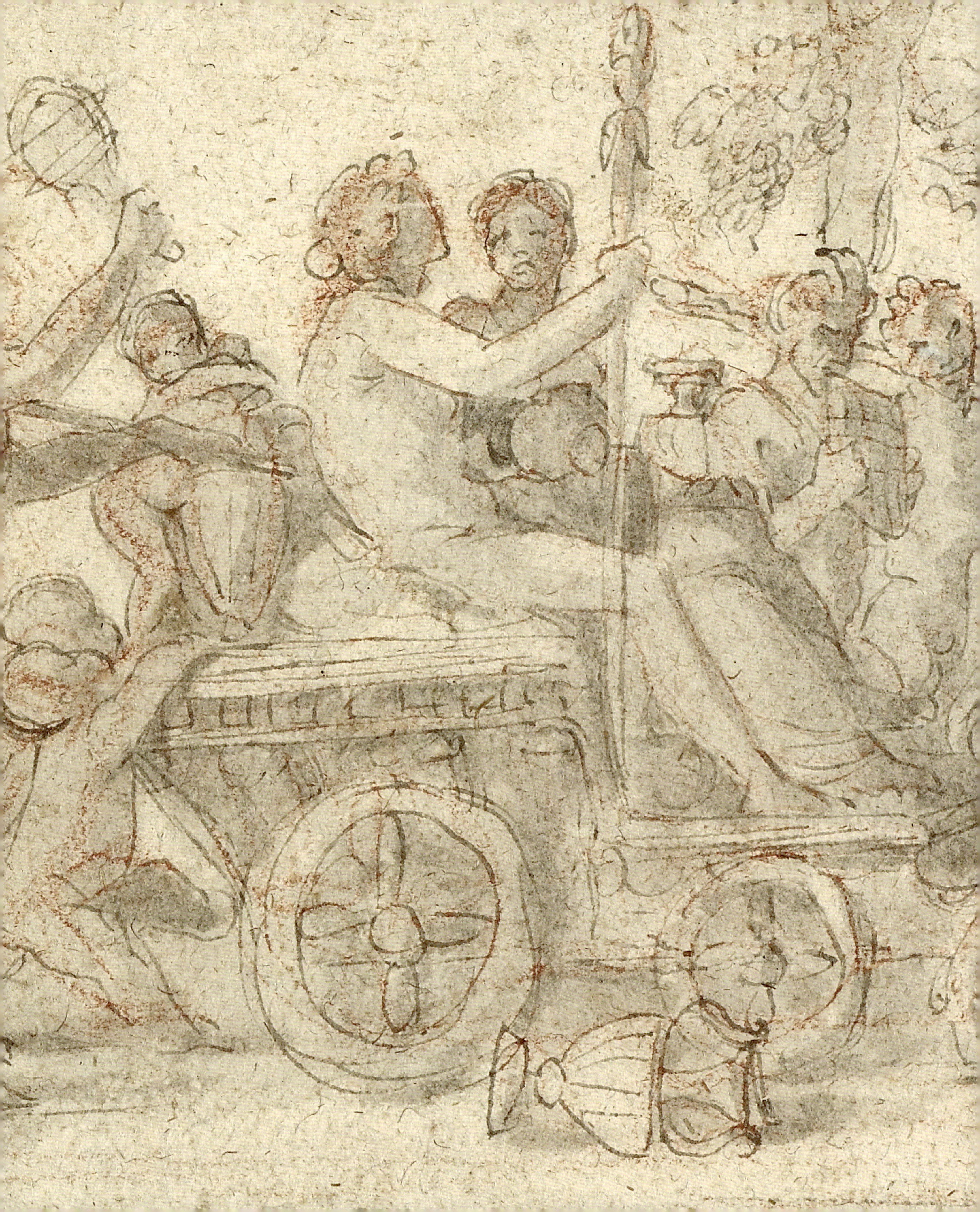

1

Nicolas Poussin

BACCHUS AND ARIADNE

ca. 1625–26

Oil on canvas

122 × 169 cm (48 × 66½ in.)

Madrid, Museo Nacional del Prado,
inv. P002312

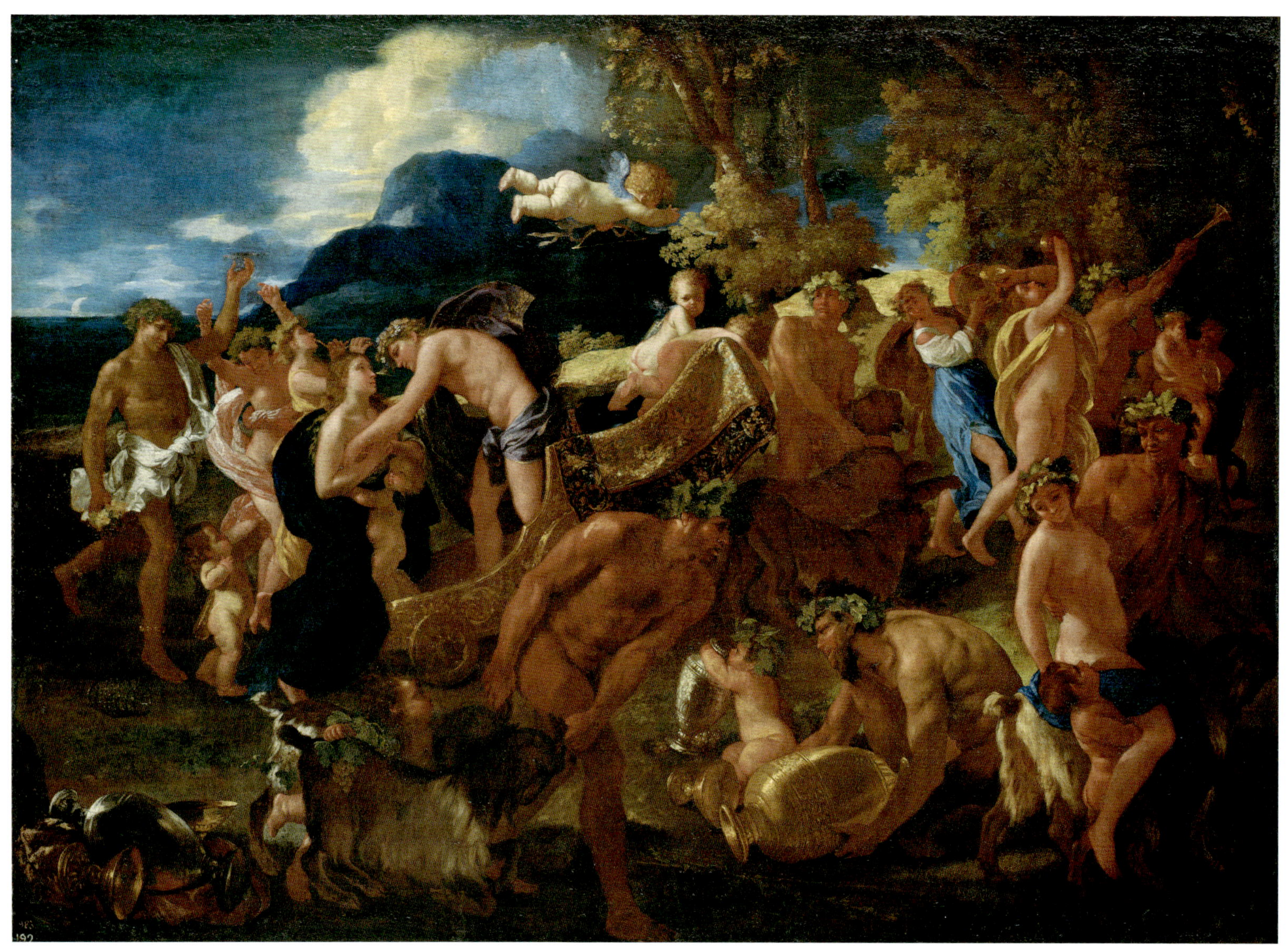

2

Nicolas Poussin

THE TRIUMPH OF BACCHUS AND ARIADNE

ca. 1627
Pen and gray-brown ink and brush and
pale gray-brown wash over red chalk on
pale buff paper
12.6 × 41.4 cm (5 × 16¼ in.)
Windsor, Royal Collection/HM Queen
Elizabeth II, inv. RCIN 911990

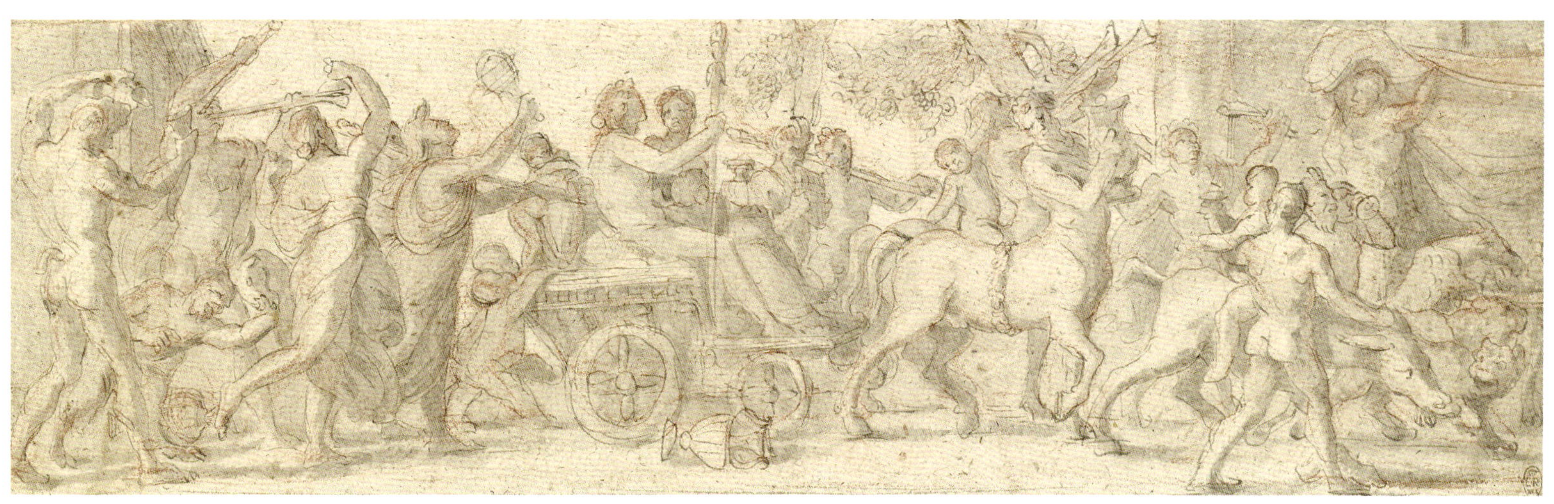

3

Salpion of Athens

KRATER DECORATED WITH HERMES CONFIDING THE INFANT DIONYSOS TO THE NYMPHS OF NYSA, AND WITH DANCING SATYRS AND MAENADS

First century BCE

Parian marble

131 × 98 × 98 cm (51⅝ × 38⅝ × 38⅝ in.)

Naples, Museo Archeologico Nazionale, inv. 6673

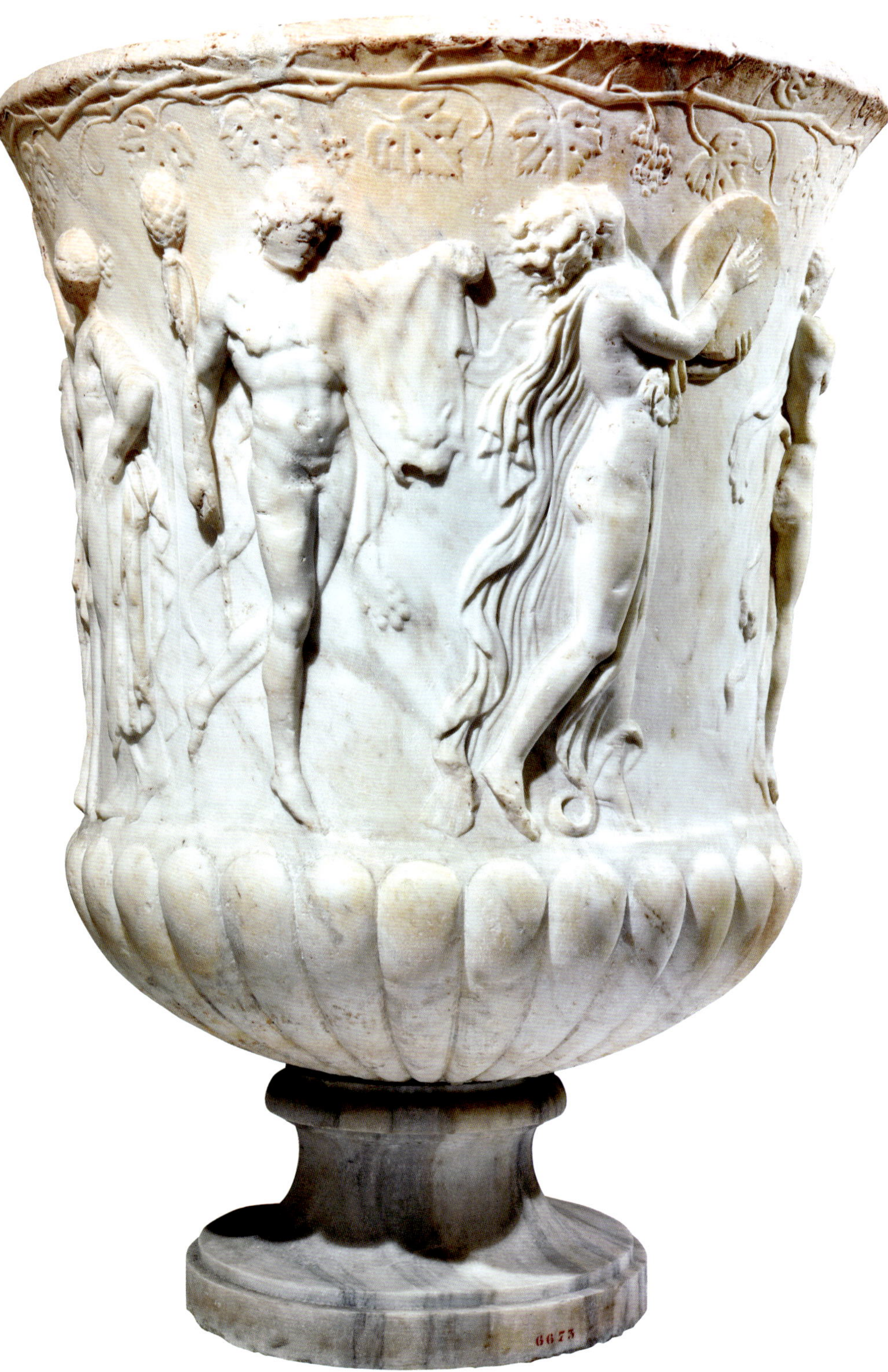

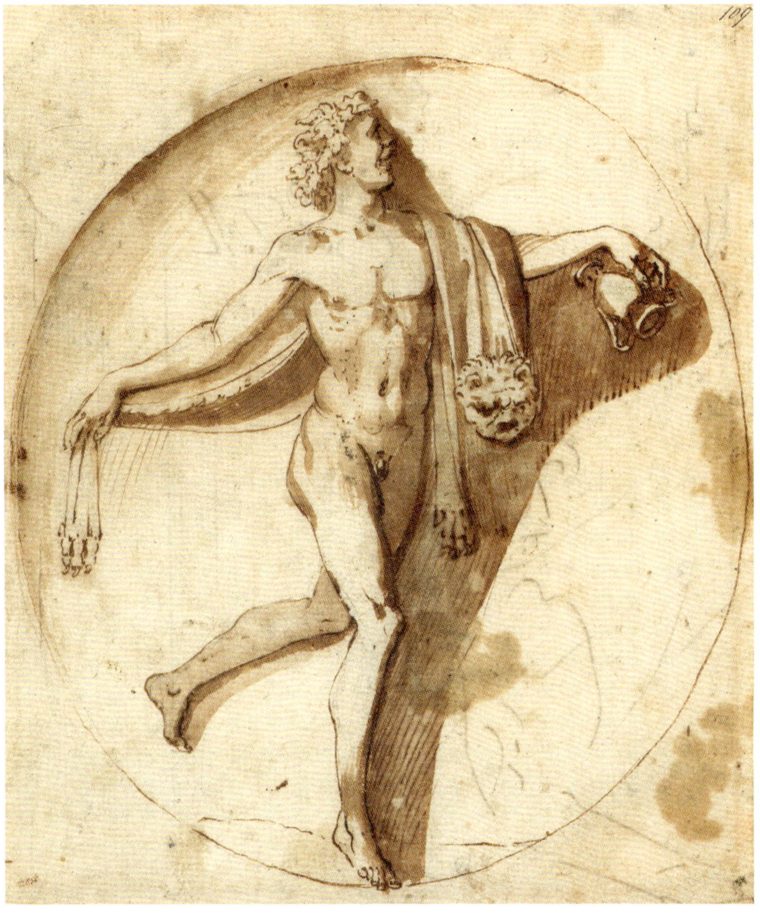

4

Nicolas Poussin

DANCING VOTARY
OF BACCHUS

ca. 1635
Pen and brown ink and brush and brown
wash over traces of black chalk on paper
15.7 × 13.5 cm (6³⁄₁₆ × 5⁵⁄₁₆ in.)
Los Angeles, J. Paul Getty Museum, inv.
86.GG.469

5

Nicolas Poussin

DANCING VOTARY
OF BACCHUS

ca. 1635
Pen and brown ink and brush and brown
wash over traces of black chalk on paper
15.5 × 13.5 cm (6⅛ × 5⅜ in.)
Switzerland, Fondation Jan Krugier,
inv. FJK100

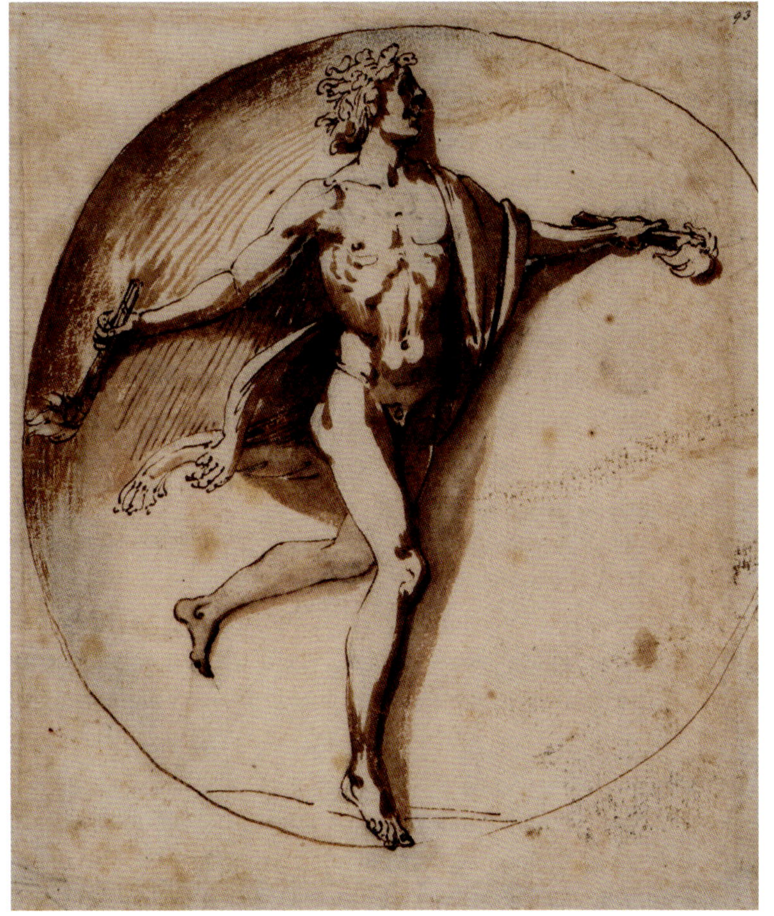

6

Nicolas Poussin

SATYRS DANCING ON A WINESKIN

ca. 1636
Pen and brown ink and brush and brown
wash over graphite on paper
24.8 × 31.8 cm (9¾ × 12½ in.)
Windsor, Royal Collection/HM Queen
Elizabeth II, inv. RCIN 911992

7

Nicolas Poussin

STUDY FOR THE REALM OF FLORA

ca. 1627
Pen and brown ink and brush and brown
wash over red chalk on pale buff paper
21.1 × 29.1 cm (8¼ × 11½ in.)
Windsor, Royal Collection/HM Queen
Elizabeth II, inv. RCIN 911983

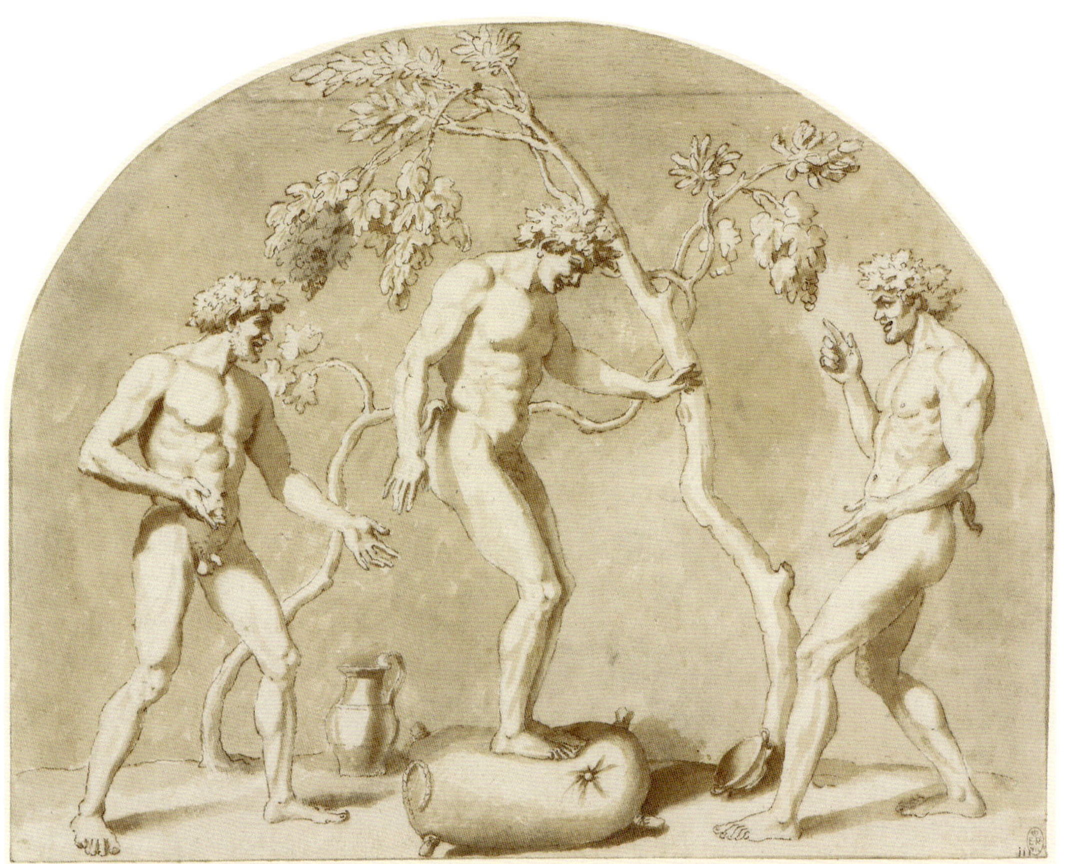

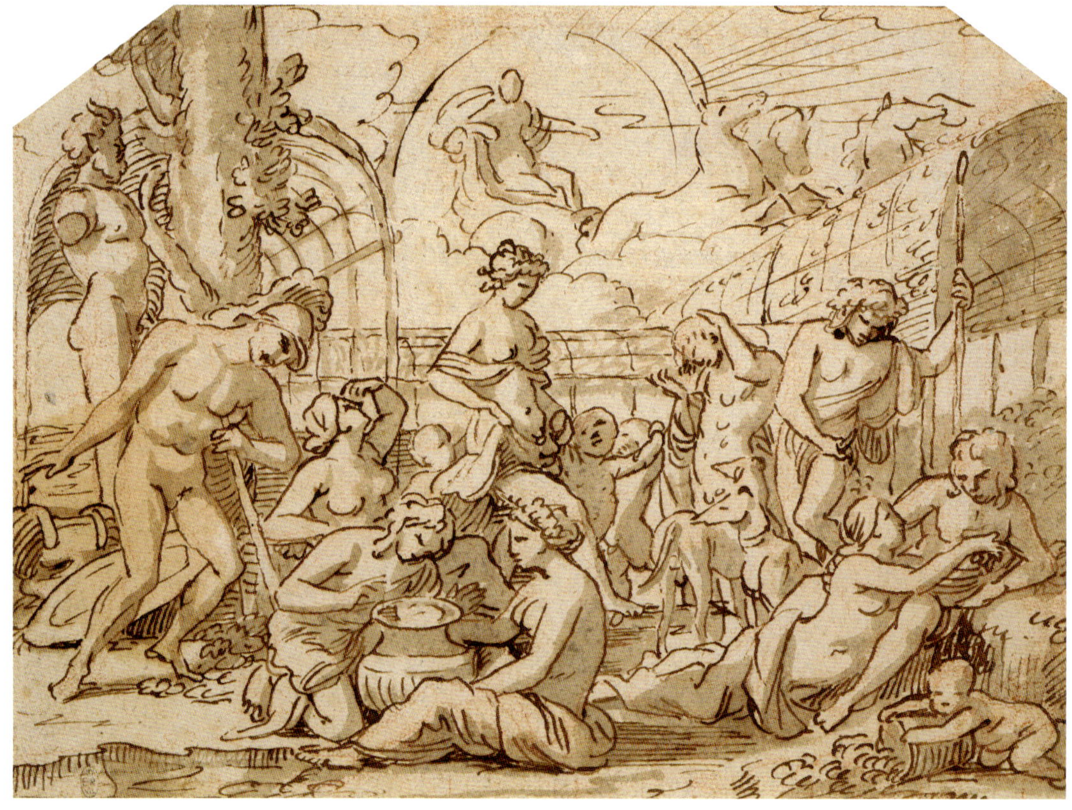

8

Nicolas Poussin

BACCHANAL WITH A GUITAR PLAYER

ca. 1627
Oil on canvas
121 × 175 cm (47⅝ × 68⅞ in.)
Paris, Musée du Louvre, Département
des Peintures, inv. 7296

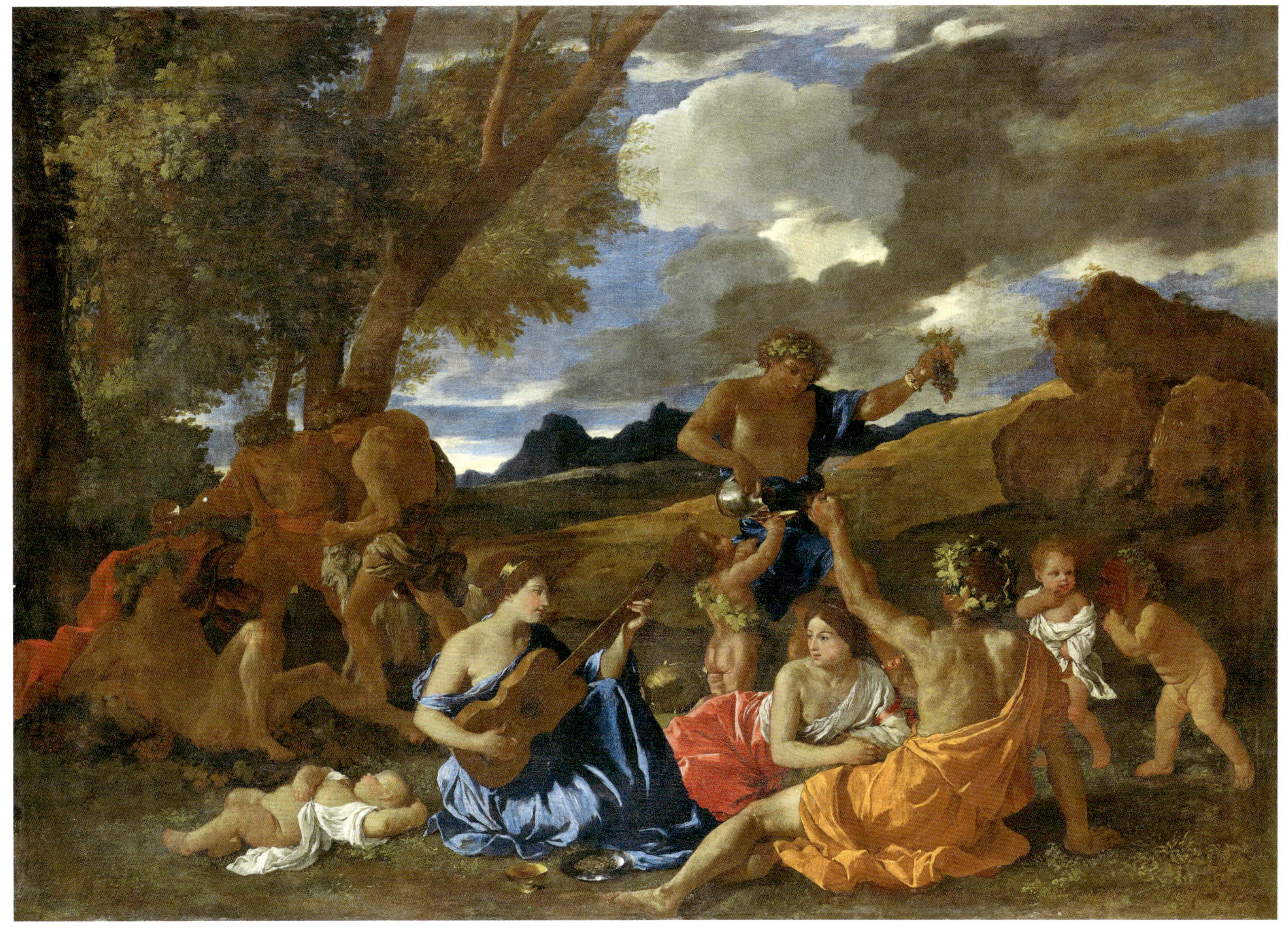

Nicolas Poussin

THE REALM OF FLORA

1630–31
Oil on canvas
131 × 181 cm (51⅝ × 71¼ in.)
Dresden, Gemäldegalerie Alte Meister,
Staatliche Kunstsammlungen, inv. 719

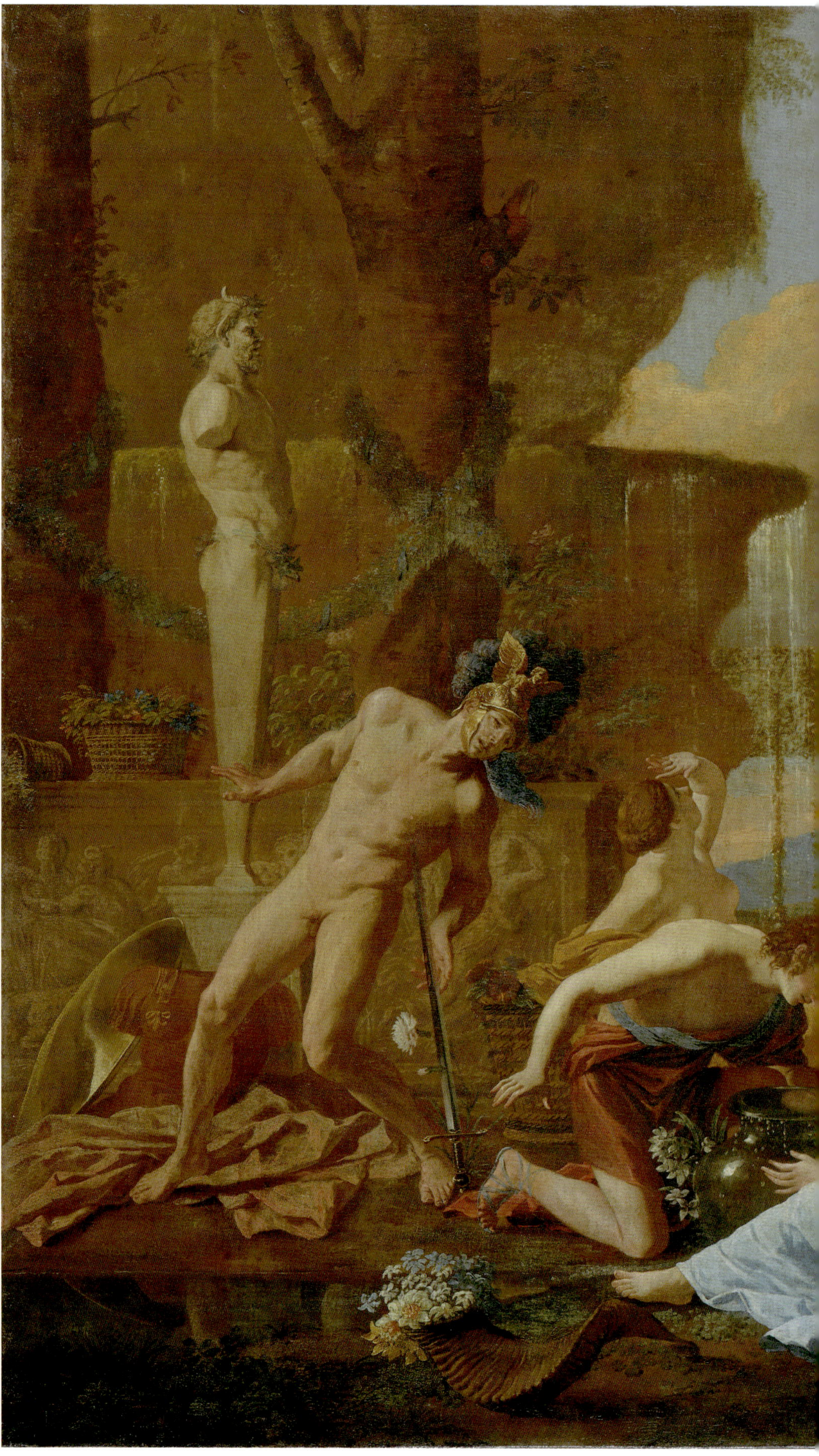

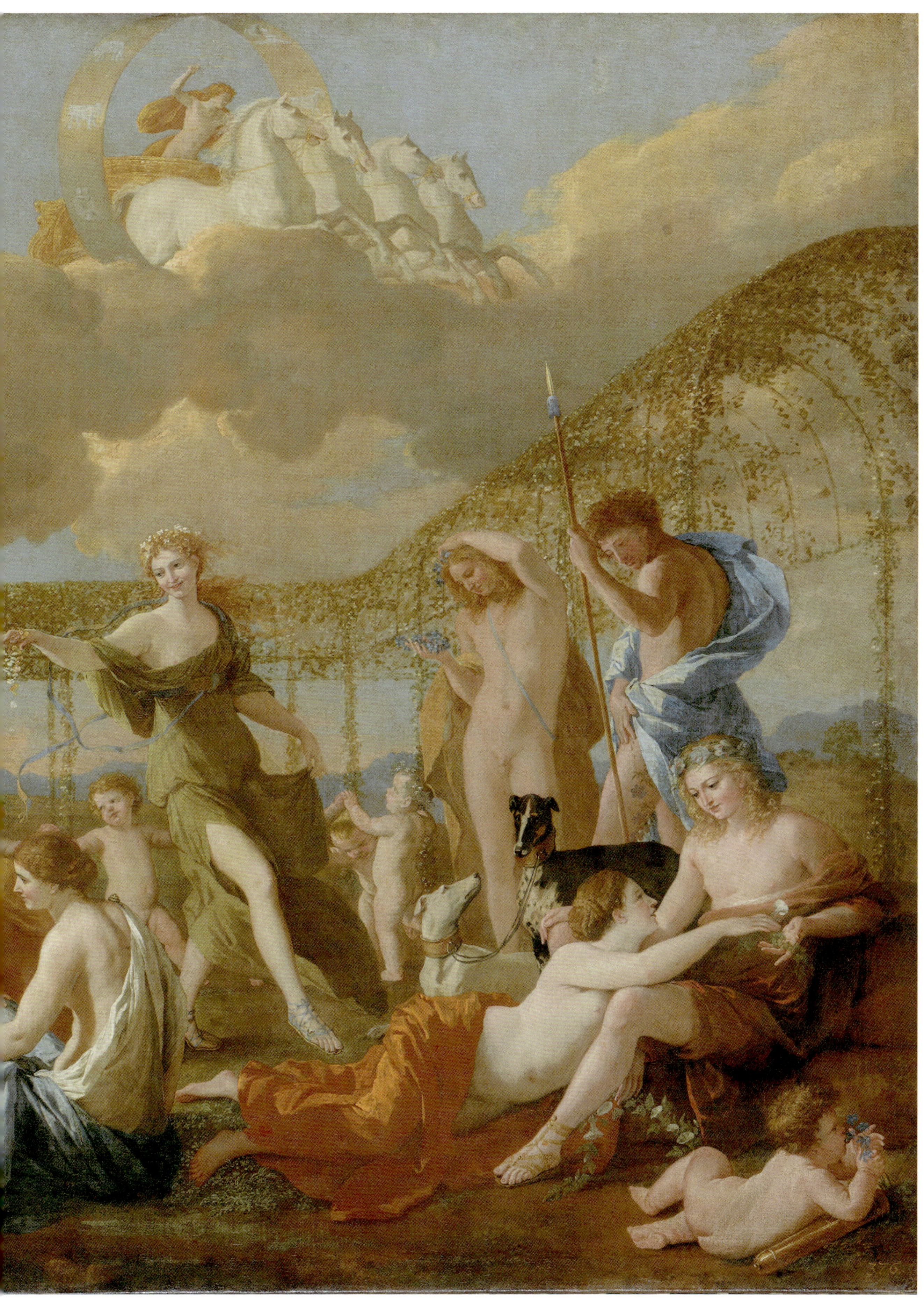

10

Nicolas Poussin

A RITUAL DANCE BEFORE A TEMPLE

ca. 1635–40
Pen and brown ink and brush and brown
wash over traces of black chalk on paper
20.8 × 31.4 cm (8⅛ × 12⅜ in.)
Windsor, Royal Collection/HM Queen
Elizabeth II, inv. RCIN 911910

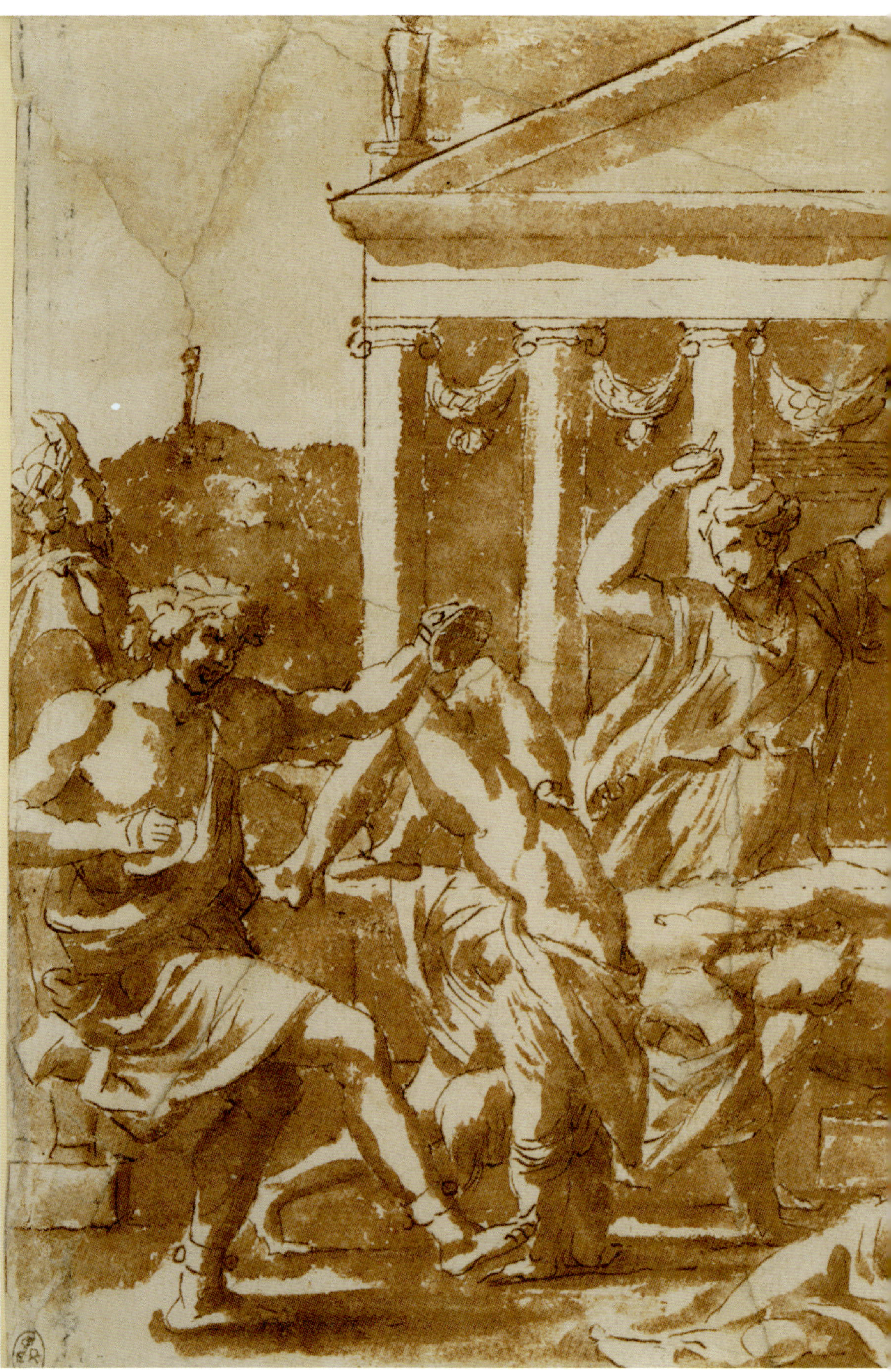

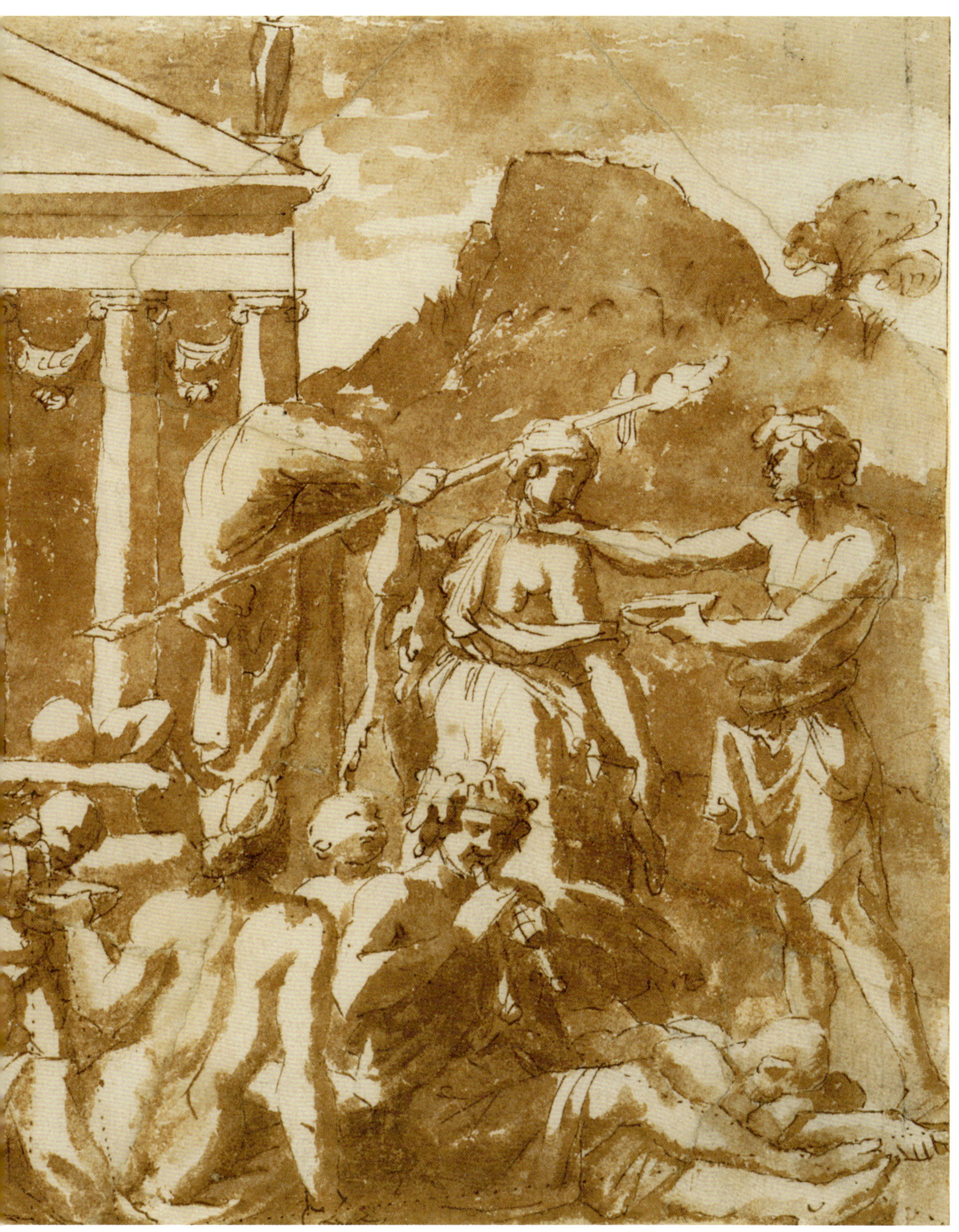

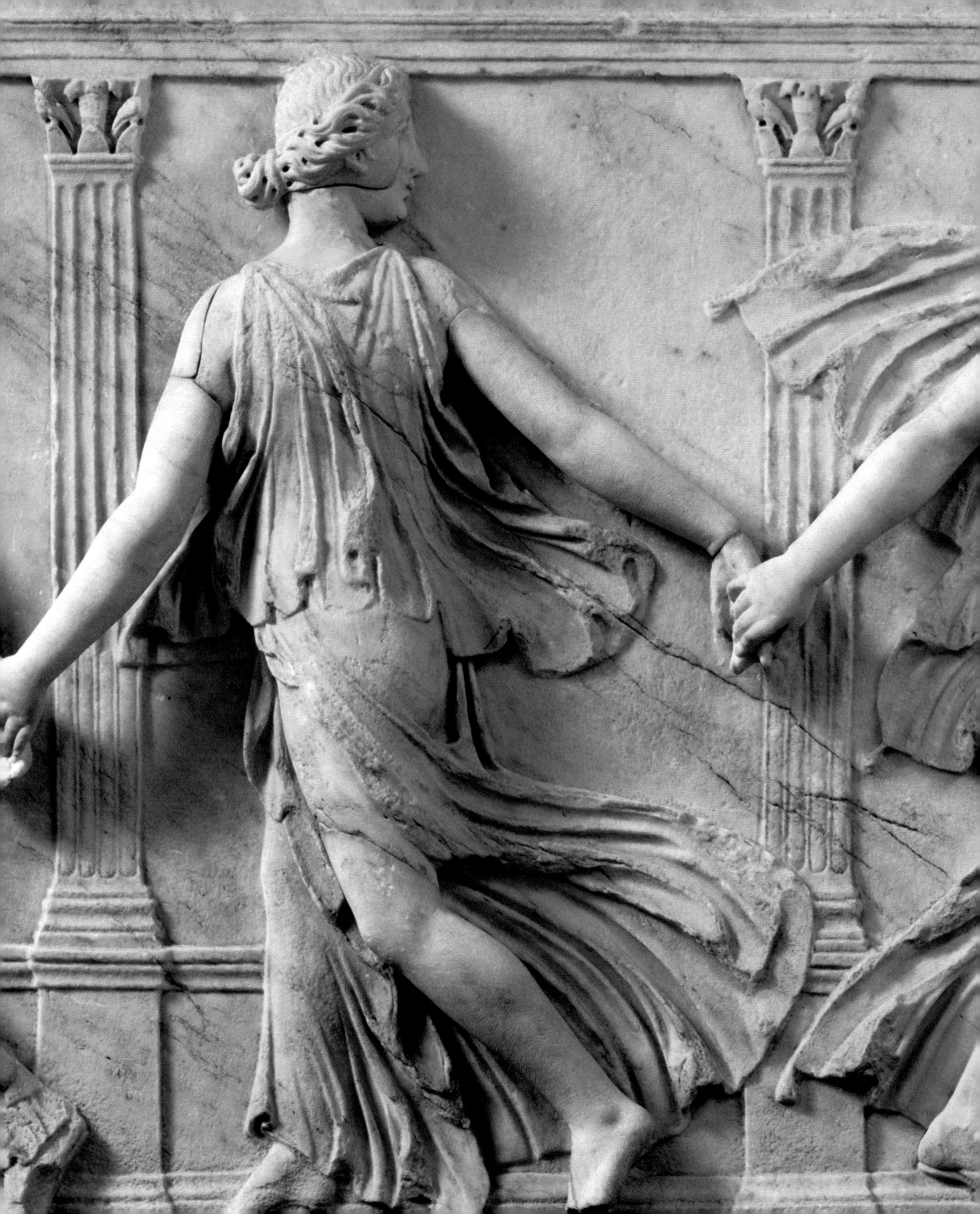

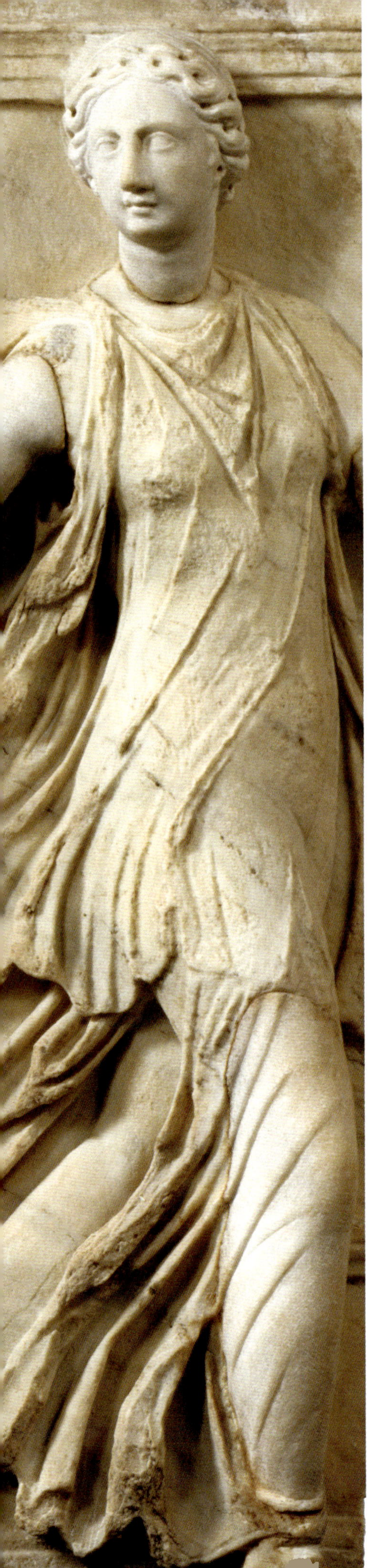

ANIMATING THE FRIEZE

FRANCESCA WHITLUM-COOPER

Five women emerge from cool marble (plate 11). Their hands linked, their heads and torsos turned in different directions, they dance their way across the stone surface. The vertical accents of their bodies are emphasized by the five Corinthian pilasters behind them, the measured division of space suggesting the measured rhythm of their steps. This second-century Roman relief has long been known as the Borghese Dancers. It was, in Poussin's day, one of the most celebrated antiquities to be seen in Rome: it belonged to Cardinal Scipione Borghese (1577–1633), the pope's nephew, who had amassed one of the city's most prestigious collections of antique sculpture, old masters, and modern painting.[1] This was the kind of antiquity one traveled to Rome to see.

Nicolas Poussin's earliest biographers tell us of his "unceasing desire to get to Rome."[2] They rehearse the history of his failed journeys, third time being the charm for an artist who reached Florence and subsequently Lyon on his first two attempts before having to turn back to Paris. Poussin knew that Rome would have a transformational effect on his career. This was the seat of the Renaissance, the closest one could get in seventeenth-century Europe to the ancient world. It was a city of innumerable artistic treasures and, thanks to the Catholic Church, a place rich in public commissions. But beyond his establishment as a fully independent artist, there is another sense in which Rome was transformational for Poussin. It was here that he began to experiment with form itself, making translations between painting and sculpture.

During his early years in Rome, with the sculptor Duquesnoy by his side, Poussin made a move toward three-dimensional art.[3] It was expected that painters would take an interest in sculpture, but Poussin went further than most of his contemporaries. "Applying [himself] intensely to the study of antiquities," he began, Bellori tells us, "to model and make sculpted reliefs."[4] According to Félibien, Poussin and Duquesnoy "together measured all the antique statues" in order to uncover the secrets of their perfect proportions.[5] Bellori even published engravings after the statue then known as the Belvedere Antinous[6] complete with Poussin and Duquesnoy's dimensions, including such detailed measurements as the distance between the Adam's apple and the clavicle, and the height of the statue's

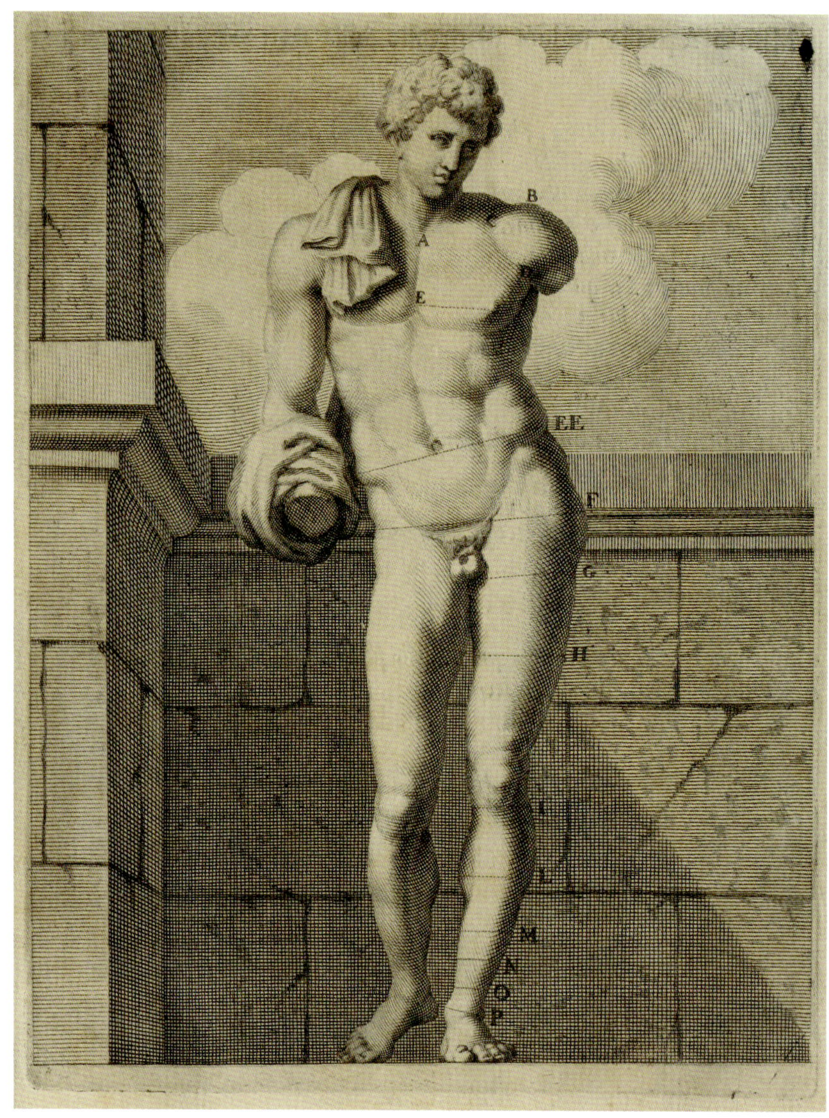

instep (fig. 9). Nor was this exploration of three-dimensional form limited to sculpture. In the case of *The Worship of Venus* (fig. 10), then at the Villa Ludovisi, Poussin copied Titian's chubby winged putti in paint as well as "model[ing] them in bas-relief out of clay."[7] Here, then, was an artist growing increasingly fluent in translating three-dimensional sculpture onto a two-dimensional surface, and vice versa.

Dance takes place in the round. It entails the movement of bodies through space, and its successful representation in paint or on paper requires an understanding of the mass and balance of forms and a sophisticated ability to render both buoyancy and weight. It is perhaps not surprising, then, that Poussin's self-directed investigation into the merits and challenges of rendering form in two and three dimensions led him in the first half of the 1630s to the repeated rendering of dance. This was not, I suggest, the mere copying of designs he saw around him—though many of the most prized antiquities of the day did indeed take on the challenge of depicting dance. Rather, this was Poussin seeking to emulate in paint the qualities he so prized in

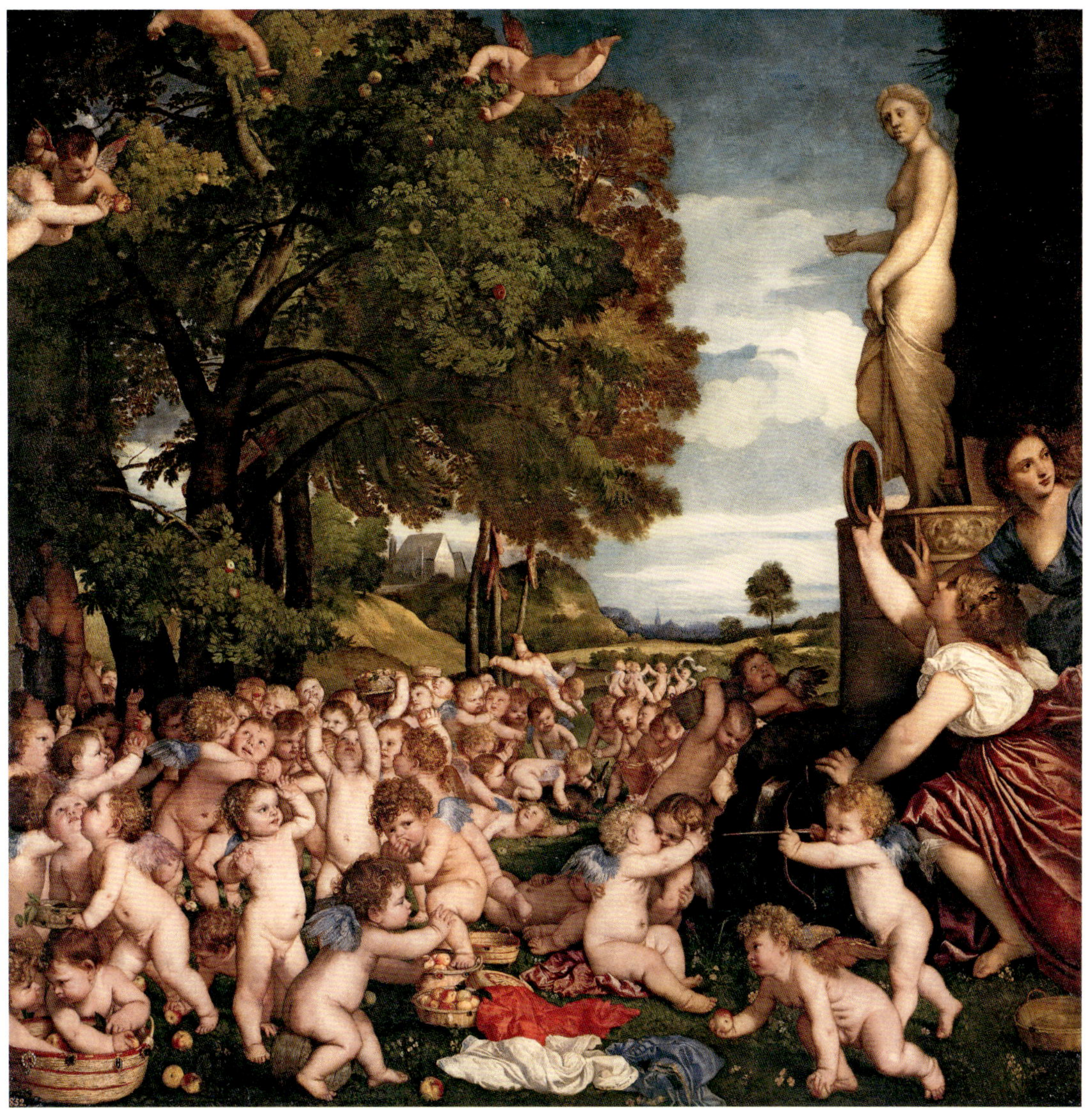

antique sculpture: volume and proportion, physicality and weight. Taking as its focus the Borghese Dancers and Poussin's fascination with the motif of chains of dancing figures, this essay argues not only that the study of antique objects informed Poussin's choice of subject but also that it directly influenced his forms and compositions as he sought to make painting more sculptural.

Félibien tells us that Poussin "often imitated with great skill and felicity all that is most pleasant in the bas-relief of dancers."[8] Of these, the Borghese Dancers was by far the most celebrated, with its chain of graceful women, all fluttering robes and out-stretched hands. Poussin's admiration for this relief is well documented: it was on his advice in 1640 that the brothers Paul Fréart de Chantelou (1609–1694) and Roland Fréart, sieur de Chambray (1606–1676), had plasters cast from the Dancers and its pendant for the French royal collections.[9] Unlike Roman sarcophagi—the other type of ancient relief with which Poussin was familiar, whose spaces could be crowded and even confusing—the Borghese Dancers is beautifully crisp and legible. With its composition "gracefully

FIGURE 10

Titian (Tiziano Vecellio) (Italian, ca. 1489/90–1576), *The Worship of Venus*, 1518–19. Oil on canvas, 172 × 175 cm (67.7 × 68.9 in.). Madrid, Museo Nacional del Prado, P000419

flowing in both directions," it has often been read as a group of women dancing eternally within a circle, and this, it seems, was what Poussin took from his study of it.[10]

Although chains of dancing putti had appeared in Poussin's work from the mid-1620s,[11] the idea of an eternal ring of dancing figures first occurs in a drawing in the Royal Collection, dated around 1628–30 (plate 12), where two men and two women skip around a wooded glade. Such rings of dancers recur throughout the first half of the 1630s, famously in *A Dance to the Music of Time* (plate 33), one of Poussin's most explicit homages to the Borghese Dancers.[12] In the Royal Collection sheet, Poussin's dancers hold hands, forming a chain of bodies, an effect emphasized by the leader of the group, who ducks beneath the raised arms of two fellow frolickers. Removed from the bas-relief sculpture of a frieze or vase, they are nevertheless caught in the same whirling continuum. The dance is watched over by a statue of Pan, god of woodlands, wildness, and shepherds. Onto its base one of the dancing women pours a libation. The careful scattering of objects in the foreground—theatrical masks, a jar of wine, a trumpet—underlines the nature of this hedonistic gathering. This is a revel, and much wine has been drunk: at far left, a seated woman fends off a satyr's lusty advances; their tussle has toppled an amphora, its spilled contents rendered by a free squiggle of ink.

It is not clear what the original purpose of this drawing was: for all the lightness of handling and subject matter, it has neither the spontaneity of a sketch nor the finish of a fully polished collector's sheet.[13] In ink and wash, Poussin conveys the spritely movement of his dancers. A small area of dark wash at the leading male dancer's hip is enough to evoke his torsion as he twists beneath the arms of the other dancers; the flexed toe of the dancing woman at left tells us that she has, for a fleeting moment, been air-bound, an effect emphasized by the paper left blank and spacious beneath her left heel. Although many elements convey a rapid, easy confidence with his medium—the statue's loosely articulated torso or the rough outlines of the satyr's feet—we need look only at the precise strokes that separate the ducking man's shoulder from his fellow dancer's elbow, or at the sliver of space between the former's raised toe and the latter's ankle, to see that Poussin has choreographed his figures with precision. Although, as we shall see, this sheet is obviously related to a painting, it is not strictly preparatory.[14] Rather, it can be seen to mark the full arrival of dance into Poussin's oeuvre, and the debt, in both subject matter and composition, to his antique sources.

In *A Bacchanalian Revel before a Term* (dated to about 1632–33), we meet the same group of dancers, fully articulated now in the bright solidity of paint (plate 13). The composition has been reversed, so that the woman with her back to us at the right of the drawing, a few dashes of ink indicating the sensual curve of her spine and shoulder blade, now faces us at the left of the painting. Her blue robe simultaneously slips down to reveal a breast and flies up behind her, as she squeezes grape juice into the bowl of an eager putto.[15] The grappling nymph and satyr now find themselves at the right of the composition, and an additional bacchante has been added, a metal vase raised in her hand as she rushes to fend off the amorous satyr. The new proximity of this unwanted embrace to the putto dipping his face into a giant jar of wine underlines the fact that these advances have been spurred on by both the vigor of the dancing and the strength of the drink.[16] There are other subtle changes to the composition: the proliferation of still-life objects in the foreground has been removed and, with the loss of the panpipes and the shepherd's crook, the garlanded statue may now be Priapus, god of fertility and gardens. The most significant difference between the drawing and the painting, however, is what might be termed Poussin's heightened impulse toward the antique.

In paint, the space the dancers occupy has been radically compressed, the arrangement of bodies tightened so that the composition unfolds in a single narrow plane. We move with the figures across the canvas as if watching a film in slow motion.[17] Where in the drawing our eye was led across the composition by overlapping limbs, in the painting the space is so tight that it is almost like watching one figure dance, turn, lunge, and tumble—an effect heightened by Poussin's careful distribution and repetition of color, from white to blue to ruddy flesh tones, before returning to blue and cream again. The precision of the choreography creates geometric slices of land, leaf, and sky between the dancers' active bodies. To an even greater extent than in the drawing, Poussin has plotted the careful intersections of limbs: the toe of the dancer in blue meets the buttock of the sleeping putto, in paint if not in space; the toe of the man in yellow reaches within a hair's breadth of the same dancer's pale leg. Perhaps the juxtaposition of the fallen nymph—with her pale gown and porcelain skin—and the equally pale statue can be read as an invitation to consider this dance as an antique object itself: the transposition of an ancient relief onto canvas, the rendering of a frieze in pictorial space.

Yet, for all its grace and classical formality, this painting is also *fun*. Poussin has taken true delight in both form and subject matter: we see "this allegedly most cerebral of masters in an unusually light-hearted vein."[18] How else but with a smile are we to view the dimpled buttocks of the putto who, having overindulged in wine, lies sleeping beneath the dancers' feet? Or the flushed face of the nymph squeezing grape juice, her hair and gown unraveling in her abandon? Such a joyful scene may well have been intended to appeal to the Roman art market. Since the early provenance of the *Bacchanalian Revel* remains unknown and no information about its commission has come to light, there is the possibility that Poussin painted it speculatively. Appealing, moderately sized pictures such as this must have played a part in building Poussin's reputation in Rome, ultimately leading patrons to commission far more ambitious dances from him just a few years later.[19] Some commentators have noted the seeming paradox between the abandon of the subject matter and the utter control of the composition,[20] but we would do well to remember the dancing figures of the antique objects Poussin had studied. If there is a "less abandoned, more controlled frenzy" in the painting than in the drawing,[21] the crispness of paint is surely intended to evoke the cold, hard contours of marble.

Having spent his early years in Rome making models out of clay, Poussin continued to think in three dimensions about his compositions, modeling wax figurines with which he choreographed them.[22] We get a sense for these figures in the *Bacchanal around a Herm* (plate 14), dated to about 1635, a scene of sacrifice and celebration. Here the round, expressionless heads of the figures and their jointed limbs readily

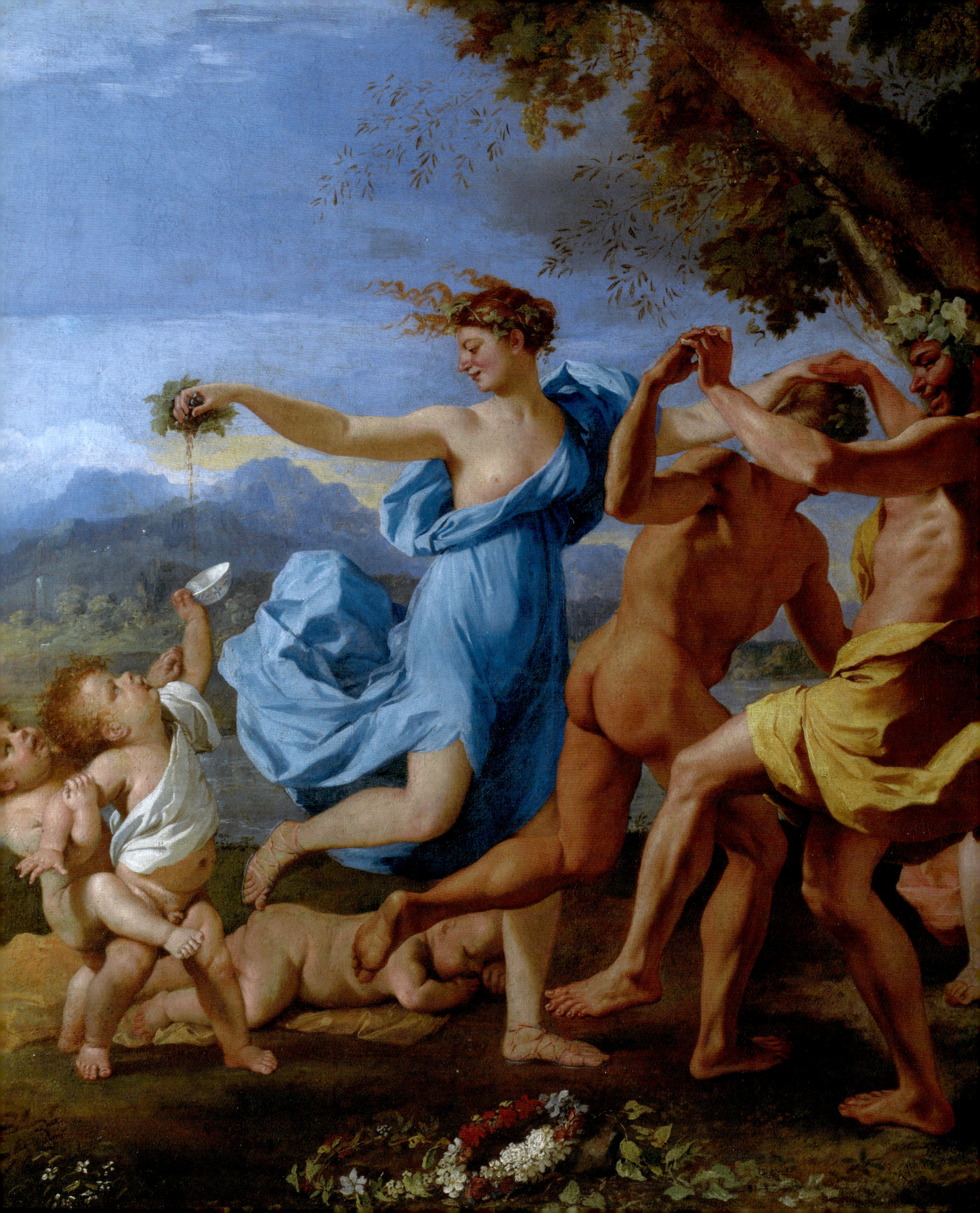

evoke both the simplicity and utility of Poussin's wax models. At left, a ring of dancers twirl in joyous abandon: the outstretched arms of the male figure and the outflung foot and raised arms of the female dancer next to him are certainly reminiscent, if not precise echoes, of the dancers in the *Bacchanalian Revel*. The broad strokes of wash do not preclude the inclusion of evocative details—at center, the garlanding of the statue is accompanied by music; at right, a frank sexual advance is warded off—but the emphasis of this working drawing is on the rhythmic fall of light and shadow, the articulation of space and volume. Poussin must have used such a set of figurines for his dancing pictures, as the dancers from the *Bacchanalian Revel* appear, rotated through 180 degrees, in the much more somber *Adoration of the Golden Calf* of 1633–34 (plate 15).

Poussin sets his scene beneath a glowering sky. We have left Arcadia, finding ourselves instead in an Old Testament drama. To the right of center, dressed in white, Aaron points at a golden statue. This is the new idol he has made for the Israelites, who, wandering in the desert, have grown fearful that their leader, Moses, will never return from his journey up Mount Sinai to meet God.[23] Aaron's gesturing hand is mirrored by the outstretched arm of a dancing woman. She and her companions have been reversed: the figure in blue who squeezed grapes into the putto's mouth at the left of the *Bacchanalian Revel* is now clad in white and green and scattering petals, her arm reaching invitingly to the right. The left foreground is given over to dancing, Poussin's redeployed Bacchic revelers reeling around the base of the statue. The right side of the painting depicts both physical and emotional movement, as the crowd surges upward and forward in states of wonder and excitement. It is only at the top left of the painting that we see Moses, descending from the mountain: angry at the fickle devotion of the Israelites, he smashes the tablets on which he has received the Ten Commandments.

The Adoration of the Golden Calf is the only religious painting by Poussin in which dancing occurs. Although it borrows its dancers from the *Bacchanalian Revel*, it is very different in both painterly and moral tone. The cloudy sky and steeply sloping rocks create a claustrophobic atmosphere and a dramatic tension quite unlike the carefree excitement generated by the bacchanalian frolics we have encountered so far. Where the *Bacchanalian Revel* is concerned with surface and light, its dancers whirling across the brightly lit foreground with little of the canvas given over to landscape, *The Adoration of the Golden Calf* concentrates on darkness and depth. In the former, dancing was an innocent pleasure; here it is idolatrous.[24] *The Golden Calf*'s coppery tone has been frequently remarked upon, yet more telling than his palette is the way that Poussin has used his colors to knit his composition together. The red, blue, and orange robes of the dancers are mirrored in the clothing of the crowd on the right. There is replication, too, in the poses of figures in the crowd: the outstretched arm of the woman in blue in the foreground at the right and the beseeching gestures of the figures on either side of her, none of whom have yet joined the dance, echo the poses of the dancers' limbs. Just as the figures in the *Bacchanalian Revel* might be read as one figure dancing, twirling, tumbling, the crowd at the right of *The Golden Calf* moves as one, surging upward, pulled with gravitational force into the statue's orbit.

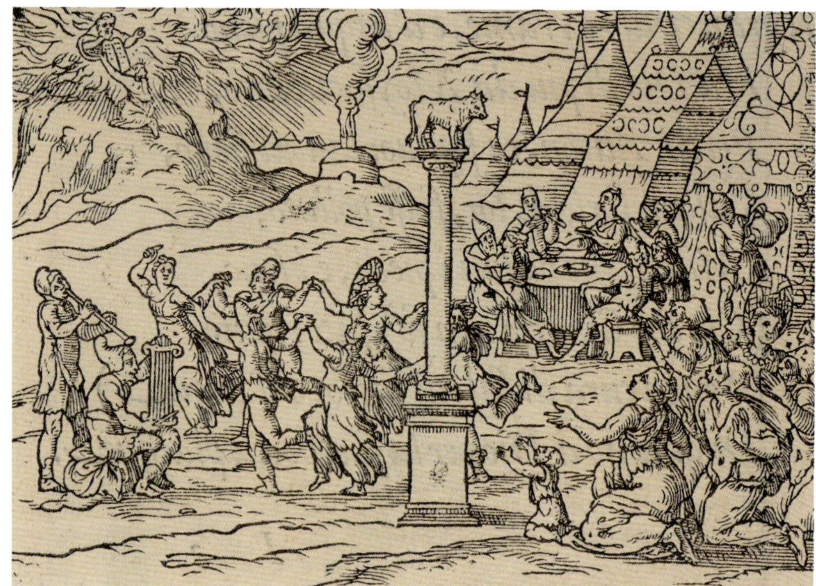

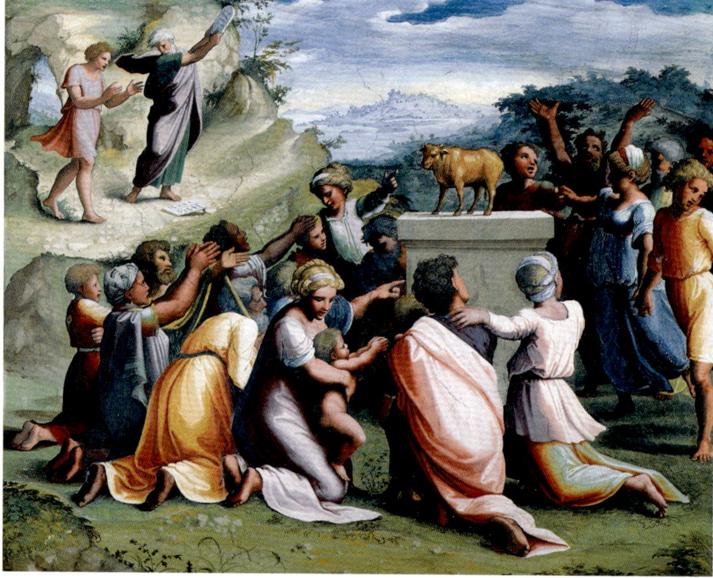

Several sources for Poussin's composition have been identified. One is an engraving of 1564 by Gabriele Simeoni, in which the Israelites dance in a circle beside (if not around) the statue (fig. 11). Another is a design by Raphael, executed in fresco by his studio in the loggias of Leo X in the Vatican, its compositional arrangement similar to that of Poussin's painting, with Moses and Joshua descending from Mount Sinai at top left and the Israelites kneeling around the golden calf on its pedestal (fig. 12). Raphael, the great Renaissance artist who had also sought to understand and return to the principles of antiquity, was "a constant in all Poussin's creations."[25] Yet in Raphael's composition, the figures are larger and far fewer than in Poussin's canvas, and the distance between the crowd and the figures of Moses and his companion is compressed: Moses feels less distant, and although there are a few hands raised in sacrilegious prayer, the Israelites can hardly be described as ecstatic. Far closer to the Raphael, in fact, is Poussin's first treatment of the Golden Calf episode, probably painted in the late 1620s and known today only through fragments and a seventeenth-century copy (fig. 13).[26] Even if the San Francisco copy is a pastiche,[27] comparison between it and the London picture vividly illustrates the far greater ambition and complexity of the latter.

Yet, what Poussin might have brought to this composition from his study of antiquity has been relatively little discussed. As in the *Bacchanalian Revel* and the Royal Collection drawing, the interlinked arms certainly allude to the Borghese Dancers—the reference is reinforced here by the placement of the figures in front of the smooth, pale plinth, as if it is the stone from which they have been carved. That Poussin has extended his chain of dancing figures from the single plane of the *Bacchanalian Revel* to a circular, encompassing movement around the statue likewise recalls such highly regarded representations of Bacchic dancing as the Borghese Vase (plate 23), on which the action, by necessity, unfurls in a continuous round. It has been said that Poussin's figures here "have that frozen appearance which is often to be seen in marble figures of dancers,"[28] a turn of phrase that underlines a crucial point:

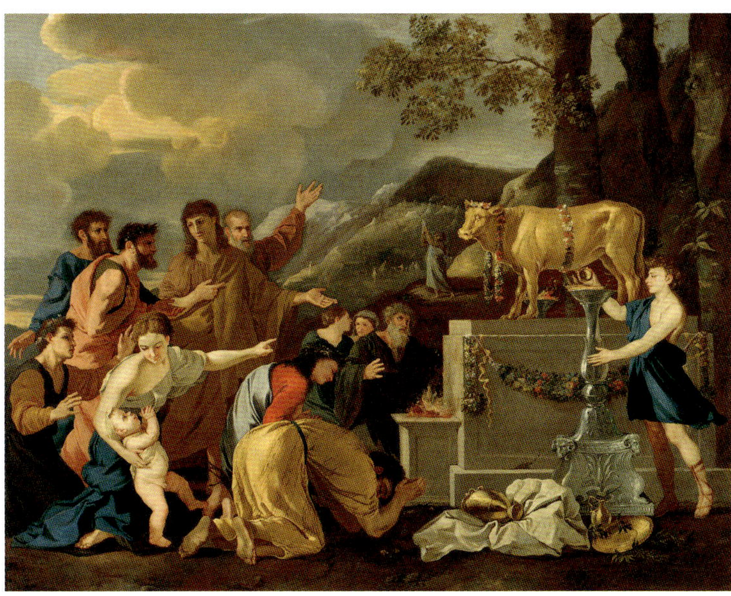

Poussin has succeeded in arresting movement, in translating the qualities of sculpture to paint. It is one of the painting's most remarked-upon idiosyncrasies that this golden calf is, in fact, a mature bull. This was no accident: Poussin was alluding to the ancient Egyptian bull-god Apis, whom some seventeenth-century syncretists (thinkers who sought to reconcile different ancient religions) connected with Bacchus.[29] *The Adoration of the Golden Calf* was one of two pictures commissioned from Poussin by Amedeo dal Pozzo (1579–1644), cousin of the antiquarian Cassiano, the painter's great Roman supporter. As Poussin does not seem to have been overly constrained in his choice of subjects or manner of treating them, his displays of erudition—such as his allusions to antiquities and the depiction of this mature bull—appear to have been for the pleasure of his learned patron.[30]

As we have seen, Poussin returned repeatedly to the motif of a chain of dancers in the first half of the 1630s. His explorations of this theme coincided not only with the development of his classical style—his passion for the antique, his investigations into the ideas of surface and depth and painting in a more sculptural manner—but also with his growing reputation, in Rome and beyond. These two strands reached their peak in the mid-1630s in his most ambitious dancing picture, the canvas that most fully articulates his fascination with bringing antique friezes to life: *Hymenaeus Disguised as a Woman during an Offering to Priapus* (plate 16).

Almost two dozen joyful women fill this vast canvas. Pillars and swags and wreaths of greenery adorned with flowers and fruit form a lavish backdrop against which they celebrate and decorate the statue that sits squarely in the center of the composition. This is Priapus, god of fertility and gardens: as in the *Bacchanalian Revel*, he is draped with crossed bands of floral garlands, but here there can be no mistaking his identity, thanks to the prominent phallus, revealed during recent cleaning. On the left, two musicians accompany the festivities on lyre and aulos. Toward the center, their companions, occupied with flowers and garlands—offerings to the god—are also decorated for the

FIGURE 13
Andrea di Lione (Italian, 1610–1685), after Nicolas Poussin, *The Adoration of the Golden Calf*, seventeenth century. Oil on canvas, 96.5 × 132.1 cm (38 × 52 in.). San Francisco, Fine Arts Museums of San Francisco, Gift of the Samuel H. Kress Foundation, inv. 61.44.30

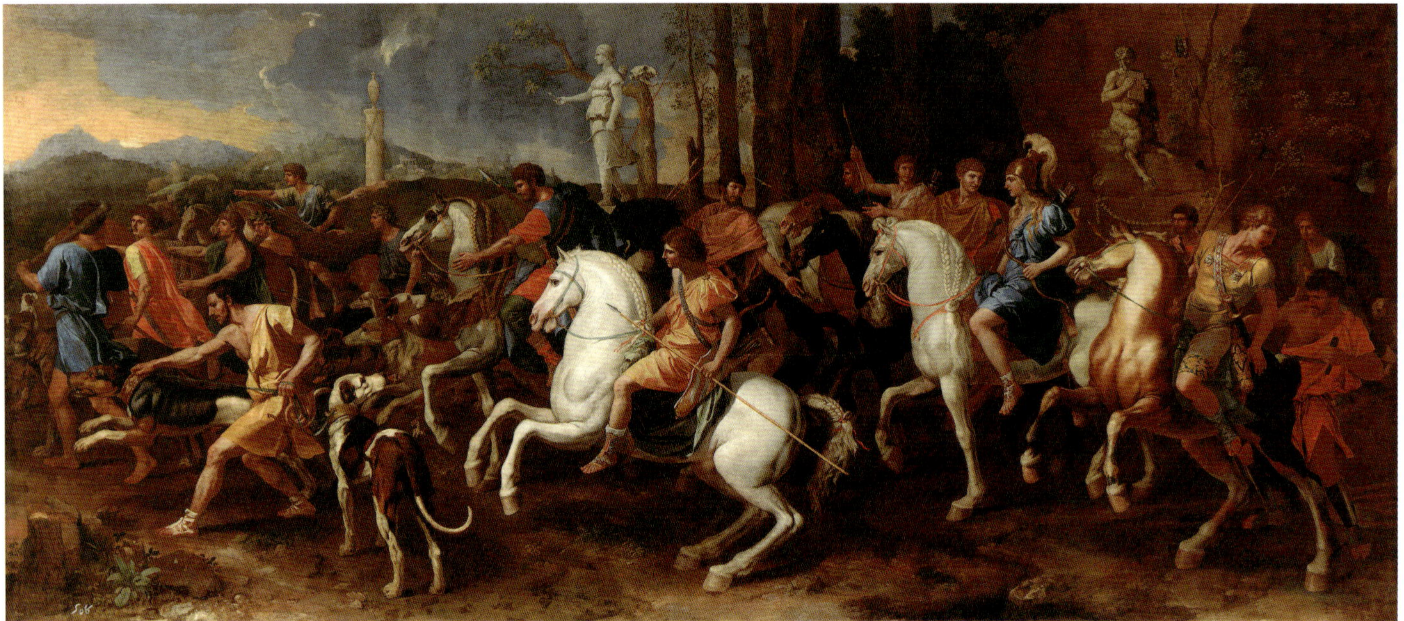

occasion with ribbons and flowers in their hair. On the right, half a dozen women dance, interlaced in a familiar kind of dancing chain. At the far right of the composition, we meet the painting's hero and only male participant: a young Athenian, Hymenaeus (later known as Hymen, god of marriage). He, too, wears flowing robes, though his chest is flatter than those of his companions, and he is the only figure wearing sandals, perhaps to disguise his male feet,[31] perhaps as the tell revealing him as an interloper who has not thought to remove his shoes on sacred ground. According to the story, which Poussin appears to have taken from Vincenzo Cartari's *Le imagini de i dei de gli antichi* (1580), a guide to classical mythology much consulted by seventeenth-century painters, Hymenaeus was so in love that he dressed as a woman in order to gaze upon his beloved, who is among the worshippers at this secret rite.[32]

Despite its breathtaking size and ambition—the *Hymenaeus* is almost four meters wide—its history has made it one of Poussin's less-known works. It was once errone- ously believed to have been in the collection of Cassiano dal Pozzo,[33] but we can now be confident that the picture was commissioned from Poussin between 1634 and 1638 for Philip IV's vast, ruinously expensive pleasure palace in Madrid: the Buen Retiro.[34] The Buen Retiro project, for which some eight hundred paintings were ultimately sourced, was masterminded by Gaspar de Guzmán, conde-duque de Olivares (1587– 1645), Philip IV's powerful first minister.[35] For a series of thirty-four scenes of Roman myth and history, Poussin painted the *Hymenaeus* and *The Hunt of Meleager* (fig. 14):[36] they were among only six paintings on this tremendous scale, probably intended to hang in long galleries overlooking the Buen Retiro's elaborate gardens.[37] Although the *Meleager* remained in Spain, the *Hymenaeus*, last documented in Spanish royal col- lections in 1811, appeared in British collections from 1896.[38] At some point, it acquired copious amounts of overpaint—"two-thirds," according to the great Poussin special- ist Jacques Thuillier, who saw it in 1981[39]—including on the key area of the statue.

A painting depicting offerings to Priapus thus became known as a dedication to Pan and even to Hymen himself for almost a century.[40] In addition to concealing its subject, the overpaint obscured the painting's quality, and it was not until its spectacular cleaning in the 2000s that the picture finally gained widespread scholarly acceptance.[41]

Poussin embraced the challenge of filling a canvas of unusual format, using its dimensions to create his most emphatically friezelike composition. Again, the main action takes place in a shallow plane, accentuated here by the dense greenery of the backdrop. Again, the rhythmic distribution of linked arms, fluttering robes, and turned heads is explicitly indebted to that of the Borghese Dancers. Yet, free from the constraints of working in three dimensions, Poussin was able to imbue each dancing figure with emphatic movement. Every dancer in the right-hand group has at least one foot raised off the ground; several rest on just the ball of a foot. In paint, Poussin did not need to worry about how to support their weight, as a sculptor would in marble. There are clear connections, too, with the Borghese Sacrifice (fig. 15), another Roman relief, pendant to the Dancers and much admired by Poussin and his contemporaries. Commonly known in the seventeenth century as the Borghese Wedding, it, too, hung at the Villa Borghese and offered a logical point of departure for Poussin's exploration of nuptial themes.[42] From the pillars in the background that divide and structure the space, to the symmetrical placement of the two figures flanking the candelabrum and the garlands they have brought as offerings, the sculpted composition finds clear echoes in the *Hymenaeus*.

Poussin's inspirations were not solely classical. An avid collector of prints,[43] he certainly seems to have consulted a celebrated engraving by the Master of the Die after Giulio Romano (fig. 16) when planning his *Hymenaeus*. Not only do we find in this print the perfectly central positioning of the herm of Priapus, but also the same baskets of fruit and flowers in the foreground and the distinctive floral swags arcing above the frieze of revelers. The gracefully turned heads and raised feet of some of Poussin's dancers seem to echo—if not precisely imitate—the twisted dancer with flowing robes to the left of the Master of the Die's Priapus.[44]

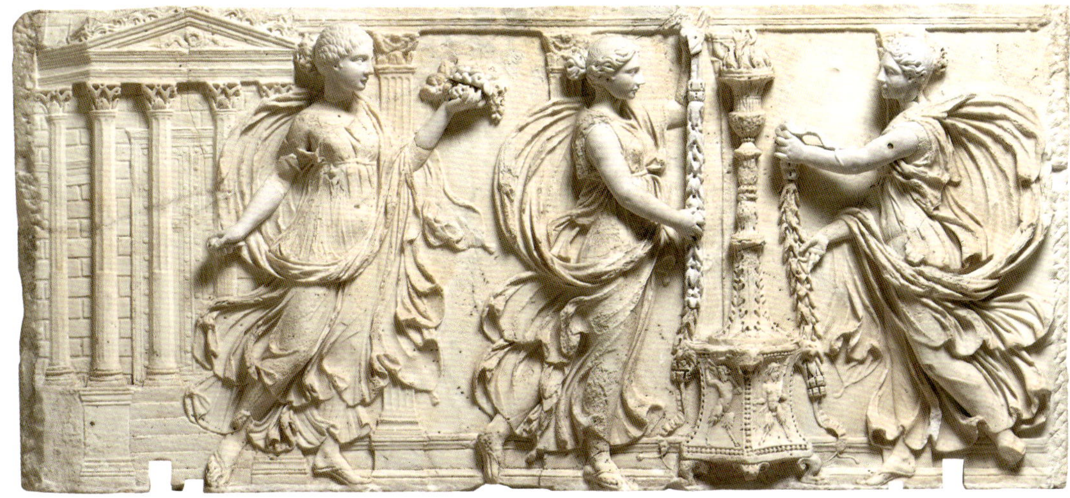

FIGURE 15
Relief known as the Borghese Sacrifice, Roman, second century CE. Marble, 68 × 150 × 14 cm (26¾ × 59 × 5½ in.). Paris, Musée du Louvre, Département des Antiquités Grecques, Étrusques et Romaines, inv. MR 822

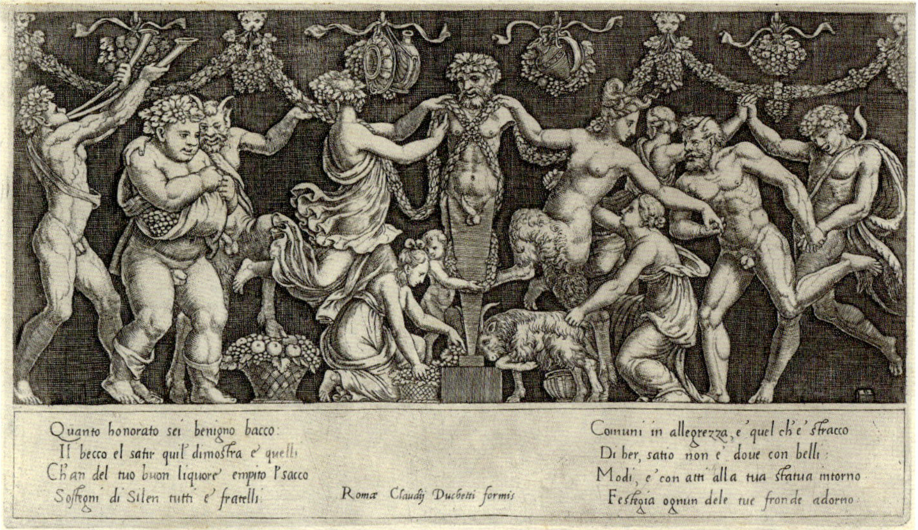

Although the pendant *Hunt of Meleager* is not strictly a picture of dancing, it presents a similarly complex choreography, as hounds, horses, and huntsmen charge across the canvas (see fig. 14). Dispensing with the friezelike frontal plane he used in the *Hymenaeus*, Poussin presents his figures here in profile, as they might have been shown in an antique bas-relief, adding sculptures in the background to emphasize this effect. Again, he has the advantage in paint, since it allows him far greater depth than that permitted by relief sculpture.[45] Poussin took his story from Ovid's *Metamorphoses*.[46] When Diana, goddess of the hunt, sent a giant boar to terrorize his father's kingdom, the young prince Meleager formed a group to track the beast down. The hunters included the beautiful Atalanta—Meleager's beloved, a virgin who refused to marry—seen here at right riding a white horse and wearing a plumed helmet, her long blonde tresses hanging down over her blue dress. Meleager is probably the figure in gold, astride the pale brown horse next to Atalanta's.[47] When *The Hunt of Meleager* and *Hymenaeus Disguised as a Woman* were last seen together in the Spanish royal collections over two hundred years ago, it would have been clear to those familiar with ancient poetry and mythology that both dealt with themes of love.

This chapter has explored how, in the early 1630s, Poussin used his knowledge of antique objects to imbue his depictions of dance with sculptural qualities; how a relief like the Borghese Dancers inspired both subject matter and compositions. Following the motif of dancers with clasped hands, it has shown not only how Poussin's compositions grew in complexity but also how their emulation of antique friezes became increasingly explicit. Beginning with the *Bacchanalian Revel before a Term*—a painting that may well have been produced for the open market—it closes with one of the most substantial commissions (in terms of sheer square footage of canvas) of Poussin's career. In this period, he looked back to antiquity but also forward, asking how he might capture in perpetuity the heat and movement of bodies. His quest was to bring to life the antique friezes he saw around him and to arrest movement in such a way that he, too, might achieve a kind of eternity. This was the challenge that Poussin took with him into one of the most significant commissions of his career: his dances for Richelieu.

NOTES

I am extremely grateful to Nicholas Penny and Letizia Treves for their close readings and thoughtful comments on an early draft of this text, and to Larry Keith for discussing condition and color change with me.

1   Displayed from at least 1617 above a doorway in the Villa Borghese, it is not clear when the Borghese Dancers was first excavated. Its citation by Raphael and his studio in the Vatican loggias (1518–19) and possibly by Mantegna in his *Parnassus* (1495–97) suggests that it was well known in Rome long before its display at the villa. Restorations to the heads and some legs were carried out by Francesco Fondi in 1617 and, in a more minor way, by Luigi Salimei in 1778. See Haskell, Penny et al. 2021, no. 29.

2   Bellori 1672, 409.

3   See Emily A. Beeny's essay "Invitation to the Dance: Poussin in Rome" in this volume.

4   Bellori 1672, 411–12.

5   Félibien 1725, 4:12. See also Wittkower 1963, 41–50.

6   This is now known as *Hermes* and is still in the Vatican.

7   Bellori 1672, 412. See also Colantuono 1989, 208–9.

8   Félibien 1725, 4:147.

9   Haskell, Penny et al. 2021, no. 29.

10   See Haskell, Penny et al. 2021, no. 29; Bober and Rubenstein 1986, 95.

11   Putti dancing with linked hands can be found decorating the vase at left of one of Poussin's *Bacchanals of Putti* (about 1626, Palazzo Barberini, Rome), as well as around the figure of Flora in the Louvre *Triumph of Venus* (ca. 1627, fig. 6), the *Study for the Realm of Flora* (ca. 1627, plate 7), and *The Realm of Flora* (ca. 1630–31, plate 9).

12   The Borghese Dancers has previously been called *The Hours* or *The Dancing Hours*. See Haskell, Penny et al. 2021, no. 29; and Beresford 1995, 44–47. For more on Poussin's dancing rings, see Beeny 2019b.

13   London et al. 1995–96, no. 25, 74–77.

14   London et al. 1995–96, no. 25, 76.

15   A preparatory sketch for these putti survives in Stockholm; see Rosenberg and Prat 1994, 1: no. 44, 82.

16   Poussin first made use of this motif in a *Bacchanal of Putti* of about 1626 (Palazzo Barberini, Rome). See Wine 2001, 291.

17   Paris 1994–95, no. 47, 210.

18   Verdi 2019, 29.

19   See my essay "Dances for Richelieu" in this volume.

20   Graham-Dixon 2003, 12.

21   Wine 2001, 291.

22   See Beeny's essay "Invitation to the Dance" in this volume, 8.

23   Exodus 32:1–19.

24   See Beeny 2019b, 32.

25   Oberhuber 1996, 67. For more on Poussin and Raphael, see Kurita 1999 and Beeny 2020.

26   The fragment, *Two Female Heads*, is in a private collection and has been on loan to the Dulwich Picture Gallery, London, for several years. The full composition is also known through a print by Jean-Baptiste de Poilly (1669–1728); see Wine 2001, 314; Rosenberg and Stewart 1987, 90–93; and Di Penta 2016, 127.

27   Paris, New York, and Chicago 1982, 371.

28   Blunt 1999, 184.

29   Dempsey 1963, 117–18.

30   Poussin contributed two paintings to the Palazzo dal Pozzo in Turin, *The Adoration of the Golden Calf* and *The Crossing of the Red Sea* (ca. 1633–34, National Gallery of Victoria, Melbourne). The two formed part of a cycle of Mosaic subjects, alongside Pietro da Cortona's *The Gathering of Manna* and Giovanni Francesco Romanelli's *The Construction of the Tabernacle* (both ca. 1635, Palazzo della Provincia, Turin). Making the point that Cortona's and Romanelli's canvases share a theme (that of religious offerings), while Poussin's do not, Wine argues that Poussin must have had some degree of freedom in the commission; Wine 2001, 319–20.

31   Rosenberg 2009, 58.

32   Cartari 1571, 193–95 and 198–200. On the subject and Poussin's sources for it, see Friedlaender 1961.

33   See Blunt 1966, nos. 163 and 176.

34   Úbeda 2005, 169–89; and Rosenberg 2009, 45–48.

35   Although Olivares oversaw the project, the commissions themselves likely came via Manuel de Moura y Corte-Real, 2nd Marquis of Castel Rodrigo (1590–1651), who was ambassador to the Holy See between 1632 and 1641, and Manuel Fonseca y Zúñiga, 6th Count of Monterrey (1588–1653), who was viceroy of Naples between 1631 and 1637. See Úbeda 2005, 171–72; and Rosenberg 2009, 53–55.

36   Poussin was the only artist to produce work for two of the palace's most significant groups of commissions. As well as the Roman pictures (others of which were provided by Domenichino [1581–1641], Jusepe di Ribera [1591–1652], Giovanni Lanfranco [1582–1647], and Massimo Stanzione [ca. 1585–1656]), he painted the *Landscape with Saint Paul the Hermit* (Museo Nacional del Prado, Madrid) for a series of twenty-five landscapes with anchorite saints, to which his friend Claude Lorrain (1604/5–1682) and his brother-in-law and only pupil, Gaspard Dughet (1615–1675), also contributed.

37   The others are *Vespasian's Triumphal Entry into Rome* and *Constantine's Triumphal Entry into Rome* by Domenico Gargiulo (1609–1675) and Viviano Codazzi (1604–1670), and *Sacrifice for a Roman Emperor* and *Roman Naumachia* by Lanfranco (all Museo Nacional del Prado, Madrid).

38   See Rosenberg 2009, 46–47. It seems likely that the painting was removed from Spain at some point during the Napoleonic Wars (1803–15), when many Spanish paintings made their way into British collections.

39   Thuillier 1994a, no. 116, 254–55.

40   See, for example, Lord Henry Beaumont sale, London, Foster, March 25, 1896, lot 80, "A Sacrifice to Pan"; and Paris 1953–54, no. 44, 90, "L'Offrande à Hymen ou la Danse des Nymphes."

41   On the conservation treatment of this picture, see Ravaud 2009.

42   See Haskell, Penny et al. 2021, under no. 29.

43   Delisle 1858.

44   Two other graphic sources cited in relation to the *Hymenaeus* are an illustration by G. B. Marliani from the *Topographia antiquae urbis Romae* (1544) and an engraving by Léon Davent after Giulio Romano titled *The Dance* (1540–56). See Rosenberg 2009, 59–61.

45   Poussin's composition here is closer to the other large-format pictures commissioned for this part of the Buen Retiro (see note 37 above), three of which depicted large crowds with multiple figures on horseback.

46   Ovid, *Metamorphoses* 8:260–450.

47   Melbourne 2014, 200.

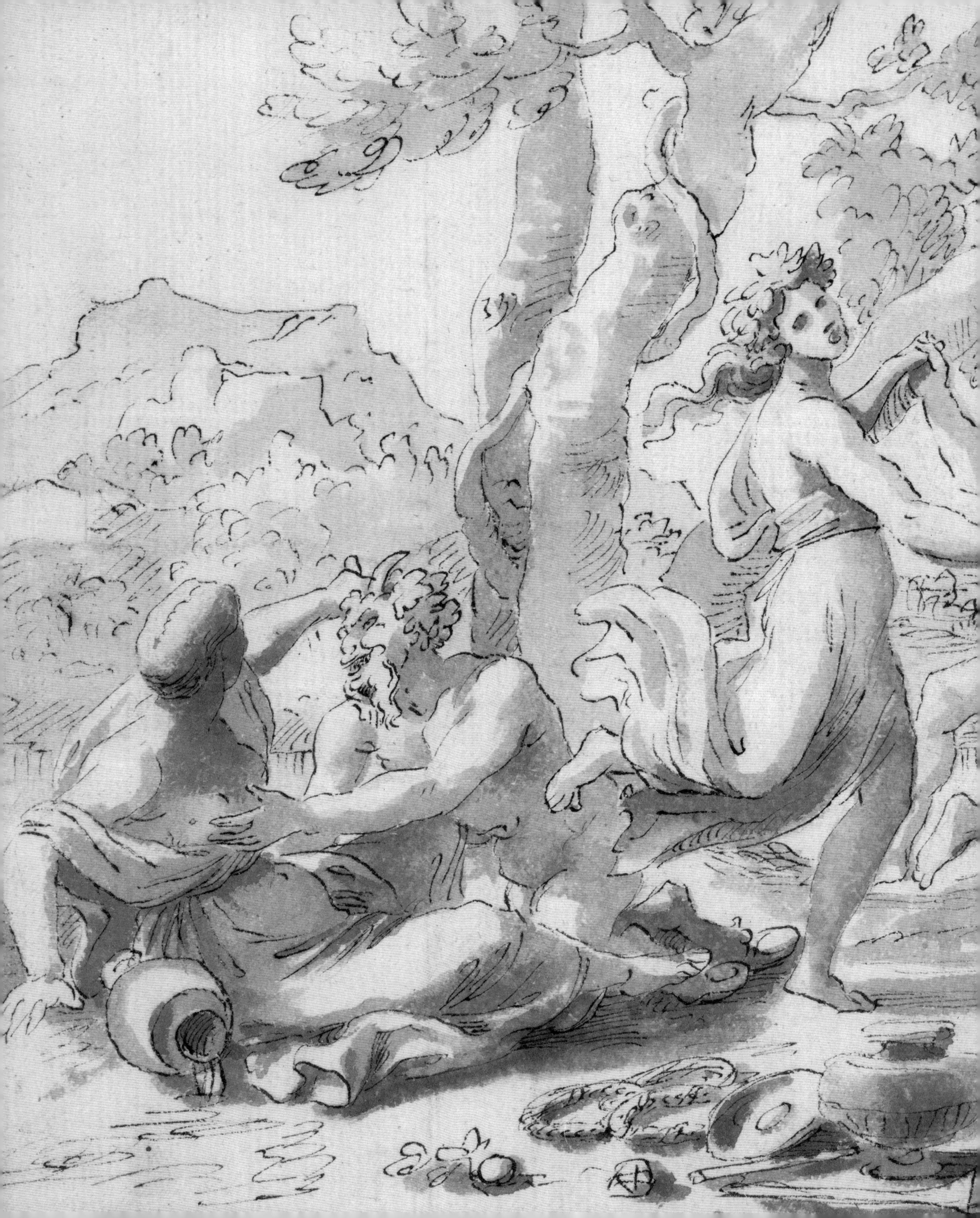

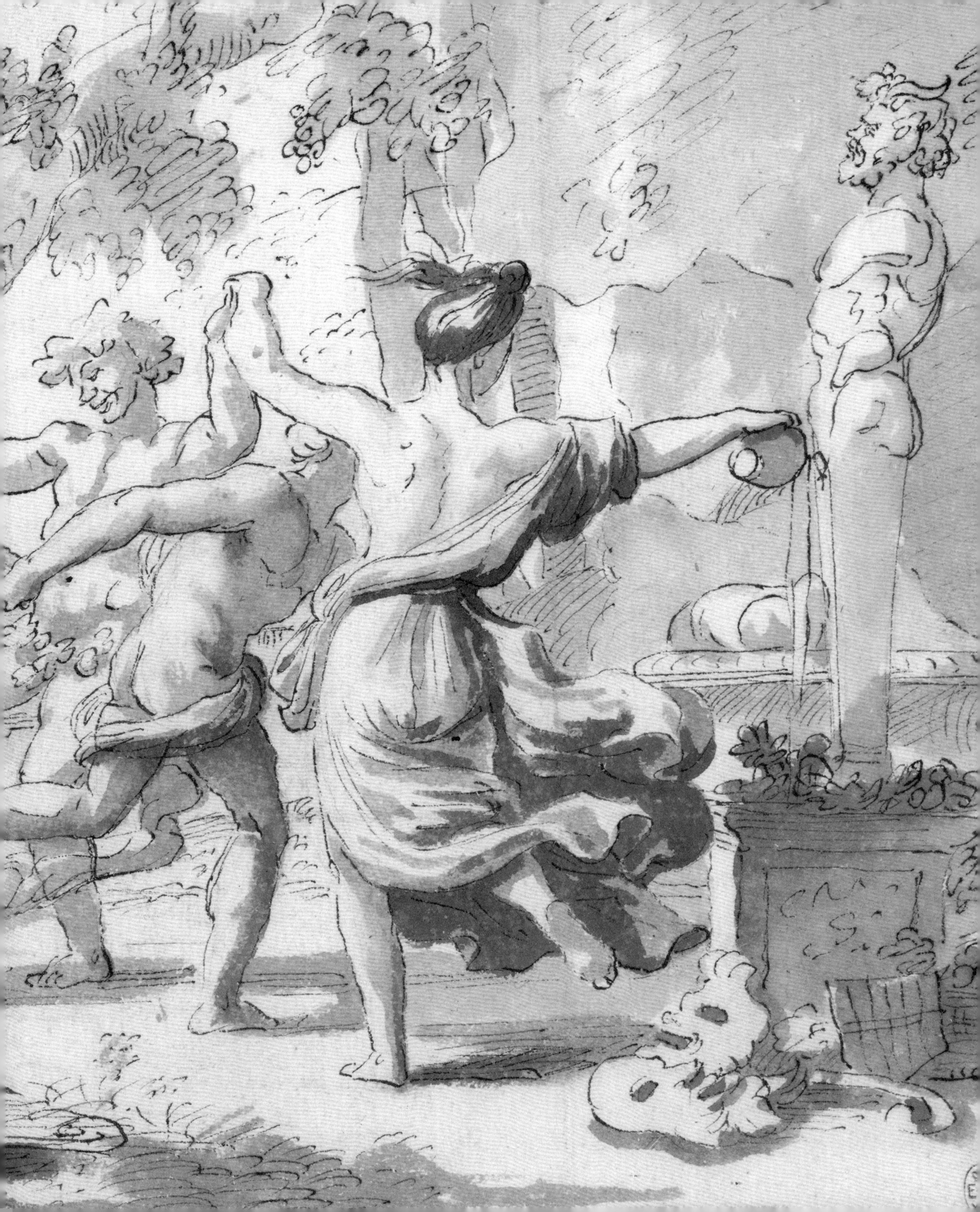

11

Roman

RELIEF OF FIVE DANCERS BEFORE A PORTICO, KNOWN AS THE BORGHESE DANCERS

Second century CE

Marble

72 × 187 × 14 cm (28¼ × 73⅝ × 5½ in.)

Paris, Musée du Louvre, Département des Antiquités Grecques, Étrusques et Romaines, inv. MA 1612

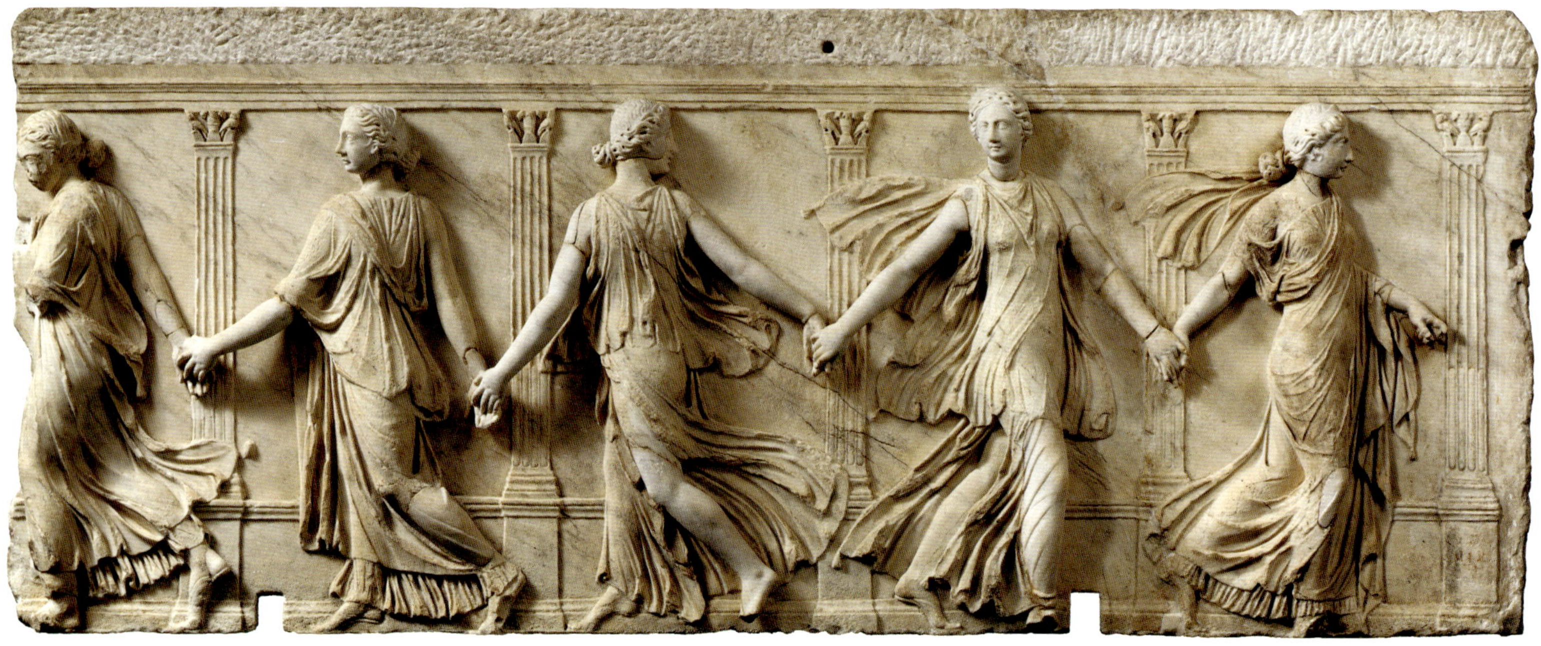

Nicolas Poussin

DANCE BEFORE A HERM OF PAN

ca. 1628–30
Pen and brown ink and brush and brown
wash over traces of graphite on paper
20.6 × 32.7 cm (8⅛ × 12⅞ in.)
Windsor, Royal Collection/HM Queen
Elizabeth II, inv. RCIN 911979

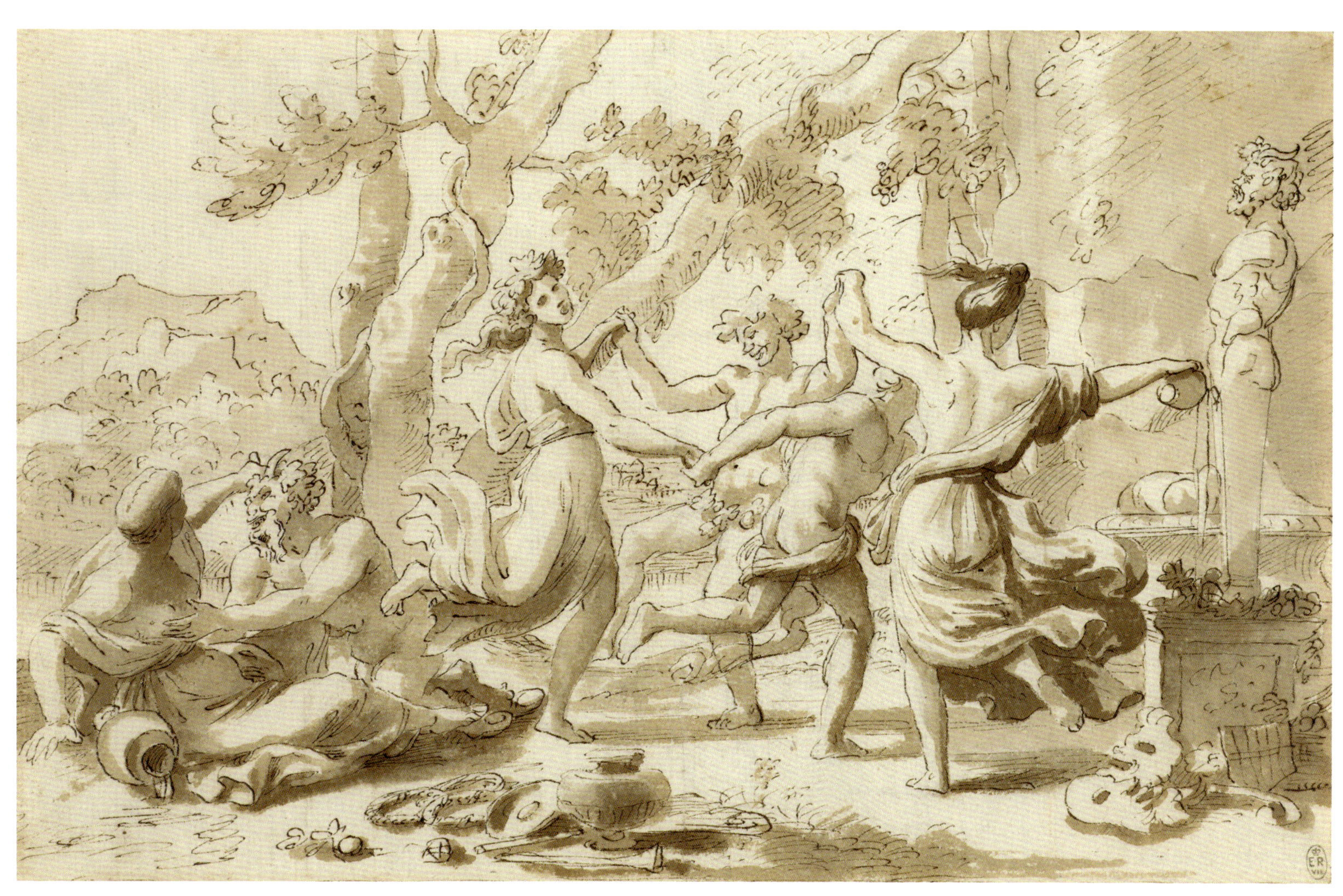

Nicolas Poussin

A BACCHANALIAN REVEL BEFORE A TERM

ca. 1632–33
Oil on canvas
98 × 142.8 cm (38⅝ × 56¼ in.)
London, National Gallery, Bought, 1826,
inv. NG62

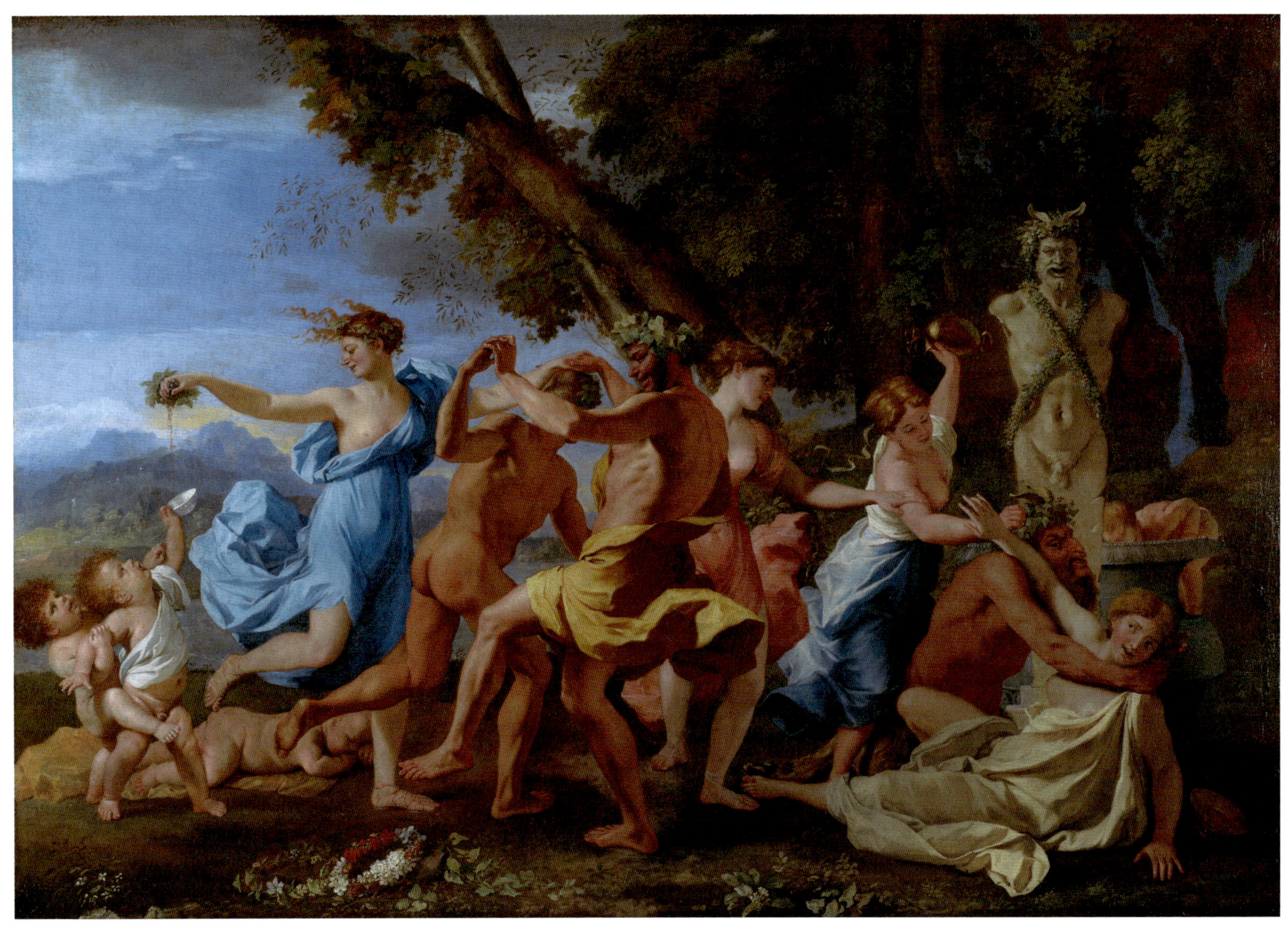

14

Nicolas Poussin
BACCHANAL
AROUND A HERM

ca. 1635–36
Brush and brown wash over black chalk
on paper
18.1 × 25.9 cm (7⅛ × 10¼ in.)
Paris, Musée du Louvre, Département
des Arts Graphiques, inv. MI 1103

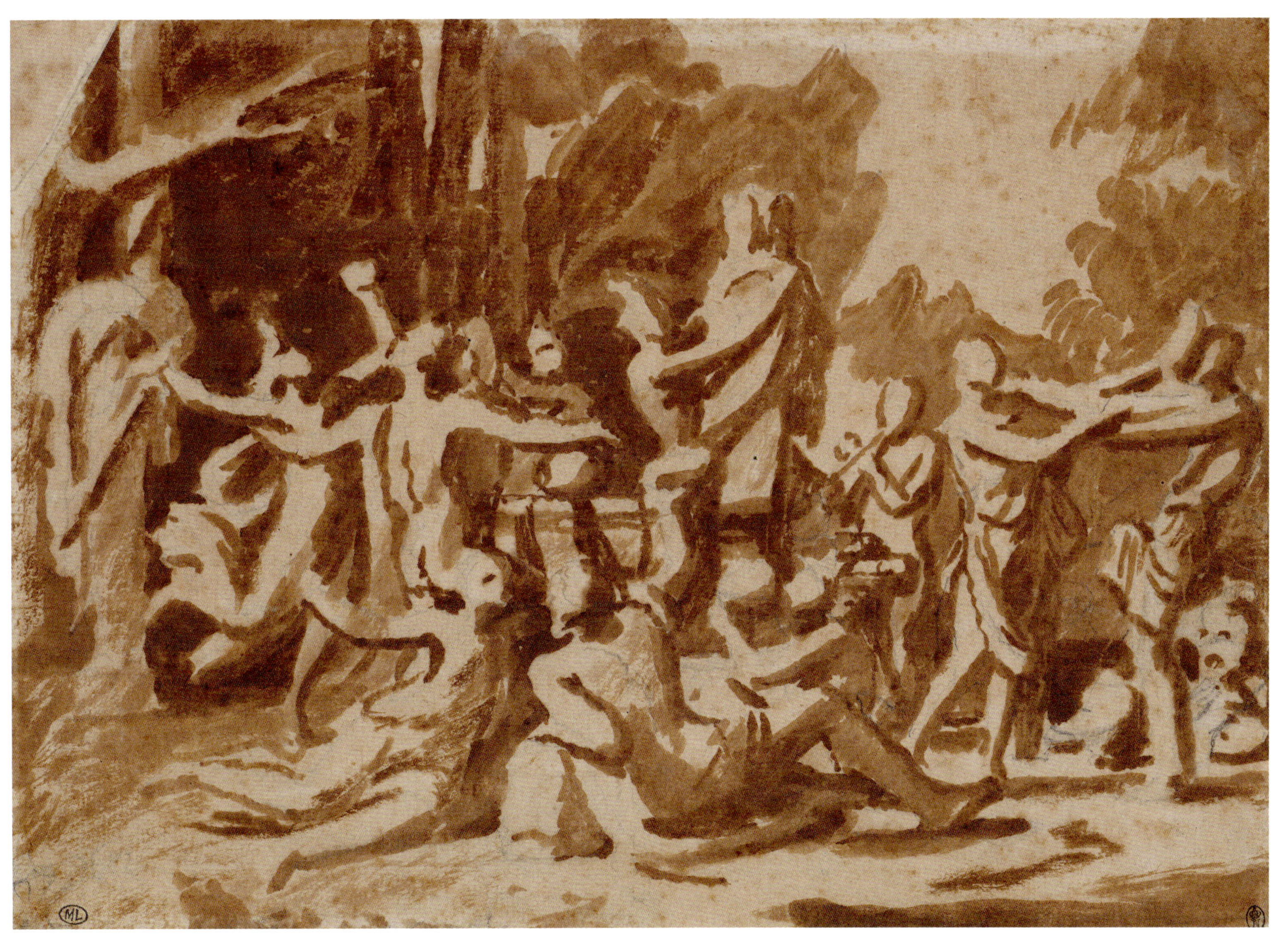

Nicolas Poussin

THE ADORATION OF THE GOLDEN CALF

ca. 1633–34
Oil on canvas
153.4 × 211.8 cm (60⅜ × 83⅜ in.)
London, National Gallery, Bought with
a contribution from the Art Fund, 1945,
inv. NG5597

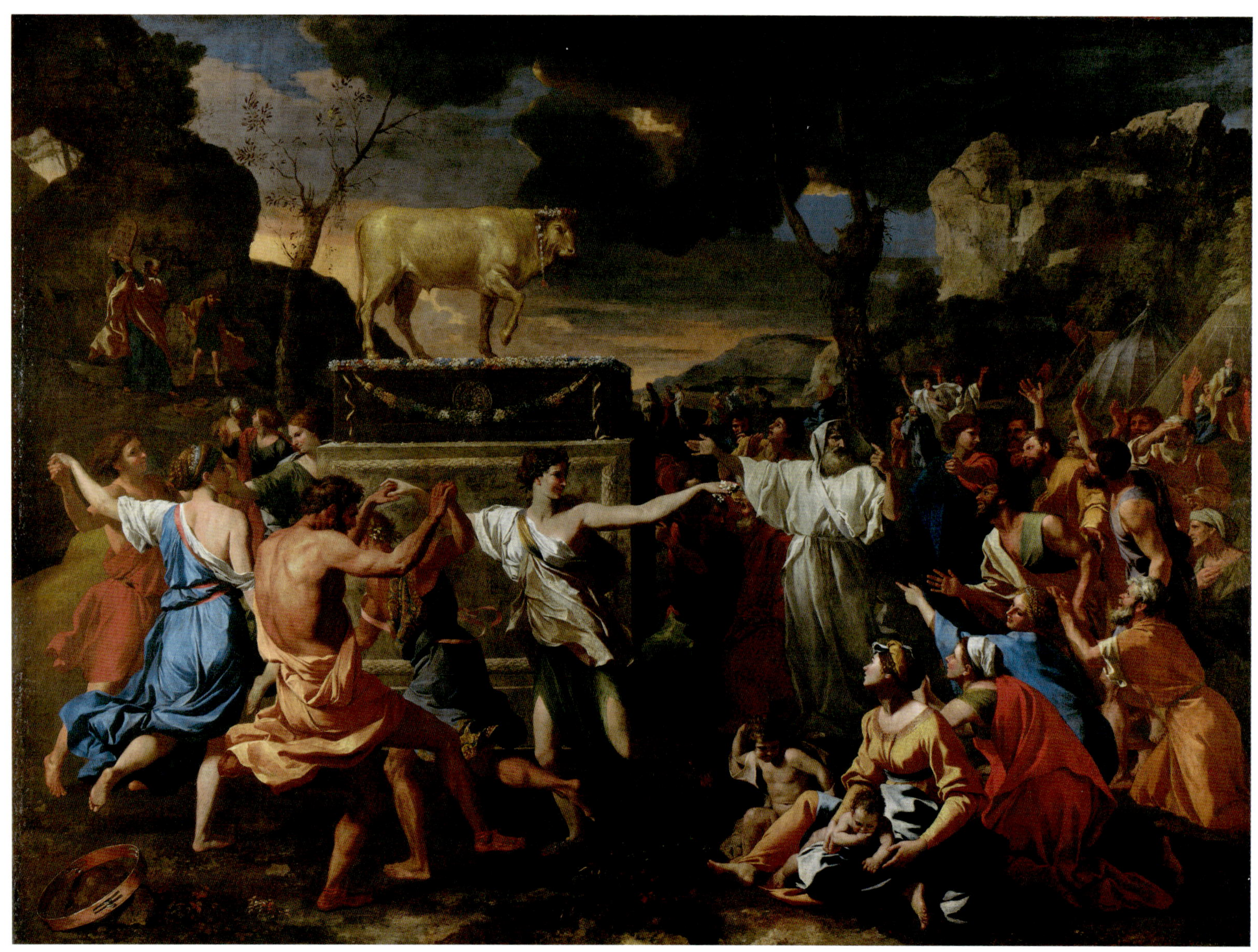

16

Nicolas Poussin

HYMENAEUS DISGUISED AS A WOMAN DURING AN OFFERING TO PRIAPUS

ca. 1634–38

Oil on canvas

166.5 × 373 cm (65½ × 146⅞ in.)

São Paulo, Collection Museu de Arte de São Paulo Assis Chateaubriand, Purchase, 1958, inv. MASP.00046

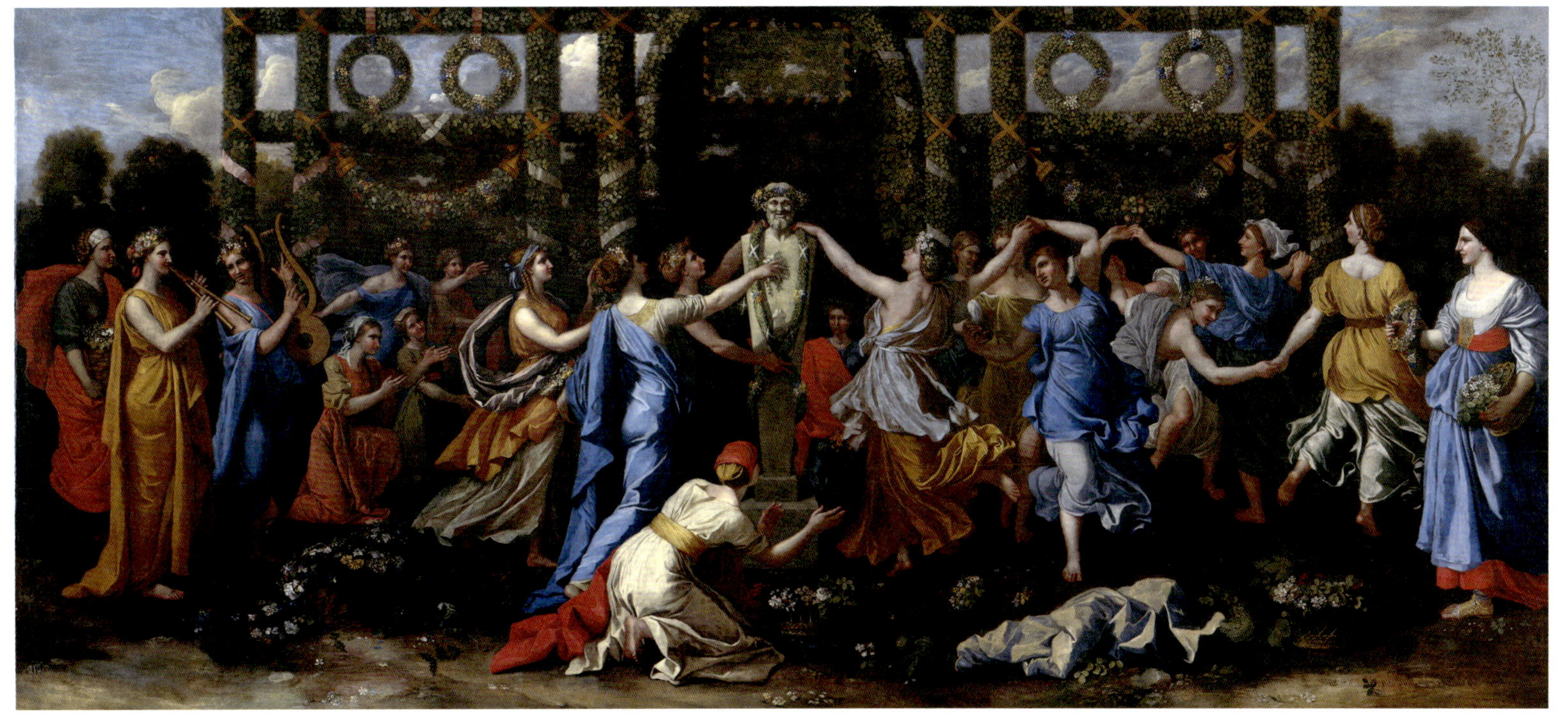

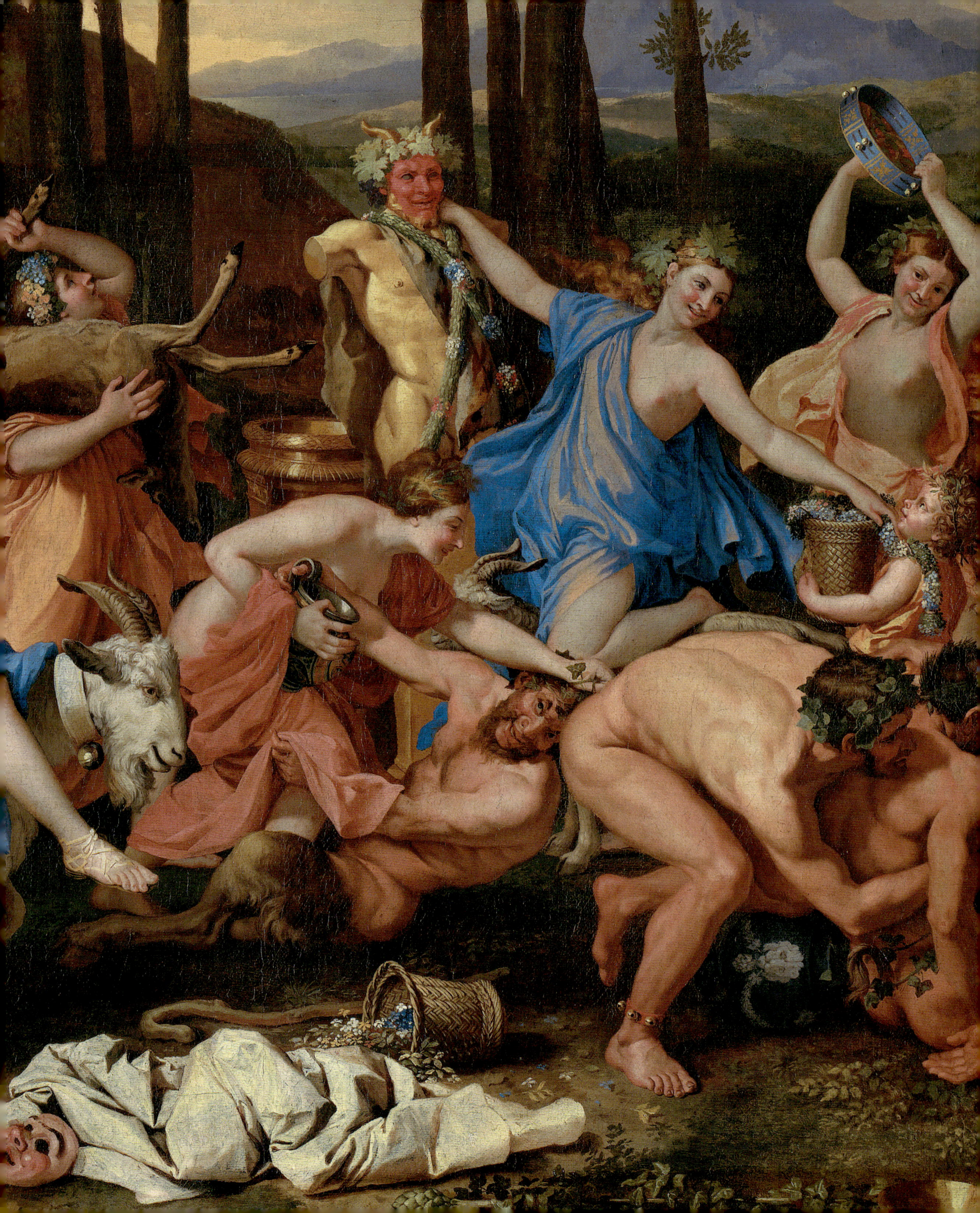

DANCES FOR RICHELIEU

FRANCESCA WHITLUM-COOPER

On May 19, 1636, the Marchese Pompeo Frangipani wrote to Cardinal Richelieu (Armand-Jean du Plessis, duc de Richelieu, 1585–1642), first minister of France and, after the king, the most powerful man in the country, to say that the new bishop of Albi had departed from Rome, carrying with him "two paintings of Bacchanals that the painter [Nicolas] Poussin has already executed according to your desire and intention."[1] These two bacchanals have long been identified as *The Triumph of Pan* (plate 17) and *The Triumph of Bacchus* (plate 18), painted for the château de Richelieu, the cardinal's newly built palace, about two hundred miles southwest of Paris.

In the first, a tightly knit group of nymphs and revelers cavorts around a horned golden statue: this is most commonly believed to be Pan, god of woodlands and shepherds and follower of Bacchus, the god of wine, although we shall see that this identification is not entirely straightforward. Theatrical masks alluding to Bacchus's role as protector of theaters and ivy-wrapped staffs carried in his rituals lie strewn in the foreground, as the statue is garlanded with flowers and a deer is carried off for sacrifice. This is a wild, even debauched moment, as exuberant dance, loud music, and strong wine cause the revelers to lurch, stumble, and throw back their heads in ecstasy.

The second triumph depicts Bacchus himself in an ornate chariot drawn by centaurs. His entourage of satyrs, maenads, and mythological characters is accompanied by trumpets, tambourines, and panpipes. A river god gazes up at the procession as the chariot of the sun god Apollo wheels through the golden sky. The subjects of these canvases, with their half-naked, drunken figures, might seem at first unusual choices for such a prominent figure of church and state as Richelieu. Yet, these bacchanals are among the most rigorously composed canvases of Poussin's career, bursting with allusions to classical antiquity. In these paintings, he makes drunkenness not only elegant but also erudite.

Almost a dozen drawings for *The Triumph of Pan* survive, more than for any other composition by Poussin. There is no firm consensus on how precisely these drawings follow one another—Anthony Blunt, the twentieth-century authority on Poussin,

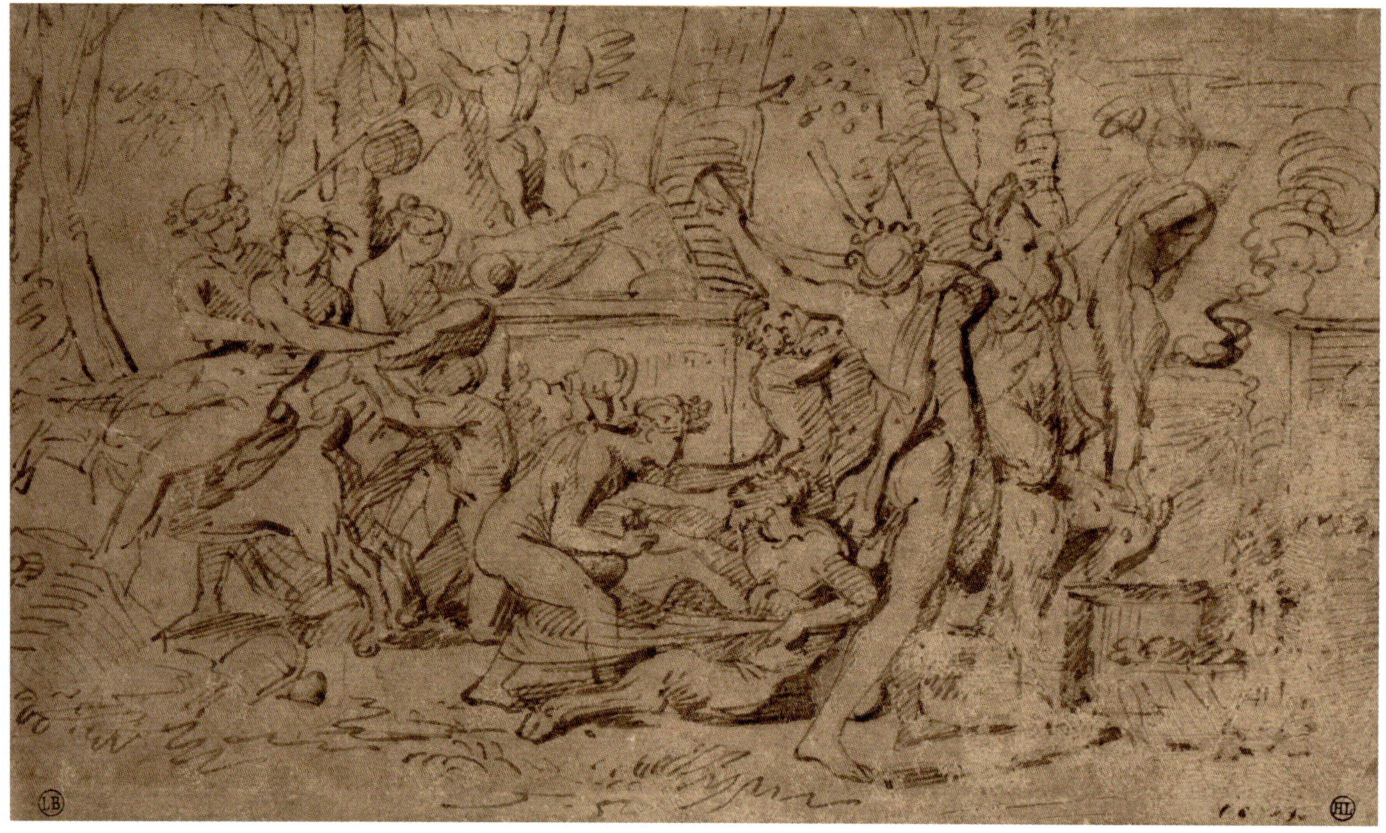

FIGURE 17
Nicolas Poussin, *Bacchanal*, ca. 1635. Pen
and brown ink over red chalk on paper, 11.1 ×
19.6 cm (4⅜ × 7¾ in.). Bayonne, Musée Bonnat,
inv. 1671; NI, 46

believed that "enough drawings [. . .] survive to enable us to study its evolution in detail,"[2] while Pierre Rosenberg, co-author of the most recent catalogue raisonné of Poussin's drawings and author of the forthcoming catalogue of his paintings, thinks it "extremely difficult to assign them an order of execution"[3]—but it is clear that this wealth of preparatory material offers an unparalleled window onto Poussin's creative process. Certain groups "reappear" across the sheets "like motifs in a piece of music."[4] The drawings have been seen as a series of "attempted juxtapositions, freely experimented modifications, harmonics developed around a theme," as if Poussin, through and across and even behind these sheets—some of which have drawings on both sides—riffs his way toward the final composition.[5] This essay will trace these motifs and harmonies, moving from the drawings to the painted triumphs.[6]

A brisk pen drawing in Bayonne (fig. 17) may be among the earliest of Poussin's experiments, for it is the only drawing to contain "the emphatically contrapposto figure" blowing a horn in the foreground.[7] This garlanded, scantily clad male figure strides across the sheet, twisting toward the altar at the heart of the composition. The centrality of this altar, and the libations being poured upon it, emphasizes that the scene is one of both worship and sacrifice. Even at this early stage, several familiar elements are taking shape: on the left, the nude woman riding a goat—whom Poussin will ultimately clothe in crisp blue and white draperies; the tussling nymph and satyr at center, her tugged skirts captured in just a few concentric lines of ink; and the herm at far right, already being decorated by a garlanded bacchante.

The scene takes place in a grove: a shepherd's crook and panpipes hang on one of the loosely hatched tree trunks, close to a putto gathering fruit. In what may be the next iteration of the theme (plate 19a), we spy another putto climbing into the tree-tops, although the forest elements are less articulated. The group around the goat has moved from the left to the right—the goat has gained fur, and there is now clearly delineated fruit in the proffered basket—while the horn player has been rotated and relegated to the background at right. Such rearrangements of figures strongly argue for Poussin's use of wax models—Blunt called them his "wax corps-de-ballet"—to work up his compositions.[8] Although the altar has receded, a figure carrying a sacrificial deer has been added in the center of the composition in dark, bold strokes.

The verso of this sheet (plate 19b) contains three more drawings: a light sketch of children at center; a study for *The Triumph of Bacchus*, in which a centaur unfurls a banner; and another study for *The Triumph of Pan* that vividly illustrates not only Poussin's use of wax models but also their value to him. The figures here are mere outlines. Poussin's concern is not for expression or detail: rather, he is looking at the relationship of bodies, the articulation of limbs, and, in the soft gray washes, the fall of light across three-dimensional forms.

In another bacchanal (plate 21), instead of grappling with the mechanics of a large composition, our artist brings into tight focus one of the key figure groups that has been present from the beginning. Here the goat has delightful shaggy fur and curling horns; even her eyelashes have been drawn in. The man who supports (or grabs at) the seated nymph now has both articulated musculature and a jocular, leering expression. The kneeling figure's muscles are picked out with careful hatching and washes. His activity is earthily rude: holding a basket of fruit and flowers on his head with his left hand, he appears to be milking the goat with his right.

The two sides of a second sheet in Bayonne (figs. 18 and 19) bring us back to the full composition and to the suggestion that "a design for an ordinary Bacchanal, with the Herm of Pan in a subordinate position, was gradually worked out into a specific Feast or Triumph of Pan, with the Herm as the central point of the design."[9] In the detailed pen drawing on the recto (fig. 18), we return to woodland, with putti climbing in fruit trees and a drunken satyr collapsing in the foreground. At center a nude woman squeezes grapes into a bowl, while at right a nymph decorates the statue, whose erection evokes not Pan but the fertility god Priapus. This may be the "ordinary Bacchanal," with overindulgence and merrymaking abounding across the sheet. On the verso, however, in a small sketch that has been cut down (fig. 19), Poussin moves toward the final form of his composition, "with the Herm as the central point of the design." The sacrificial deer has been reinstated, and we see—albeit in reverse—the outstretched arms of the figure that will ultimately become the blue-clad, ivy-garlanded nymph decorating the statue. This version of the composition is developed in a sheet at Windsor (plate 20b) that moves progressively closer to the finished painting.

The larger of the two pen and ink studies on this sheet is the only surviving drawing with proportions corresponding to those of the painting.[10] Although the herm is not yet in the center of the composition, key features have been introduced, such as the space allotted to the still-life elements in the foreground and the vertical accents of

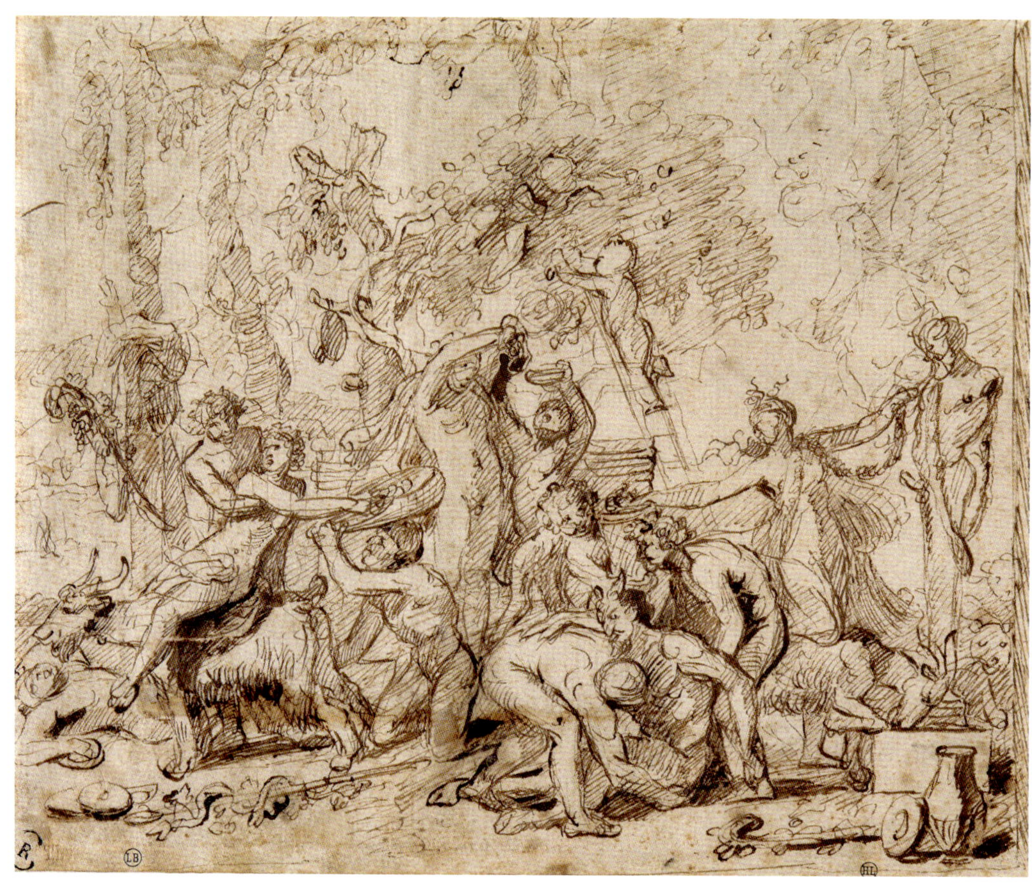

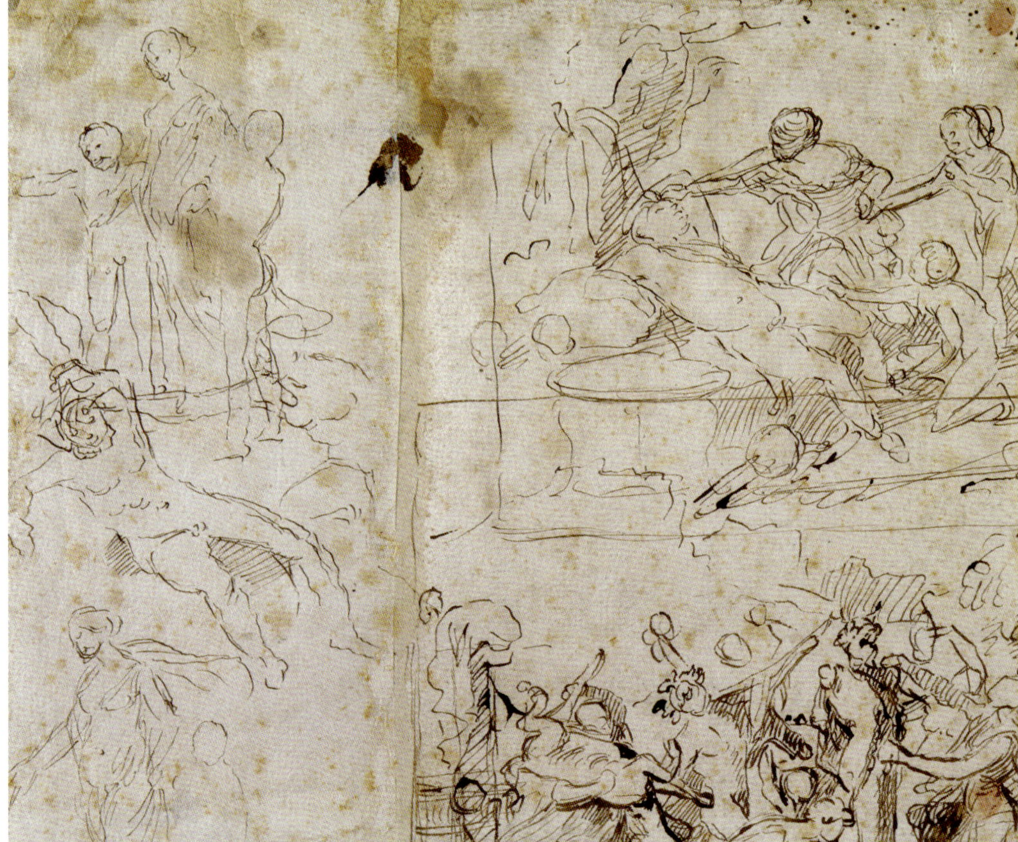

FIGURE 18
Nicolas Poussin, *Bacchanal*, ca. 1635. Pen and brown ink on paper, 17.4 × 21.2 cm (6⅞ × 8⅜ in.). Bayonne, Musée Bonnat, inv. 1672; NI 47, recto

FIGURE 19
Nicolas Poussin, *Bacchanal and Studies for a Group Approaching a Sleeping Silenus*, ca. 1635. Pen and brown ink on paper, 17.4 × 21.2 cm (6⅞ × 8⅜ in.). Bayonne, Musée Bonnat, inv. 1672; NI 47, verso

the trees and column. The second, more schematic study (see plate 20b), occupying a smaller portion of the paper, is in many respects the closest to Poussin's final composition, with dancing bacchantes at right raising cymbals in the air, the sacrificial deer, the man blowing the trumpet at left, and the herm at center. In the background, swags of greenery are slung between the tree trunks, neatly dividing the composition into quarters and emphasizing the newfound symmetry of the arrangement. These swags directly recall a print by the Master of the Die after Giulio Romano (see fig. 16) that was also an important source for Poussin's *Hymenaeus* (plate 16).

"No literary source exists for this painting, which was entirely Poussin's own invention";[11] "very little in this work is original to Poussin."[12] It is one of the paradoxes of *The Triumph of Pan* that two such seemingly contradictory statements can hold true. Poussin's designs, for all their inventiveness, revolved around rich borrowings from antiquity, as underlined by Bellori: "Among the other paintings [. . .] were some made for Cardinal de Richelieu, particularly four Bacchanals and the triumph of Bacchus, and various fantasies, and wild dancing; these compositions derive precisely from the study of antique marbles and from his poetic invention."[13] For Passeri the Richelieu bacchanals confirmed Poussin's status as "always the most diligent investigator [. . .] of bas-reliefs, columns, vases and other recollections of antiquity."[14] In Rome, Poussin had access not only to some of the most celebrated "antique marbles" of his day but also to the Museo Cartaceo—or Paper Museum—of his friend and patron Cassiano dal Pozzo. For example, Poussin may have looked to Dionysian sarcophagi or to Cassiano's drawings after them for the elegant reveler astride the goat (fig. 20), while the impish figure of the cloaked boy at right imitates the celebrated Borghese Gladiator (fig. 21).[15]

The arrangement of figures in *The Triumph of Pan* is one of those in which Poussin comes closest compositionally to that in an antique bas-relief, so tightly are his figures and the objects they carry knitted together. This is demonstrated in another drawing at Windsor, where the figures are depicted in more or less their final poses (plate 22). The paper itself is integral to the composition, the bright white of the unmarked areas of the sheet forming the bulk and mass of their bodies. Behind them the background is marked in a rich, deep wash, giving this highly polished sheet a jewellike effect reminiscent of an antique cameo. The purpose of this drawing is puzzling: it was not sent to Richelieu as a preliminary design for approval, nor do its distinctly different proportions suggest it played a role in *The Triumph of Pan*'s development.[16] It may have been a sheet produced for a friend or patron in Rome once the painting had been finished.

Infrared reflectography (IRR, an imaging technique that makes visible carbon-rich materials used to draw the design of a painting) shows very few changes to the underdrawing of the figures of *The Triumph of Pan*—not surprising, perhaps, in a picture over whose composition Poussin clearly labored. More surprising, however, are the changes to the background revealed in part by IRR and, more dramatically, by X-ray fluorescence (XRF) scanning (a technique that allows the mapping of the distribution of different chemical elements, helping us understand how an artist has used particular pigments).[17] The XRF element distribution map for mercury reveals that, in prepara-

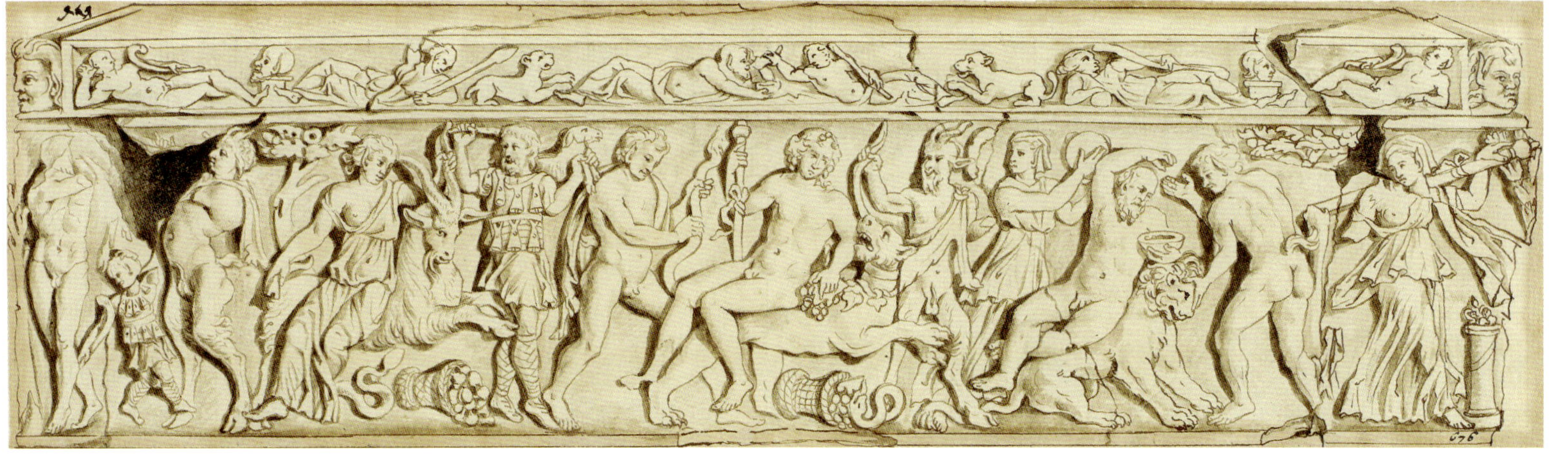

FIGURE 20
Drawing after the Dionysian Sarcophagus in the Capitoline Museum, Rome, from the Cassiano dal Pozzo Collection. Pen and brown ink and grayish-brown and black wash over black chalk or graphite on paper, 19.9 × 41.1 cm (7⅞ × 16⅛ in.). Windsor, Royal Collection/HM Queen Elizabeth II, RL 8324 (*Bassi Relievi Antichi* 3 album, folio 2)

FIGURE 21
Fighting Warrior, known as the Borghese Gladiator, ca. 100 BCE. Signed by Agasias of Ephesus, Greek, fl. ca. 125–ca. 75 BCE. Marble, 199 cm (78 in.). Paris, Musée du Louvre, Département des Antiquités Grecques, Étrusques et Romaines, MR 224

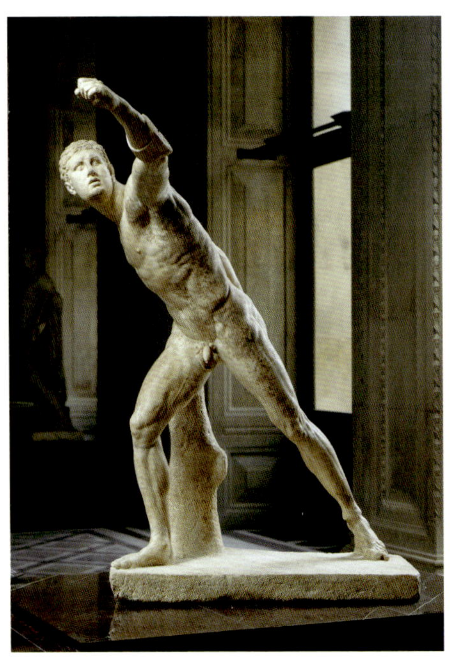

tion for adding the central frieze of figures, Poussin laid in a loosely applied layer of paint containing vermilion: this may have looked similar in effect to the brown wash around the figures in the highly finished Windsor sheet (plate 22), for it seems to be a localized application in the central area of the composition.[18] XRF imaging also reveals that, at the earliest stage of painting, the background consisted of an elaborate, plant-festooned architectural feature very close to that seen in the São Paulo *Hymenaeus* (fig. 22; see plate 16). This architectural form had a central recess, with swags of foliage slung between uprights to either side of it, as in the Windsor sketch and the Master of the Die print (see plate 20b; see fig. 16). Poussin did not get very far in working up the structure of this elaborate backdrop: it seems to have been planned but not executed, abandoned after the drawing and blocking-in stages, with the screen of trees in the finished painting added later to disguise signs of the architectural forms.

The information provided by these investigations, alongside the wealth of preparatory material, presents intriguing possibilities for the identification of the herm, which has long been debated. The Marchese Frangipani's letter of May 1636 is typical of early accounts of the commission, insofar as it refers to "Bacchanals" generally rather than to the specific subjects of these paintings. Almost all the major authorities on Poussin have acknowledged the possibility that the deity described as Pan might equally be Priapus.[19] One recent proposition argues that the herm is in fact Dionysus (the Greek, and rather more violent, version of Bacchus), pointing to both the Dionysian friezes used as sources and the specificities of this herm—the draped animal hide, the red mask, the golden paint—which are characteristic of Dionysus, not Pan or Priapus.[20] However, the new discoveries enabled by technical imaging strengthen the argument in favor of Priapus, given the onetime closeness between the London and São Paulo compositions.[21] Possibly the notion of "a design for an ordinary Bacchanal"[22] needs to be revisited. Perhaps it was not only the herm's placement that changed across Poussin's drawings, from "a subordinate position" to "the central point of the design": the herm's identity may also have morphed as the composition developed.

Although fewer preparatory sheets survive for *The Triumph of Bacchus*, it is still possible to trace Poussin's process from vibrant sketch to the stately, bas-relief effect

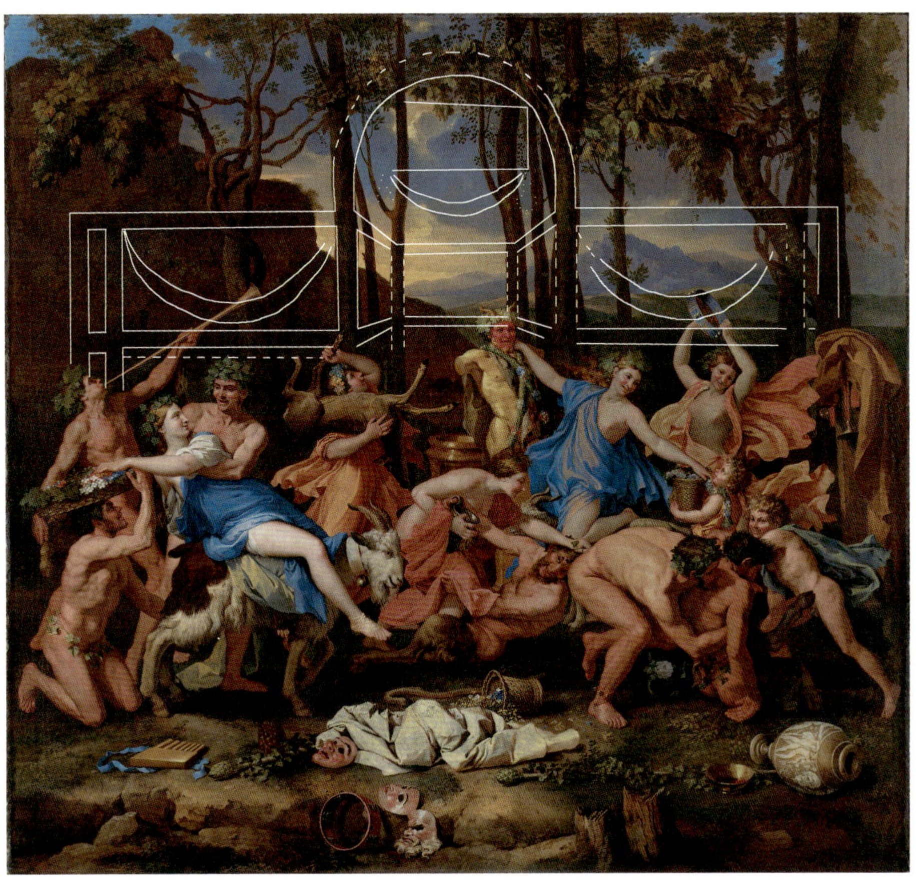

of the final painting. The earliest drawing for the composition is that at Windsor, on the recto of the two studies for *The Triumph of Pan* (plate 20a). Sharing a sheet with two sketches after ancient sculpture—a bas-relief with caryatids or dancers raising their arms and a winged lion—Bacchus's triumphal parade moves diagonally toward us across the paper. The composition celebrates his victories in India, for his entourage contains all manner of exotic creatures, from elephants to a camel to a giraffe to the spotted leopards who pull his chariot. Bacchus sits in splendor, radiantly nude at the center of the sheet, drawn mostly in outline with only a little shading to suggest an animal skin draped over his arm. By contrast, the procession around him, led by a dancing bacchante clashing a pair of cymbals, feels frenetic, even chaotic, with raised arms and the pouring of wine depicted with overlapping forms and frenzied hatching.

The second preparatory drawing for *The Triumph of Bacchus* marks a crucial departure (fig. 23). Gone is the striking if somewhat disorderly diagonal, replaced with a composition that runs strictly parallel to the picture plane, emulating both antique bas-reliefs and works like Annibale Carracci's Palazzo Farnese fresco of the subject (see fig. 4).[23] The elephants and camels now find themselves alongside mythological creatures.[24] Silenus, who appeared in the first drawing astride an ass and supported by two followers, has been eliminated,[25] and two centaurs lead the procession; Bacchus's chariot is now driven by a small winged putto. On the verso of the Uffizi study for *The Triumph of Pan*, we find a study for the centaurs, waving a banner rather

FIGURE 22
The Triumph of Pan (plate 17): a tracing of features seen in the infrared reflectogram and macro-XRF element maps that relate to an earlier stage of the composition, overlaid onto a visible image of the painting

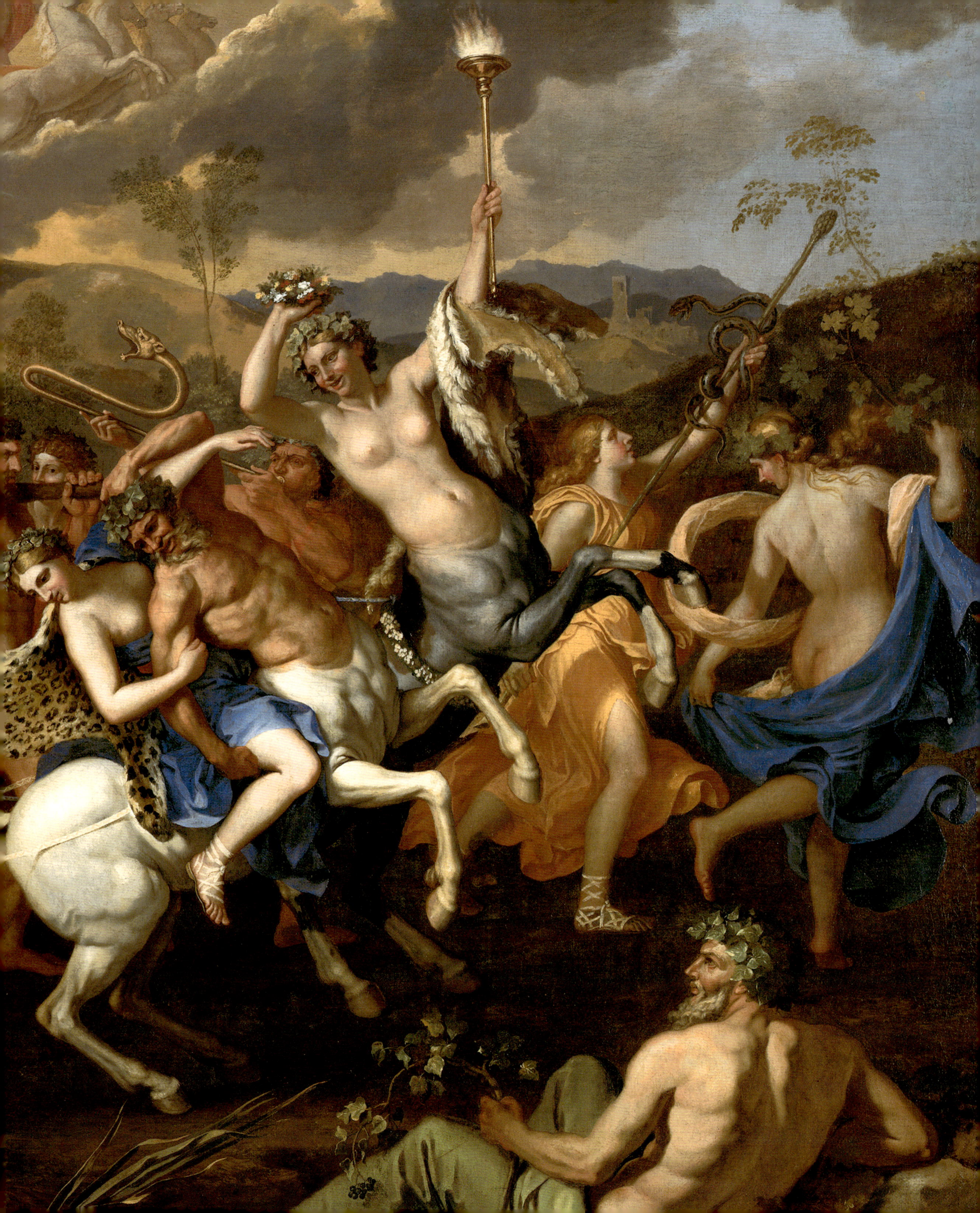

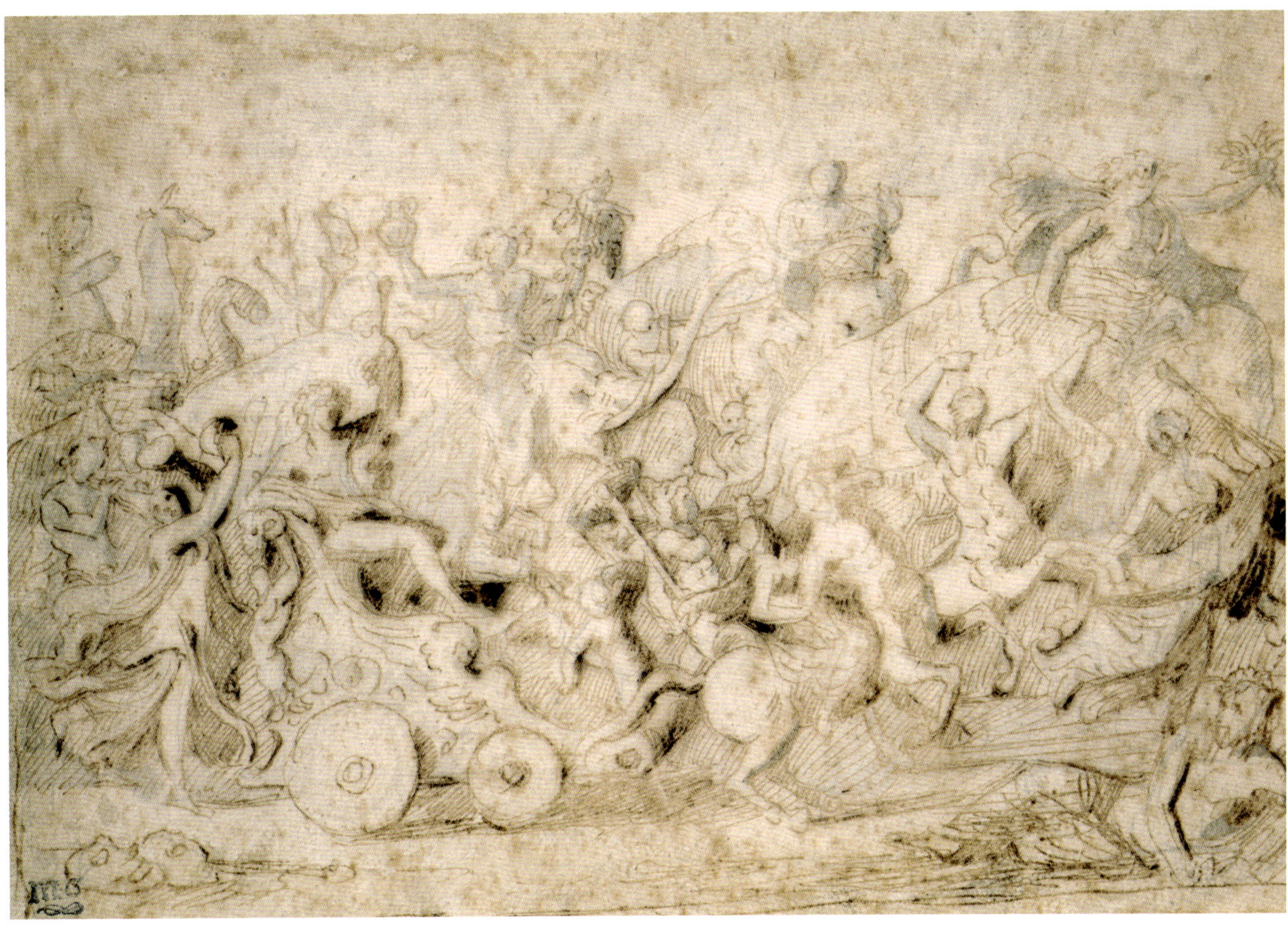

than the flaming torch of the final composition (see plate 19b). Since several sheets bear drawings for both *The Triumph of Pan* and *The Triumph of Bacchus*, the two compositions must have been conceived and executed simultaneously.

Where the revelers in *The Triumph of Pan* are generic, those in *The Triumph of Bacchus* include several identifiable mythological personages (see plate 18). Besides the triumphant god himself, wreathed in ivy and clutching a staff, we spy Pan, blowing his famous pipes and carrying a shepherd's crook. Next to him we find Silenus, Bacchus's drunken companion, grinning and holding aloft a torn vine complete with bunches of grapes. Ahead of him marches Hercules, looking grim and determined: he has stolen the sacrificial tripod of the sun god Apollo, seen above wheeling across the sky. The exotic animals of the drawings do not appear in the painting, though the animal skins remind us of the impending frenzy—maenads (female followers of Dionysus, whose name literally translates to "raving ones") were known to rip animals to shreds during their rites. Leaving behind the dense, chaotic energy of the preparatory drawings, Poussin presents his bacchanalian procession as a stately, friezelike arrangement of figures in space. Yet he also creates a greater sense of physical extension and exertion than in *The Triumph of Pan*, with the dramatically rearing centaurs, the

FIGURE 23
Nicolas Poussin, *Study for the Triumph of Bacchus*, ca. 1635. Pen and brown ink over traces of black chalk on paper, 15.7 × 22.7 cm (6¼ × 9 in.). Kansas City, The Nelson-Atkins Museum of Art, Purchase: William Rockhill Nelson Trust, inv. 54–83

bacchante in orange thrusting her snake-wrapped thyrsus ahead of her, and the sinu-
ously curving spine of the nude with blue drapery.

This figure is a direct quotation from the Borghese Vase (plate 23), one of the
antiquities that Félibien tells us Poussin "often imitated with great skill and felicity."[26]
Standing over a meter and a half tall, this monumental vase is a magnificent example
of Imperial Roman taste in garden ornament. Discovered in the gardens of the Roman
historian Sallust in the 1560s, it was in Poussin's day one of the most celebrated
antiquities. Beneath trailing vines, a Bacchic procession winds its way around the
vase: Dionysus presides over the revels, as satyrs and maenads whirl in an endless
parade of inebriation and ecstasy. As in *The Triumph of Bacchus*, music plays an
important role: one man plays an aulos, an antique double pipe, while the bacchante
that Poussin quotes in his painting dances to a tambourine. Farther along, a satyr
collapses after too much drink and is helped by his friend—this staggering pair surely
inspired the drunken faun in the right foreground of *The Triumph of Pan*. The sense
of movement here is emphasized by the vase's physical form: this procession has
no obvious beginning or end. While that is not strictly true for Poussin's composition, whose format imposes clear starting and end points, there are strong parallels
between stone and paint in the flowing draperies and active poses of the figures,
whose heady, evanescent excitement is captured equally on canvas and in marble.

These explicit references to antiquity were certainly intended to flatter Poussin's
patron. From 1630 until his death in 1642, the all-powerful Cardinal Richelieu was
engaged in an extremely ambitious building project, transforming his family's modest
manor into a "magnificent Château,"[27] comprising vast castle buildings as well as a
town—also named Richelieu—in which he could house those nobles closest to him in
a private court.[28] Since the early 1630s, he had been engaged in the wholesale transport of classical sculpture from Rome to France to decorate the château.[29] Although
filled with "so many precious and rare examples from Antiquity,"[30] the château was
also home to Renaissance sculpture (most notably Michelangelo's *Rebellious Slave*
and *Dying Slave*, today in the Musée du Louvre, Paris) and paintings, the most significant of which was the group that Richelieu acquired in the late 1620s from the
sixteenth-century *studiolo* (private study) of Isabella d'Este in Mantua, comprising
works by Andrea Mantegna, Lorenzo di Ottavio Costa, and Pietro Perugino.[31] It was
among these celebrated paintings, in perhaps the most prestigious room in the château, the Cabinet du Roi (king's cabinet), that Poussin's triumphs found their home.[32]

The Cabinet du Roi was a sumptuous space: at 10 by 12 meters, with ceilings
5 meters in height, its decorations included paintings ("admirable Pictures, as many
by Old Masters as by the modern ones") as well as caryatids and panels painted with
fleur-de-lys and battles and triumphs of the marine gods.[33] Although Bellori and
Félibien mention four bacchanals for Cardinal Richelieu, the earliest accounts of this
richly decorated room describe three pictures by Poussin hanging in it:[34] *The Triumph
of Bacchus* and *The Triumph of Pan* flanked a window opposite the door; above that
doorway, between Costa's *Allegory of the Court of Isabella d'Este* and Mantegna's *Parnassus*, hung "a banquet of Silenus."[35] This depiction of Silenus, it is important to note,
does not appear to have been sent with the "two Bacchanals" from Rome to Paris in

May 1636. Although part of the same decorative scheme, Poussin's *Triumph of Silenus* was distinct from its other elements.

The three Poussin triumphs remained in the Cabinet du Roi until some point in the first half of the eighteenth century, when they were replaced by copies.[36] These copies tell us not only that the dimensions of *The Triumph of Silenus* differed from those of *The Triumph of Pan* and *The Triumph of Bacchus* but also that its composition matches that of a painting that entered the National Gallery's collection in 1824 and has long been considered to be "after Poussin" (plate 24).[37] It depicts another bacchanalian revel by a stand of trees in a rocky landscape. At left the drunken figure of Silenus is supported by revelers: one leg slung over a tiger, he resembles the figure in the first study for *The Triumph of Bacchus*. At center two revelers dance and make music as a satyr drinks deeply from a cup of wine. A companion behind him, suffering from over-indulgence, sprawls sleeping on a blue cloth. At right a female satyr straddles a goat, and two centaurs punish an amorous donkey, branding its head with a torch.

The painting has been rejected by many—though not all—Poussin scholars on the grounds of both perceived quality and compositional weakness.[38] Compared to *The Triumph of Pan* and *The Triumph of Bacchus*, it is as if some final layers of paint and detail have been omitted. While each pine needle in the garland of the kneeling satyr has been carefully picked out, elements such as the donkey and tiger and the musculature of some of the secondary figures, seem to consist of little more than underlayers, without the further paint layers that would soften the contours of the schematic *ébauches* (rough outlines) beneath. The composition, similarly, does not feel as rigorous as those of the other two triumphs.[39] However, recent conservation treatment and technical analysis now offer a fresh perspective on this much-debated picture. Without the distorting effects of discolored varnish, it is apparent that the *Silenus* and *Pan* are closer in both style and tonality than was previously recognized. IRR and XRF scanning have revealed several changes made during painting, under-mining the argument that *The Triumph of Silenus* is a copy after an already finished work. Likewise, comparison of the pigments used in both paintings reveals very similar—indeed idiosyncratic—mixtures and components that are difficult to explain across two unconnected paintings. These findings, in addition to the recent revelation that all three paintings were painted on canvas cut from the same bolt, argue strongly for the London *Silenus* having been produced in the same workshop as the other two triumphs.[40] Since there is no evidence that Poussin had studio assistance,[41] and since there is nothing in the early provenance of the London picture to preclude its being the original,[42] the logical conclusion is to treat it as autograph.[43]

Yet, how are we to explain the discrepancies in design and execution between the *Silenus* and the other triumphs? One way is to acknowledge that it was always intended to hang separately from the other two pictures, and that it was almost cer-tainly delivered later. We must also consider how busy the late 1630s were for Poussin: the two Buen Retiro pictures alone would have been a colossal undertaking (see plate 16, fig. 14), even for someone with studio helpers. While the Richelieu commis-sion must have been important for Poussin—indeed, the bacchanals were effectively an audition for his reluctant return to Paris in 1640—he does not appear to have had any great loyalty to France during this period.[44] If the *Silenus* was indeed commissioned and sent later, it is possible that it received less attention from Poussin, either in the rush to deliver it to Richelieu (far too terrifying a figure to keep waiting) or because other, more lucrative projects were then occupying his attention.

Dance, drunkenness, revelry: these are the elements that unite the three Richelieu bacchanals, but what, given the power and gravity of its patron, was the series intended to signify? Various interpretations have been put forward.[45] These range from the idea that the inclusion of Hercules in *The Triumph of Bacchus* was intended to flatter Richelieu, who was associated with Hercules elsewhere in the château's decoration,[46] to the argument that contemporaries would have recognized parallels between Dionysus and Christ befitting Richelieu's position as France's most powerful cardinal.[47] Other suggestions figure the triumphs as statements about Richelieu's prowess as a collector,[48] or as a celebration of Louis XIII's political and military might.[49] Yet, however compelling these suggestions, we must acknowledge that any underlying meaning uniting the series appears to have been lost by the time Vignier published his description of the château in 1676. Although Vignier does not offer a reading of the room's meaning, its bright colors, gilded ceilings, and "peerless glory" come vividly to life.[50] Four decades after Poussin's pictures arrived in France, the series clearly still inspired awe.

Poussin painted one other triumph during the 1630s, the exquisite and enigmatic *Triumph of Neptune and Amphitrite*, now in the Philadelphia Museum of Art (plate 25). In the conventional reading of this scene, Neptune, Roman god of the sea, emerges from the water astride four charging seahorses: he clasps his trident in his hand, looking lovingly at the sea goddess Amphitrite, who rises on a shell borne by dolphins, her pale flesh and pink and gold fluttering draperies contrasting beautifully with the pale blue sea and sky. Overhead, putti scatter flower petals: one holds a torch, symbol of marriage, as another aims love's arrow at Neptune's heart. However, the painting has also been read as a depiction of *The Birth of Venus*, with the goddess of love emerging from the waves, as her chariot, driven by Cupid and drawn by a team of doves, approaches through the sky at left. The possibility that it depicts Galatea—one of the Greek goddesses of calm seas—has also been suggested, thanks to the composition's obvious debt to Raphael's *Triumph of Galatea* fresco at the Villa Farnesina.[51]

This painting's provenance has been almost as hotly debated as its subject. Both Bellori and Félibien referred to it as a *Triumph of Neptune*, and both associated it with Richelieu, specifically with the other triumphs in the Cabinet du Roi.[52] Certainly it is easy to see how such a composition would have been intensely flattering to Richelieu, not only in its direct citation of Raphael but also given his role as *grand-maître, chef et surintendant général de la navigation et du commerce de France* and his enormous success in rebuilding the French navy.[53] While not, in a literal sense, a depiction of dance, the lunging figures and swirling draperies might also have alluded to the *Ballet de la marine*, an entertainment mounted by Richelieu—a major patron of French ballet—in 1635 to celebrate the restoration of French naval prowess.[54] Yet, in spite of these tantalizing suggestions, *The Triumph of Neptune* does not appear in either Vignier's 1676 account of the château de Richelieu or the posthumous inventory of the cardinal's possessions, or in the possession of any of those to whom he was most likely to have given the picture.[55] Until archival evidence comes to light, the radiant picture, while in its own watery way balletic, cannot be read as one of Poussin's dances for Richelieu.[56]

In the four hundred years since they were painted, the Richelieu bacchanals have accrued renown and acclaim. Richelieu must have been pleased with them, since he orchestrated Poussin's recall to the French court and capital in 1640, a move that helped to establish the artist's reputation as the leading painter of the French school. Their compositions have been swooned over by artists as diverse as Gian Lorenzo Bernini (1598–1680)[57] and Pablo Picasso (1881–1973).[58] Today they are lauded as masterpieces of their respective galleries.[59] Yet Poussin did not paint pictures like these again. In the later 1630s he moved away from dancing pictures and their lighthearted subject matter. This was the moment in which he turned toward the first series of The Seven Sacraments, which could not be more different in tone from these joyful compositions. Did Poussin, after all the time and effort that went into composing the Pan and the Bacchus, grow tired of his subject matter? Blunt, on seeing The Triumph of Pan for the first time, apparently felt that it had been "painted without love."[60] The bacchanals came late in Poussin's career as a painter of dance, effectively marking the end of his engagement with the theme.[61] A little over a decade after his arrival in Rome, Poussin left behind the dancing nymphs and whirling bacchantes that had for so long occupied his mind and his canvases. In Blunt's words, "The pure rhythm of the dance was not rational enough for the master in his later phase."[62] As he looked toward the 1640s, a new, more sober Poussin was about to emerge.

NOTES

My thanks to Letizia Treves for her comments on an early draft of this text, and to my colleagues in the National Gallery Conservation and Scientific Departments—Larry Keith, Hayley Tomlinson, Marika Spring, Catherine Higgitt, and Rachel Billinge—for sharing their expertise with me.

1 Quoted in Pintard 1960, 33n7; see also Chastel 1960, 2:56–57.

2 Blunt 1979a, 99.

3 Paris 1994–95, no. 56, 229.

4 Rosenberg and Prat 1994, no. 83.

5 Prat 2013, 39.

6 In doing so, it follows the "hypothetical chronological order" proposed by Wine 2001, 355.

7 Wine 2001, 355. See also Rosenberg and Prat 1994, no. 85.

8 Blunt 1979a, 103.

9 Friedlaender and Blunt 1939–74, 3:24.

10 Wine 2001, 357.

11 London 1995, no. 29, 203.

12 B. Cole 2008, 99.

13 Bellori 1672, 423.

14 Passeri 1772, 353.

15 For more on Poussin's possible sources, see B. Cole 2008, 71–79; and Wine 2001, 354.

16 This drawing entered the Royal Collection in an album assembled by Cardinal Camillo Massimi, an amateur artist and friend of Poussin. See London et al. 1995–96, 10–11, and no. 37.

17 I am grateful to colleagues in the Conservation and Scientific Departments at the National Gallery who undertook the technical study of *The Triumph of Pan* (NG6477), in particular Rachel Billinge, who undertook the IRR; Catherine Higgitt, who led the macro-XRF scanning and produced the overlay; and Marika Spring for investigation of the paint stratigraphy and pigment analysis.

18 Although this mercury-containing layer is currently only visible in the central area of the painting, it is possible that it extends further.

19 Rosenberg 2011, 134. For a summary of related debates, see also Wine 2001, 353.

20 See B. Cole 2008, 90–98; and B. Cole 2012, 242–65.

21 This closeness is particularly fascinating given the political rivalry between Richelieu and Olivares, who were bitter enemies, and whose armies were actively engaged against each other in the Franco-Spanish War (1635–59).

22 See note 9 above.

23 It is interesting to note that Annibale, too, moved from a rowdy, diagonal composition drawing toward the friezelike form of his final painting. See London et al. 1995–96, 103.

24 For varying accounts of these figures and of the painting's iconography, see Dempsey 1966a; Bull 1995; Robin 1998; and Bastet 2006.

25 He is thus described in Ovid (*Fasti* 1.399).

26 Félibien 1725, 4:147.

27 Vignier 1676, i.

28 For more on the château and its environs, see Orléans and Tours 2011.

29 Olson 2010 discusses Richelieu's transport of art and antiquities in detail, and suggests how Poussin may have responded to it. For more on Richelieu as collector, see Boyer et al. 2009.

30 Vignier 1676, ii.

31 These paintings are Mantegna's *Minerva Expelling the Vices from the Garden of Virtue* and *Parnassus*, Costa's *Allegory of the Court of Isabella d'Este*, Perugino's *Combat of Love and Chastity*, and finally Mantegna and Costa's *Reign of Comus* (all Musée du Louvre, Paris). For more on the *studiolo*, see S. J. Campbell 2004.

32 Vignier 1676, 61.

33 Vignier 1676, 61. Much has been written about the decoration of the Cabinet: for some of the most recent literature on the decor and its relationship to the paintings, see Bastet 2006, Pierguidi 2011, and Bassani Pacht and Kerspern 2011.

34 Bellori 1672, 423; and Félibien 1725, 4:27. For a 1646 account by Willem Schellinks and Lambert Doomer, see Van den Berg 1942. The château's first governor, Benjamin Vignier, published his account in 1676, though it may have been substantially written ten years earlier; see Vignier 1676.

35 For a summary of various reconstructions of the Cabinet, see Wine 2001, 358–60. An illustrated layout can be found in Orléans and Tours 2011, 315.

36 Today in the Musée des Beaux-Arts, Tours. See Wine 2001, 350 and 360; and Orléans and Tours 2011, 320–22, 326, nos. 125, 126, 129.

37 See Wine 2001, 380; and Davies 1957, 159.

38 See Davies 1957, 159; Blunt 1966, no. 138; Thuillier 1994a, no. 111, 254; Verdi in London 1995, 202; and Wine 2001, 380. Wine notes that Mahon rejected the painting in conversation (Wine 2001, 383n40). Hugh Brigstocke believes it to be autograph at least in part, as do Rosenberg ("despite its disastrous state of conservation") and Joannides: Brigstocke 1996, 209–210; Paris 1994–95, 226; for Joannides's opinion, see Glanville 2016. I am grateful to Hugh Brigstocke for a thought-provoking discussion in front of *Pan and Silenus*, March 2020.

39 I am grateful for Richard Verdi's thoughts on this, in conversation, March 2020.

40 See Erdmann et al. 2013; and Twilley et al. 2015.

41 Save Gaspard Dughet, Poussin's brother-in-law and only documented pupil, who was predominantly a landscape painter and an unlikely candidate for this picture.

42 See Wine 2001, 380.

43 My thanks to my colleagues in the Conservation and Scientific Departments at the National Gallery who undertook the conservation treatment and technical study of this picture and without whose work it would not have been possible to reach this attribution: Larry Keith, Hayley Tomlinson, Marika Spring, Catherine Higgitt, Rachel Billinge, David Peggie, and Joanna Russell. These findings are discussed at greater length in Whitlum-Cooper 2021.

44 It has been suggested that Richelieu's request for pictures from Poussin was a direct response to Olivares's commission for the Buen Retiro (see my essay "Animating the Frieze" in this volume), made in a competitive spirit after hearing that Poussin was working for the Spanish crown; see Bonfait 2015, 42.

45 These are succinctly summarised by Wine 2001, 360–61; and Bastet 2006, 172–75.

46 Bull 1995.

47 Both were sons of god, born of virgins, both died and descended to the underworld before being resurrected. See B. Cole 2012, 261–63.

48 Olson 2010.

49 Bastet 2006.

50 Vignier 1676, 61–65.

51 See Sommer 1961; Levey 1963; Dempsey 1965; Dempsey 1966b; Flemming 1996; Weir 1998; Bull 2001; and Berger 2007. See also Rosenberg 2022 for a summary of the debate.

52   Bellori 1672, 423; and Félibien 1725, 27.

53   Montreal and Cologne 2002–3, no. 117, 276–77.

54   See Beeny 2016, 222–24.

55   Montreal and Cologne 2002–3, no. 117, 276.

56   See Rosenberg 2022.

57   See Thuillier 1994b, 18.

58   Galassi 1996, 90–97.

59   Scott 2008, 34, 74; and Langmuir 2004, 232.

60   Letter from Hugh Brigstocke to Gabriele Finaldi, November 8, 2019. NGA (National Gallery Archive) Dossier NG6477. Thanks to Hugh Brigstocke for sharing this with me.

61   Poussin would paint only one more dancing picture, *Bacchanal before a Temple*; see Beeny's essay "Invitation to the Dance" in this volume, 11–13.

62   Blunt 1951, 9.

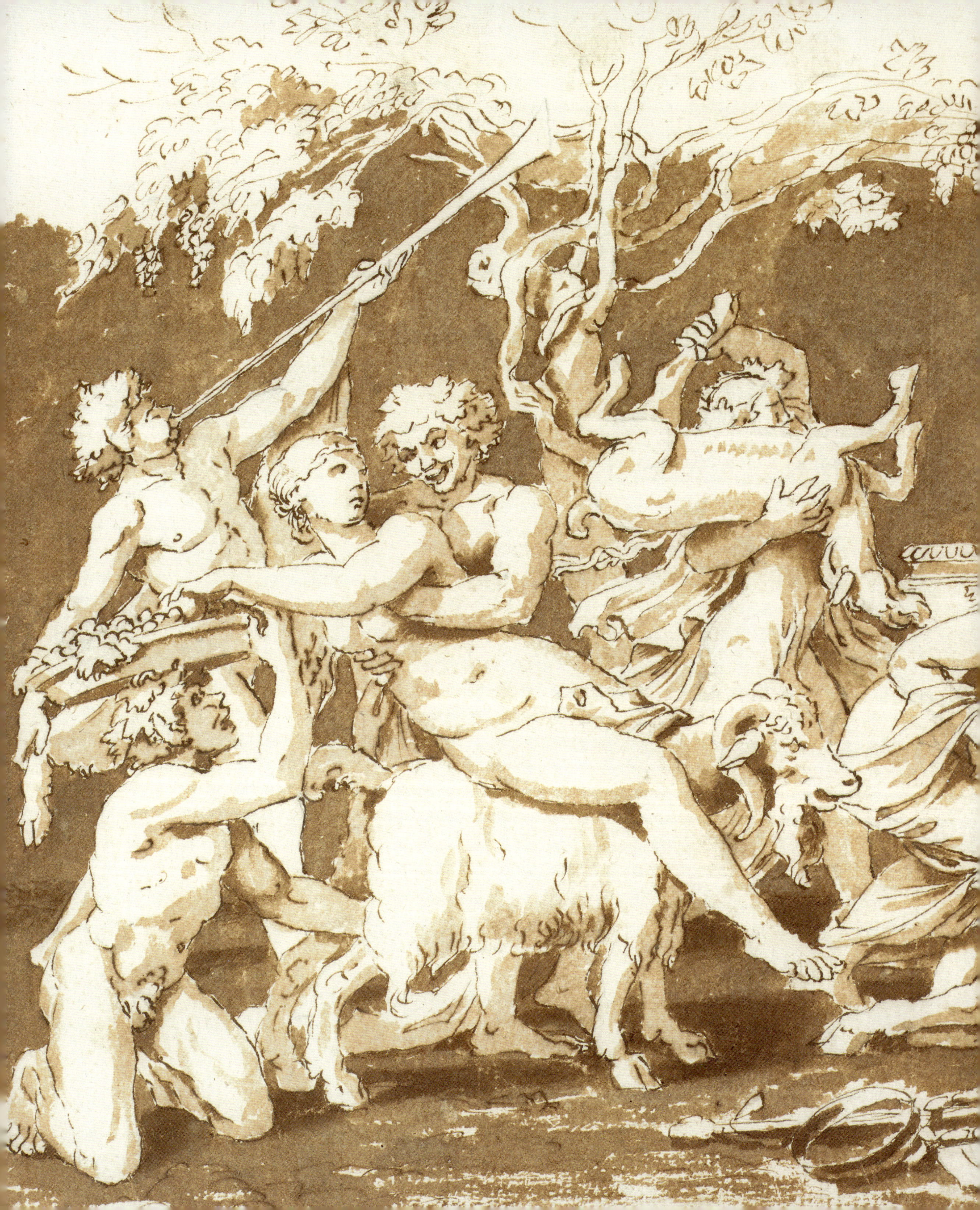

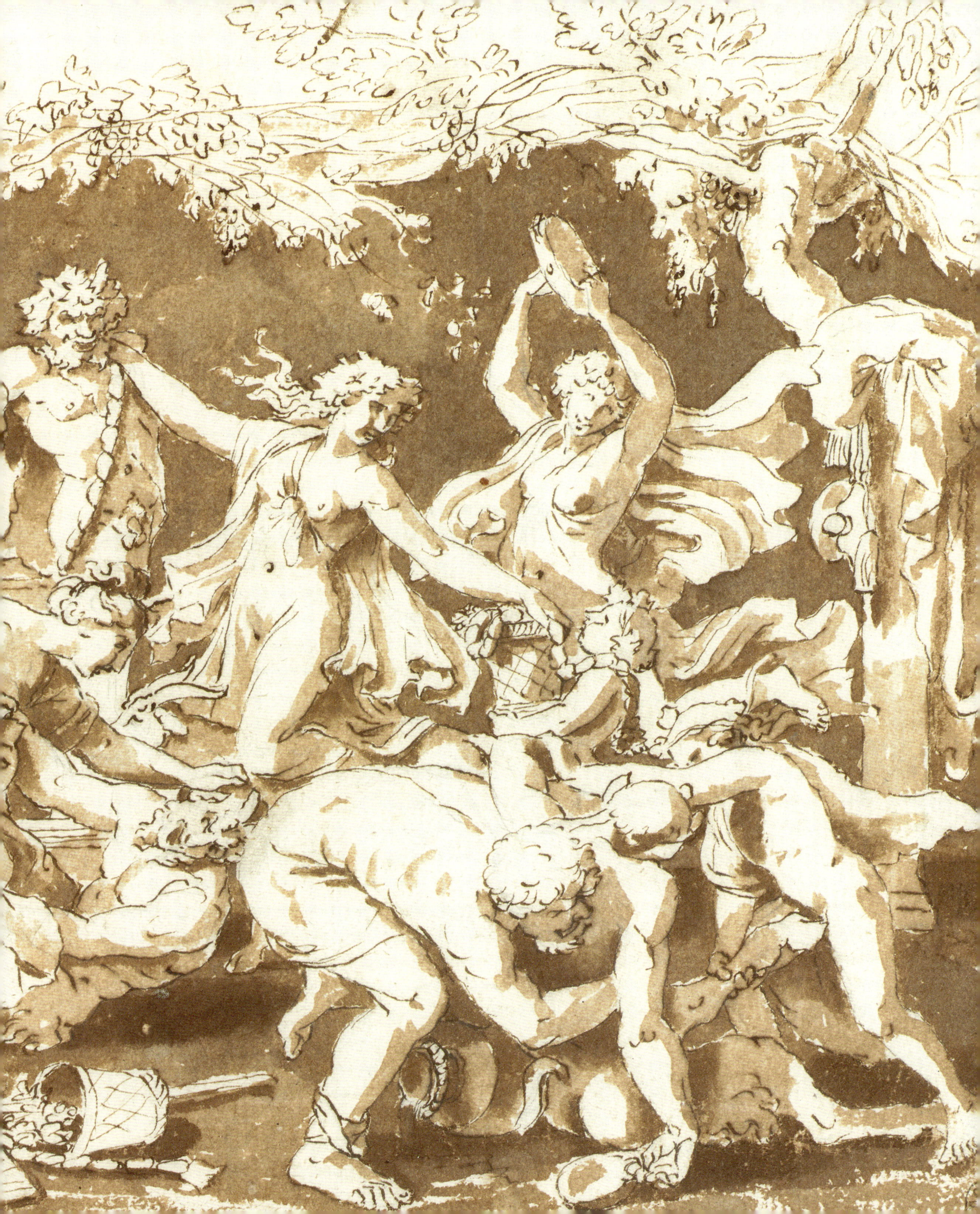

Nicolas Poussin
THE TRIUMPH OF PAN

1636
Oil on canvas
135.9 × 146 cm (53½ × 57½ in.)
London, National Gallery, Bought with
contributions from the National Heritage
Fund and the Art Fund, 1982, inv. NG6477

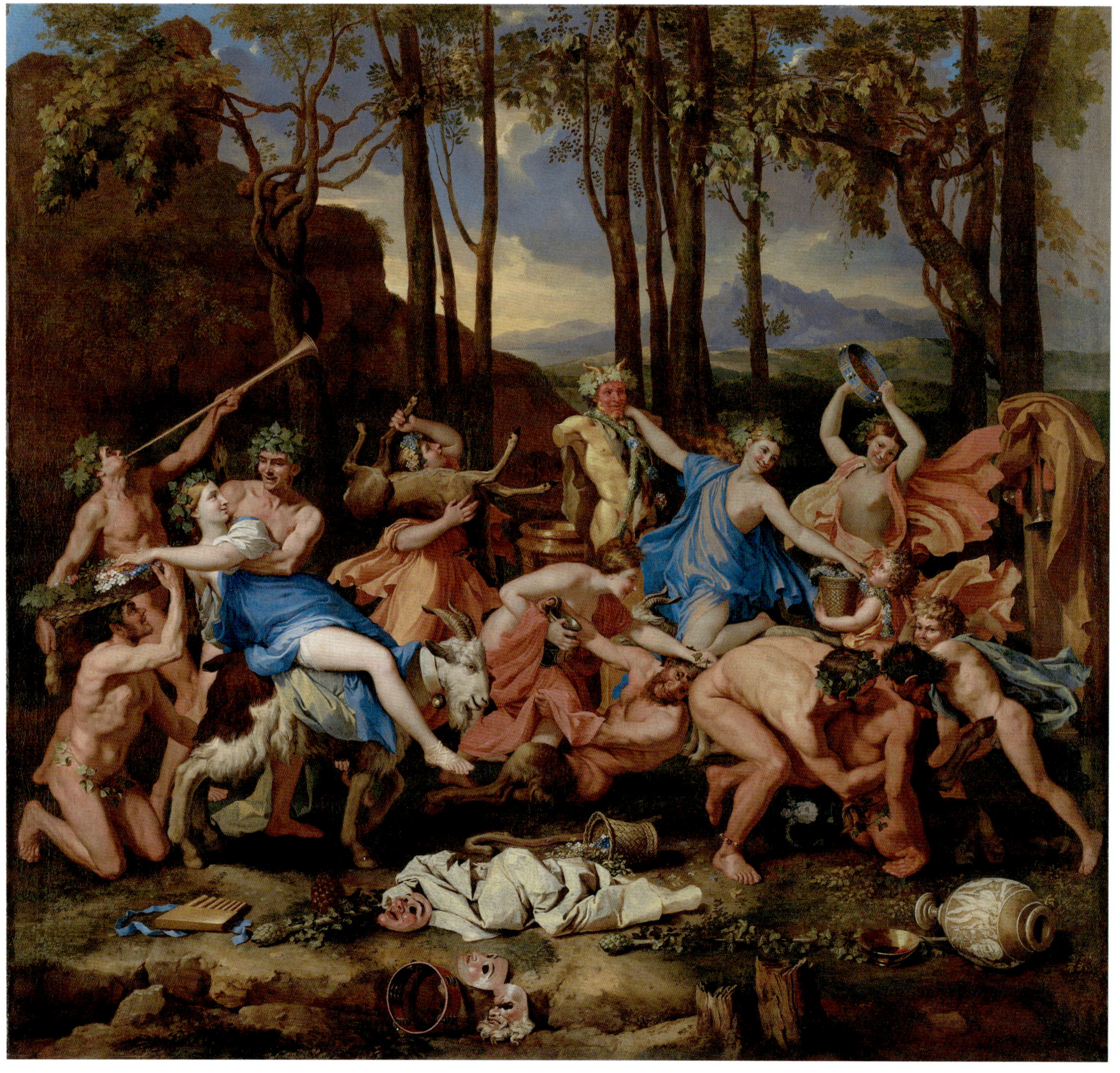

18

Nicolas Poussin
THE TRIUMPH OF BACCHUS

1635–36
Oil on canvas
128 × 151.8 cm (50⅜ × 59¾ in.)
Kansas City, The Nelson-Atkins Museum
of Art, Purchase: William Rockhill Nelson
Trust, inv. 31–94

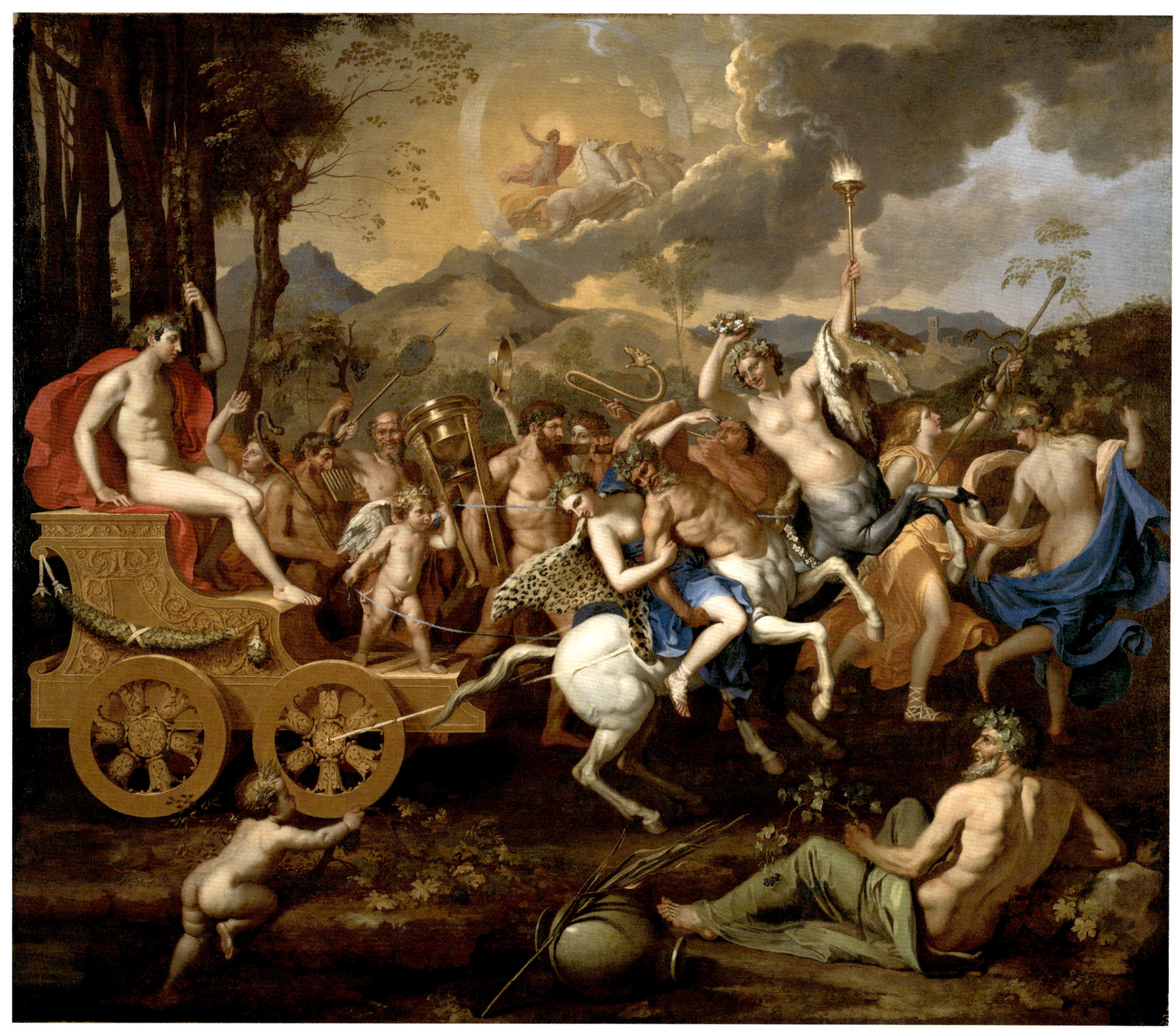

19A, 19B

Nicolas Poussin

STUDY FOR THE
TRIUMPH OF PAN

(recto)

STUDIES FOR THE
TRIUMPH OF PAN
AND THE TRIUMPH
OF BACCHUS

(verso)

ca. 1635

Pen and brown ink over black chalk on
paper (recto); pen and ink and brush and
pale gray-brown wash on paper (verso)
12.9 × 20.7 cm (5⅛ × 8⅛ in.)
Florence, Gallerie degli Uffizi,
inv. GDS 905 E

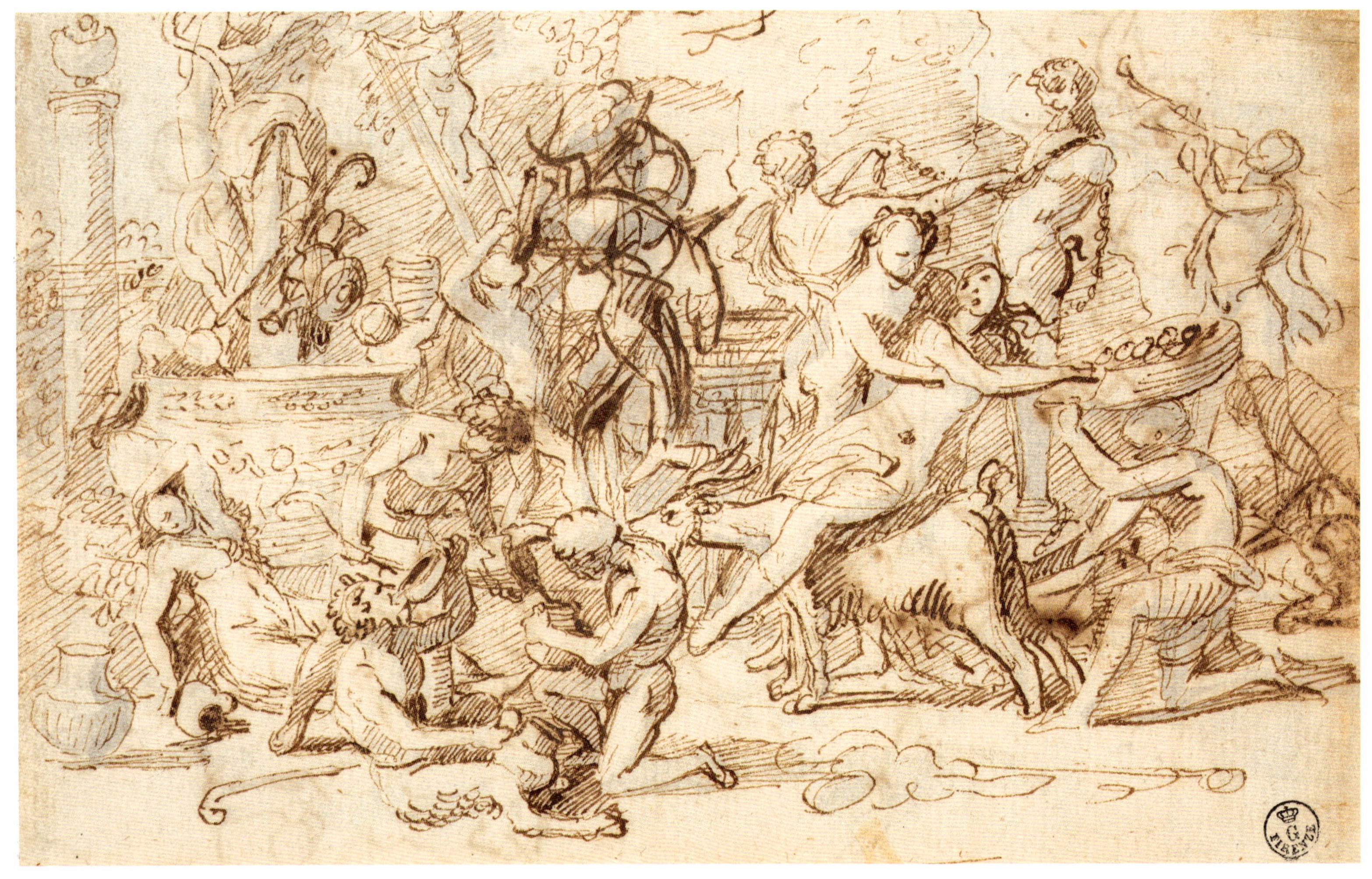

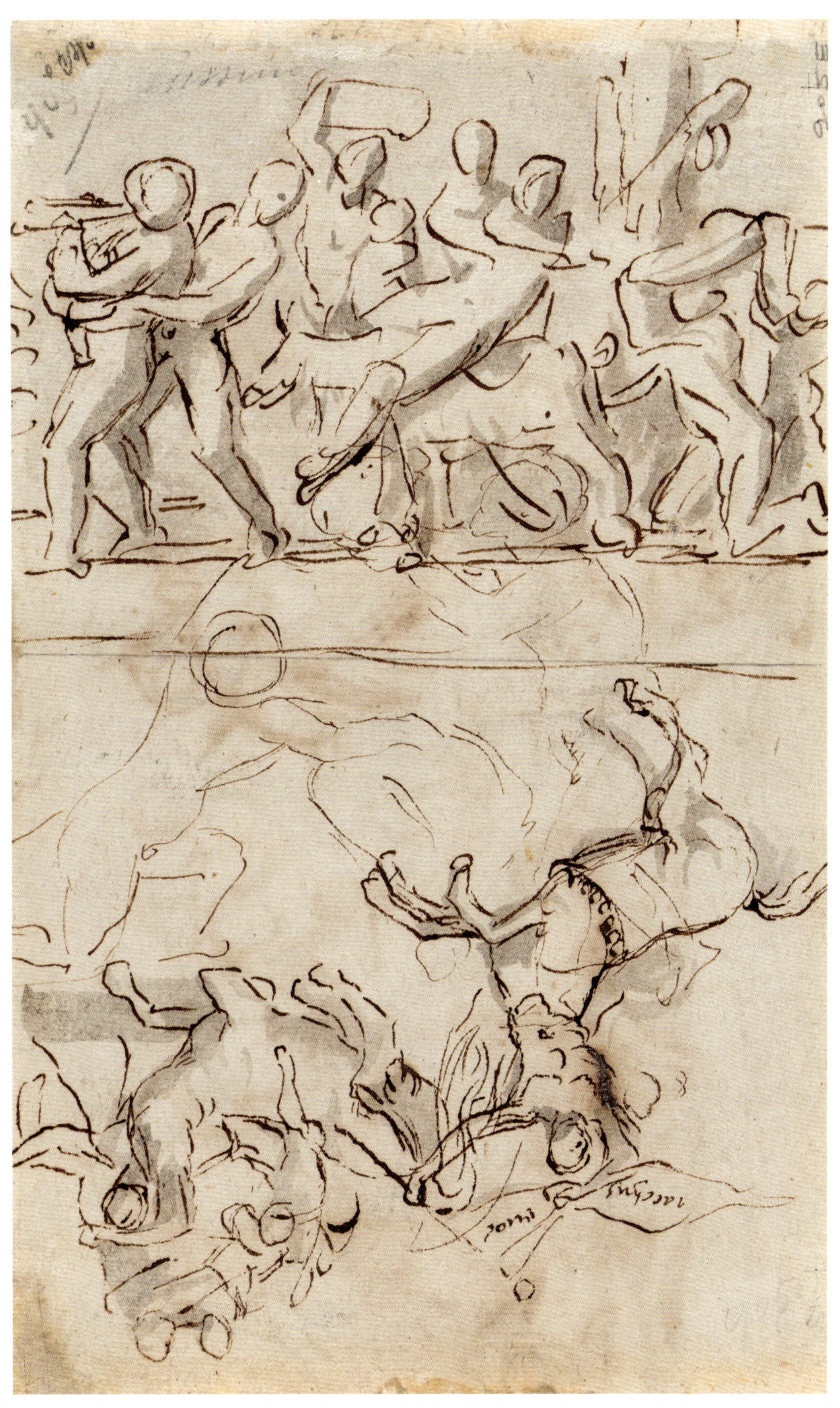

20A, 20B

Nicolas Poussin

STUDY FOR THE
TRIUMPH OF
BACCHUS

(recto)

STUDY FOR THE
TRIUMPH OF PAN

(verso)

ca. 1635
Pen and brown ink on paper (recto); pen
and brown ink over traces of black chalk
on paper (verso)
20.2 × 31.4 cm (8 × 12⅜ in.)
Windsor, Royal Collection/HM Queen
Elizabeth II, inv. RCIN 911905

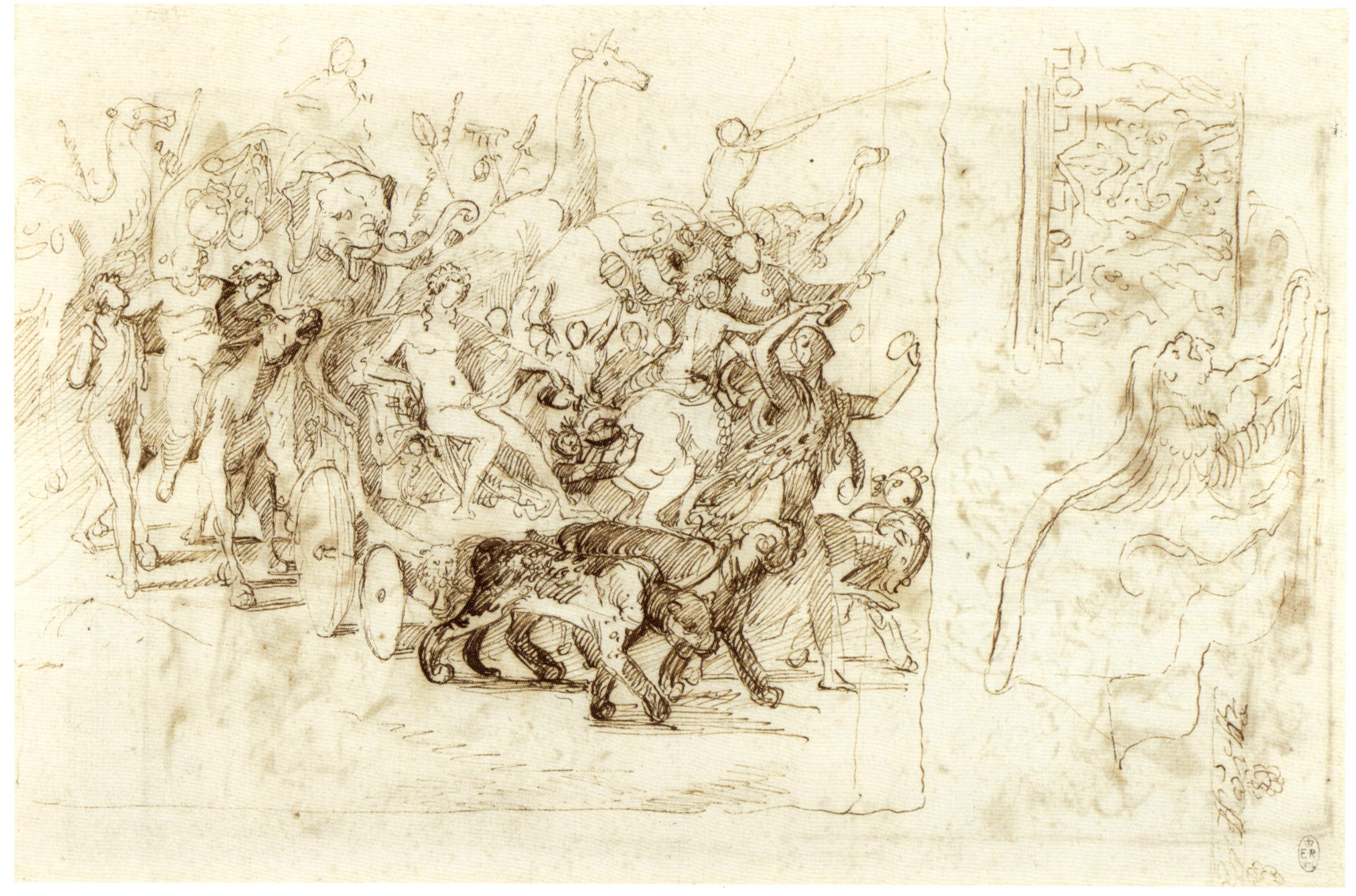

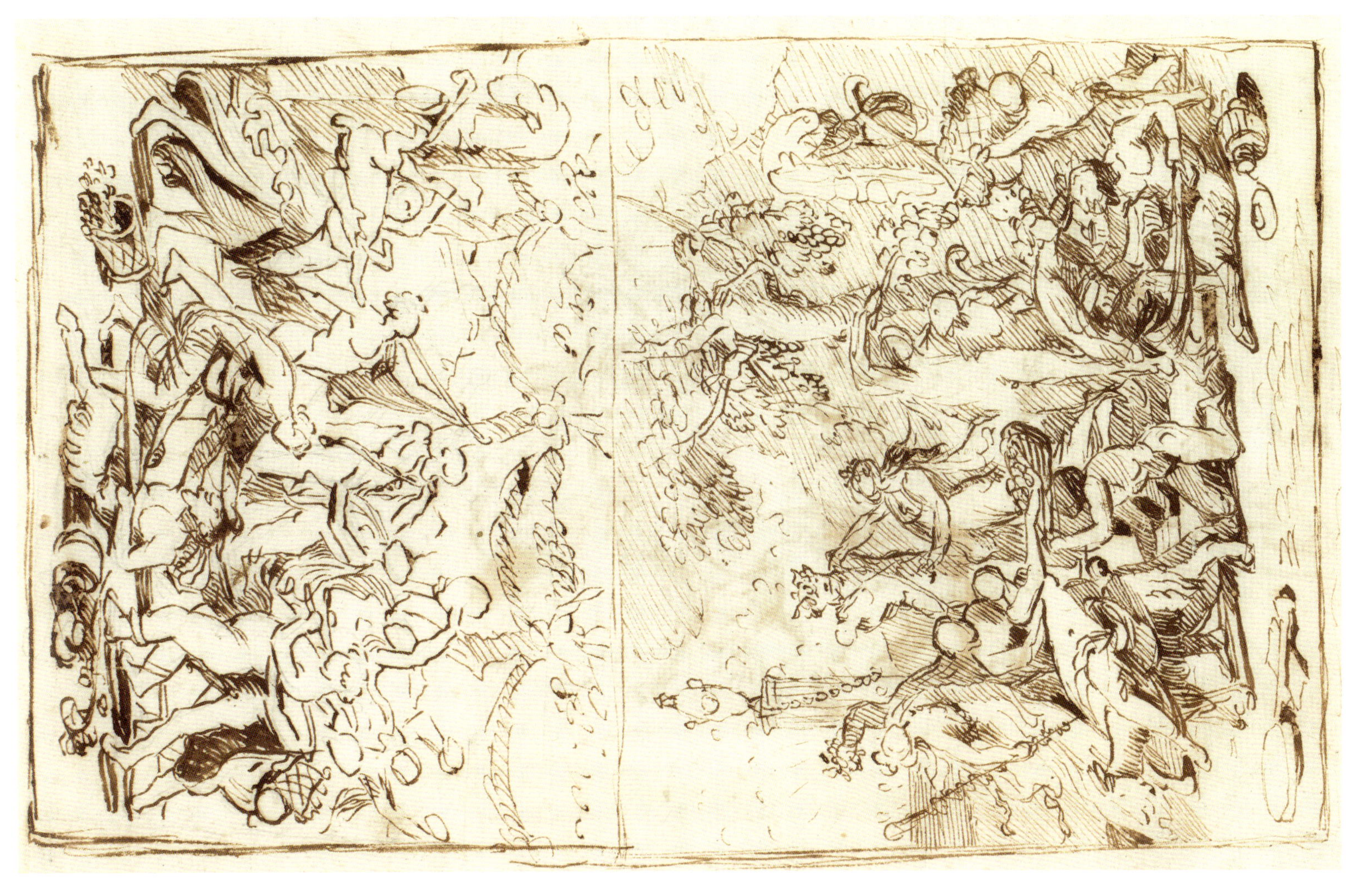

21

Nicolas Poussin
BACCHANAL

ca. 1635
Pen and brown ink, brush and
brown wash, over faint black chalk
underdrawing on paper
13.3 × 20.6 cm (5¼ × 8⅛ in.)
New York, The Metropolitan Museum of
Art, Purchase, David T. Schiff Gift, 1998,
inv. 1998.225

22

Nicolas Poussin
THE TRIUMPH OF PAN

ca. 1635–36
Pen and brown ink and brush and brown
wash over traces of black chalk and
stylus on paper
22.8 × 33.8 cm (9 × 13¼ in.)
Windsor, Royal Collection/HM Queen
Elizabeth II, inv. RCIN 911995

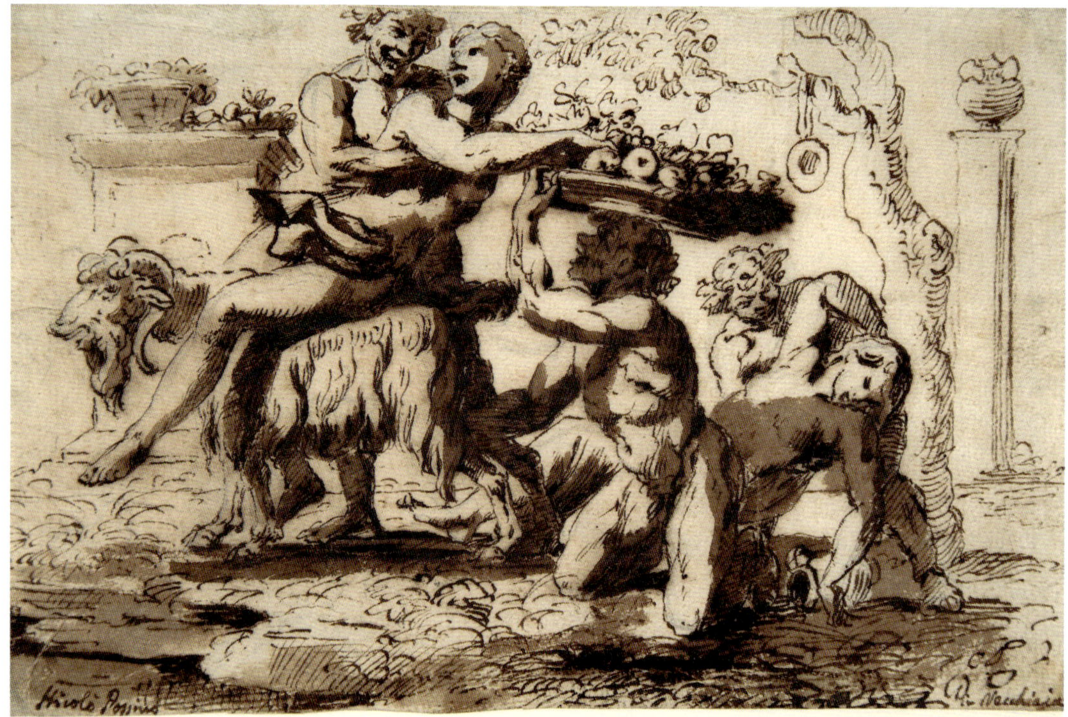

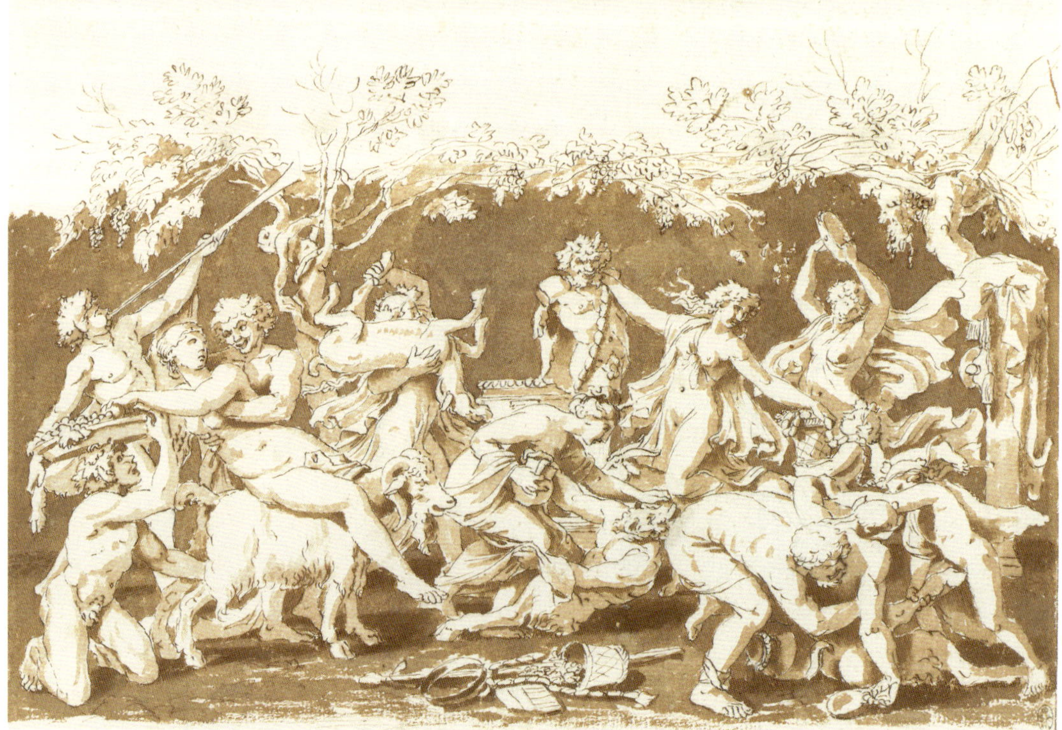

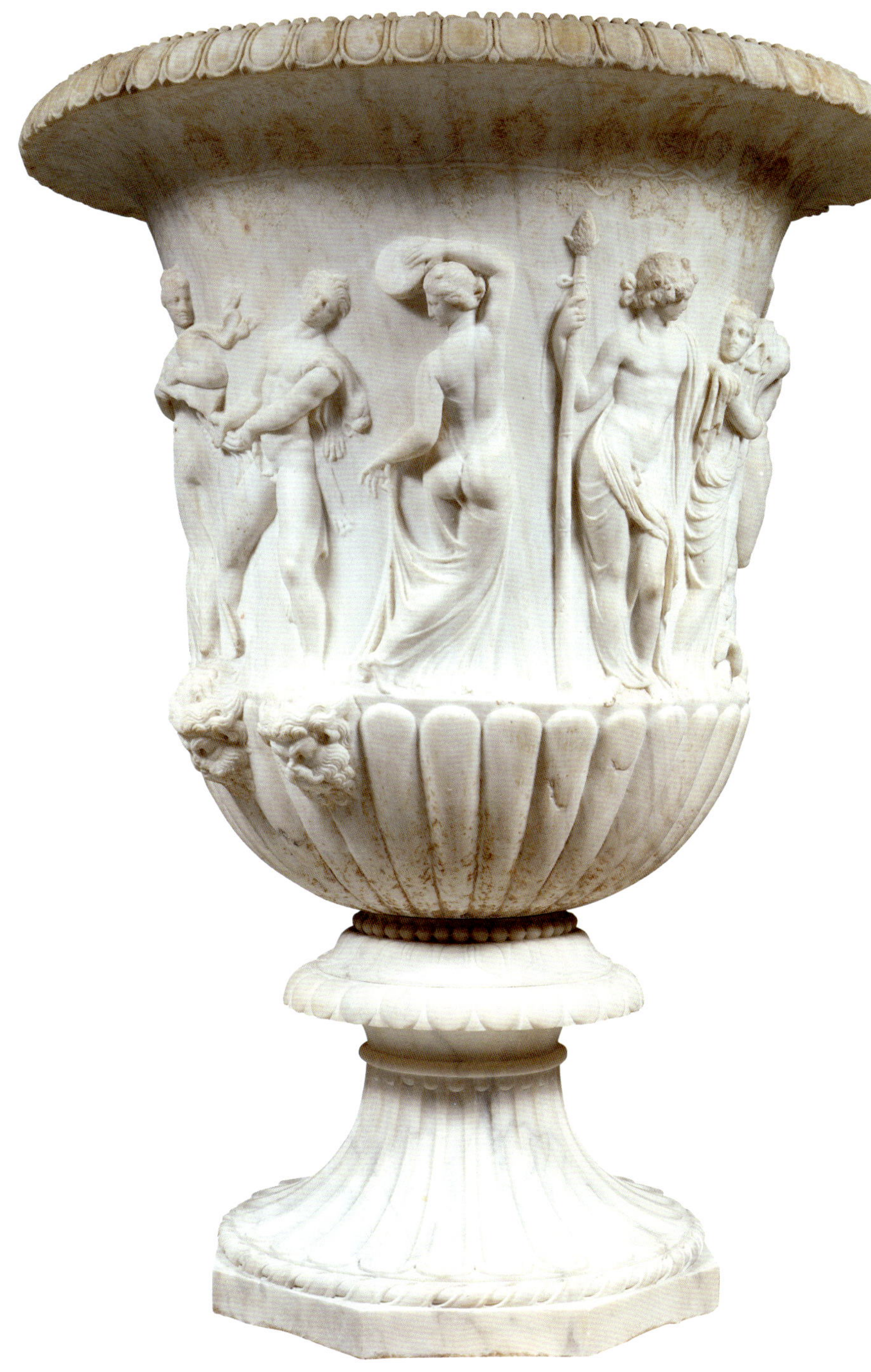

23

Attic workshop

KRATER DECORATED WITH A PROCESSION OF DIONYSOS, KNOWN AS THE BORGHESE VASE

First century BCE

Marble

172 × 135 × 135 cm (67¾ × 53⅛ × 53⅛ in.)

Paris, Musée du Louvre, Département des Antiquités Grecques, Étrusques et Romaines, inv. MR 985

24

Nicolas Poussin

THE TRIUMPH OF SILENUS

ca. 1636

Oil on canvas

142.9 × 120.5 cm (56¼ × 47½ in.)

London, National Gallery, Bought, 1824,

inv. NG42

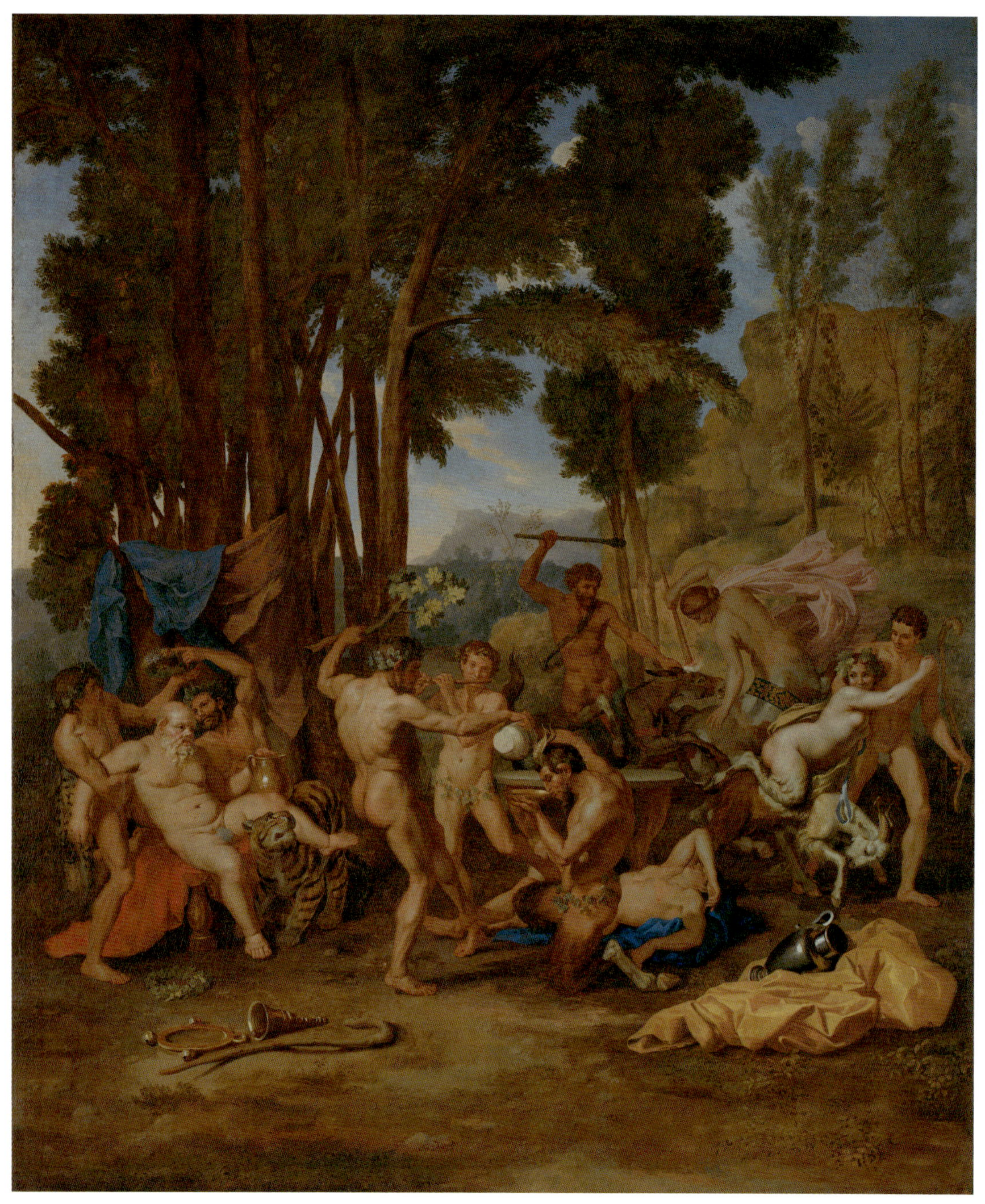

25

Nicolas Poussin

THE BIRTH OF VENUS,
also known as
THE TRIUMPH OF NEPTUNE AND AMPHITRITE

ca. 1634–35

Oil on canvas

97.2 × 108 cm (38¼ × 42½ in.)

Philadelphia Museum of Art,
The George W. Elkins Collection,
1932, inv. E1932–1–1

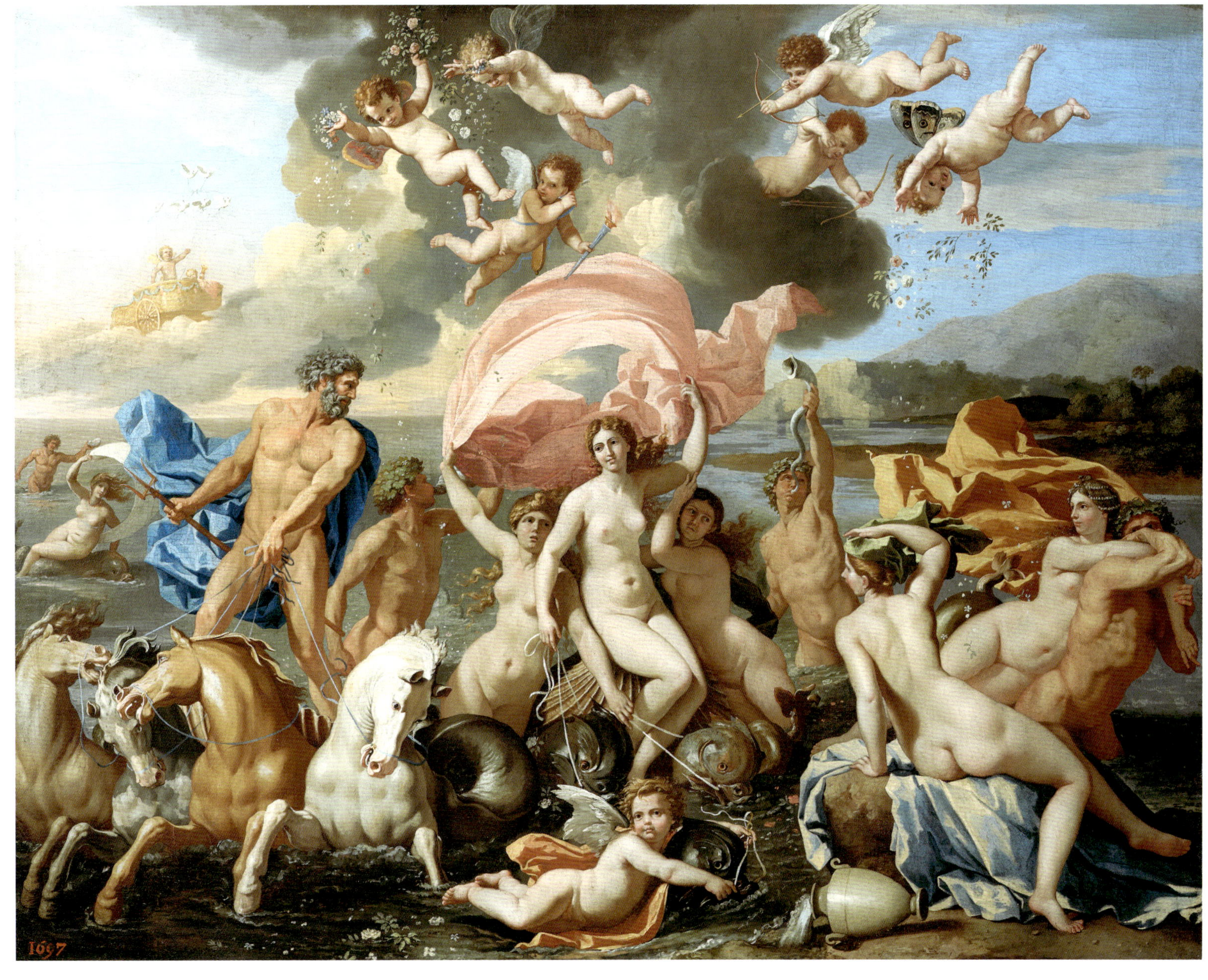

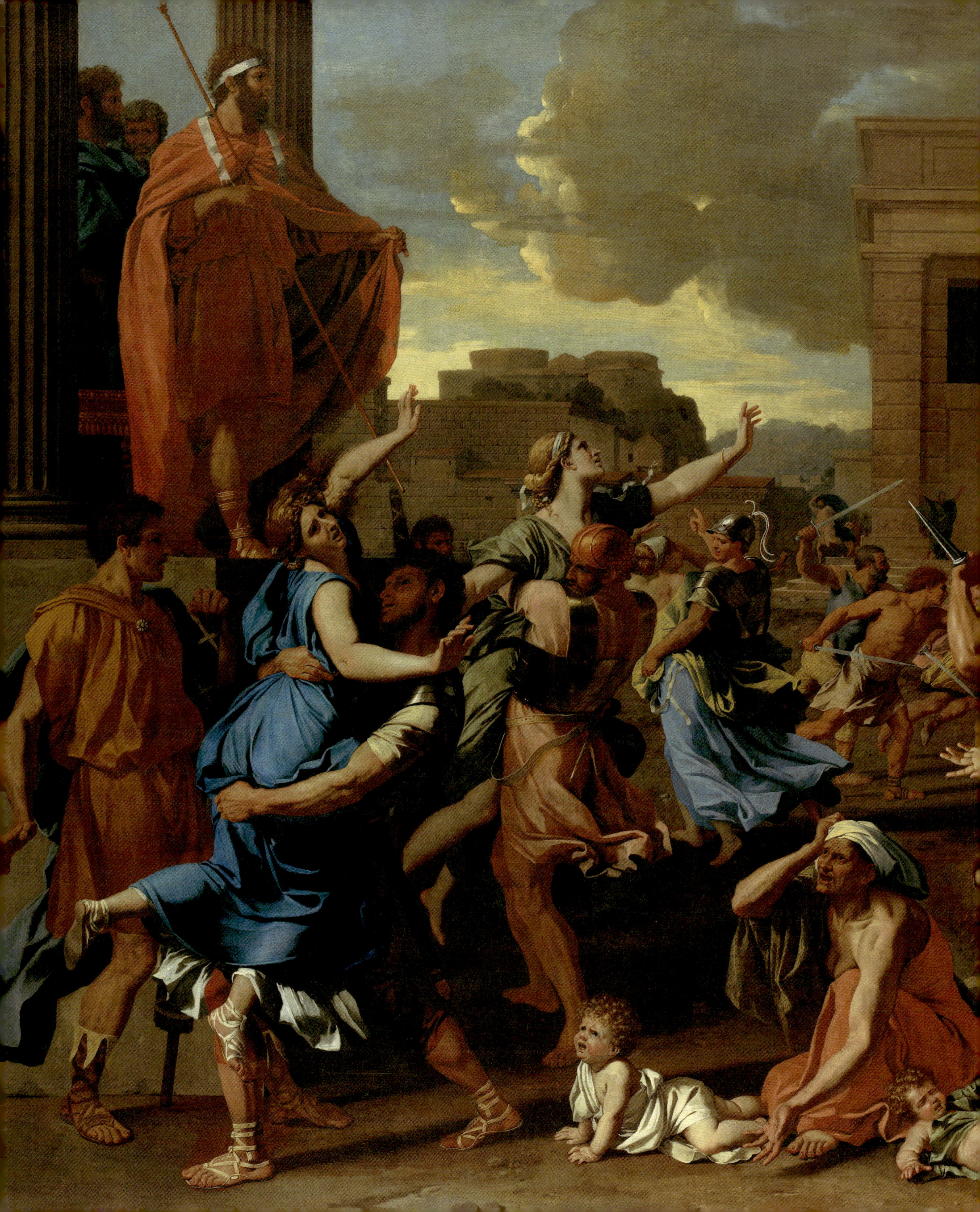

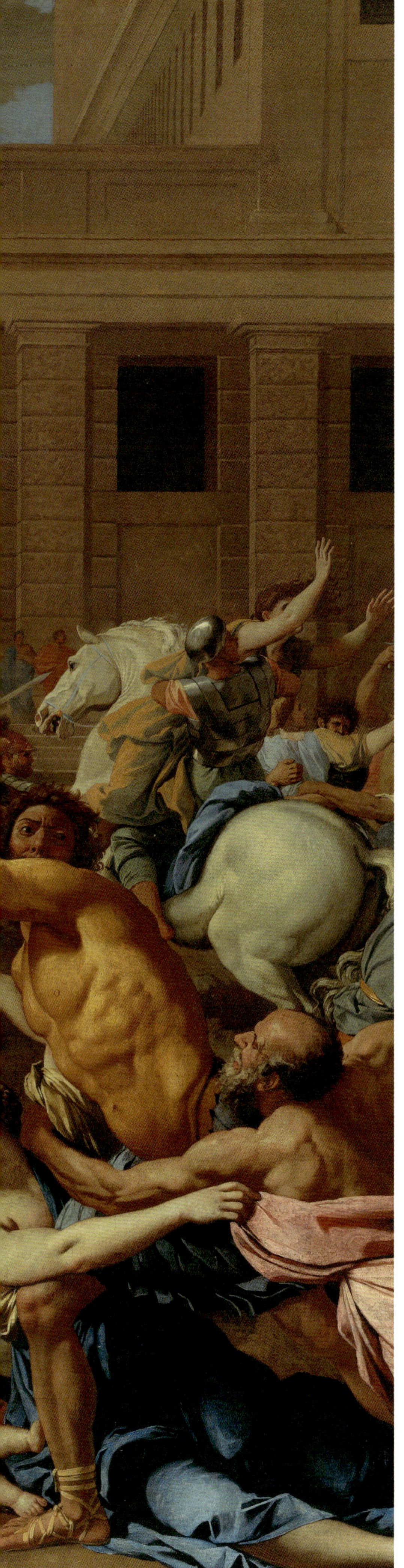

CHOREOGRAPHING VIOLENCE
THE ABDUCTION OF THE SABINE WOMEN

EMILY A. BEENY

It is a little slip of paper (plate 26). Smaller than a postcard, yet here we find what may be Nicolas Poussin's most potent drawing, terrible in its concision, astonishing in its modernity—as if the artist had reached ahead three centuries to tear a page from a sketchbook of Paul Cézanne. Two figures are locked in a violent struggle. One hoists the other in the air, binding her in a fierce embrace. The other attempts to resist, planting her palm on her captor's face and kicking uselessly behind her. A single dilution of wash, swiftly and precisely applied, carves three-dimensional forms from the flat page and confirms Poussin's reliance on his wax figurines to invent the tangled pose of these two figures, placed in the raking light of the toy theater and transcribed with chalk, pen, and brush.

The composition is strikingly similar to that of a drawing Poussin made in the margin of Leonardo da Vinci's *Trattato della pittura* (fig. 24): an illustration of the hero Hercules wrestling the half-giant Antaeus.[1] There, though, both figures are male; their evenly matched strength is the source of the drama. Even in the radically abbreviated language of our postcard drawing, however, the captive figure is legibly female—her body soft and pliant, overpowered in her captor's grip, her eyes and mouth three terse, despairing *Os*. Here is an image of rape.

The sheet belongs to a group of closely intertwined works—four surviving drawings and two of Poussin's most celebrated paintings (plates 26–31)—that treat the abduction of the Sabine women, a foundational episode in the story of ancient Rome recounted by the historians Livy and Plutarch as well as the poets Virgil and Ovid.[2] The newly founded city of Rome lacks a female population—so goes the story—therefore King Romulus and his men kidnap women from the neighboring Sabine tribe as wives to bear their children and furnish future generations of Romans. Commonly known as the "Rape of the Sabines" (from the Latin *raptio*, meaning kidnapping), the story is one of abduction for the purpose of sexual assault.[3]

Poussin's depictions of this theme, it hardly needs saying, are images not of dance but of violence, and yet their complex, dramatic choreography has attracted endless

79

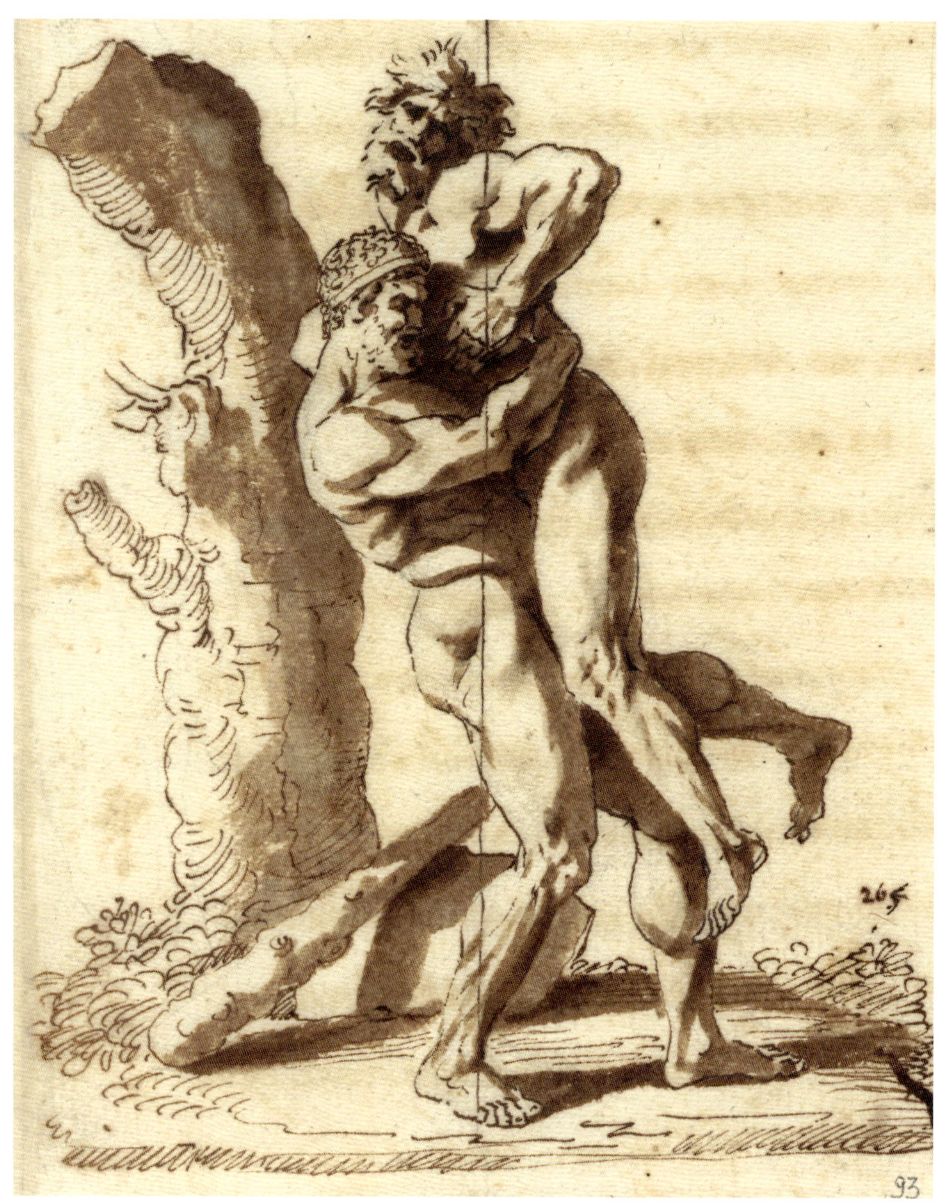

comparison to ballet.[4] That is no accident. More explicitly than any other group of works in Poussin's oeuvre, this constellation of drawings and pictures shows us the lessons the painter took away from his early exploration of dance, and the determining effect of his choreographic method on the power and the meaning of compositions where no dancing takes place.

One story, two meanings
The two finished paintings share basic compositional features: a stagelike urban setting, a presiding figure in Romulus at left, and great masses of figures rushing violently in opposite directions. Thanks to Poussin's reuse of his wax models, the pictures also share a number of individual gestures and poses: the soldier clutching a woman in blue at left in the Louvre composition (plate 31) corresponds quite precisely to a soldier

FIGURE 24
Nicolas Poussin, *Hercules and Antaeus*, in a manuscript copy of Leonardo da Vinci's *Trattato della pittura*. Brown ink and brown wash on paper, 13.7 × 10.8 cm (5⅜ × 4¼ in.). Milan, Biblioteca Ambrosiana, Ms. H 228

clutching a woman in blue at left in the Metropolitan Museum painting (plate 30); a Roman tearing at the gown of a Sabine in the right foreground of the Louvre picture corresponds to a Roman grabbing a Sabine in the middle distance at far right in the Metropolitan Museum composition; the rearing horse in quarter profile in the right middle distance is identical in the two pictures; and so on.

Yet, these works operate on quite different aesthetic and emotional registers. In doing so, they impart diverging meanings to their shared figural vignettes and common subject. The Louvre painting (plate 31), with its deep space, dramatic contrasts of light and shadow, and insistently naturalistic treatment of individual faces, offers an image of drastic chaos and despair, while the Metropolitan Museum picture (plate 30)—for all the violence of its subject—is an image of extraordinary restraint. Its shallow, luminous composition, orderly disposition of bodies, and masklike treatment of faces produce an effect powerfully reminiscent of a classical frieze. If one work presents the rape as a tragedy, the other casts it in the providential light of Roman history.[5]

It is tempting to explain these differences as a function of the painter's stylistic development: that is, to place one picture after the other in the sequence of Poussin's production and to organize the associated drawings accordingly. But the order in which he made these objects has formed the subject of much scholarly disagreement and—despite archival discoveries bearing on the dating of both paintings in the decades since they were last exhibited side by side—remains open to debate.[6] As discussed below, the Metropolitan Museum picture was almost certainly completed between June 1633 and July 1634,[7] but the Louvre picture appears to have been painted roughly between 1634 and 1635.[8] The two periods obviously overlap. Nor is the sequence in which Poussin made the related drawings certain. Both compositional studies (plates 28, 29) share features with each of the finished paintings,[9] and the more detailed figure studies (plates 26, 27) might conceivably have been executed either before or after the compositional drawings. In short, Poussin seems to have produced all of these works within a brief window and may well have had several underway at once during the first half of 1634, moving his wax figurines around the box like pieces on a chessboard, and making drawings to work out the pictorial implications of these movements before putting brush to canvas.

If it cannot be explained as a function of stylistic development over the course of several years, how do we account for the difference between the two pictures? An answer may lie in the identities of the patrons who paid for them: one a man of god, the other, essentially, a soldier. Bellori tells us that Poussin painted the picture today in the Louvre for Luigi Alessandro Omodei (1608–1685), a young legal scholar, member of the college of prelates, and future cardinal.[10] By contrast, the patron of the Metropolitan Museum picture, as Félibien informs us, was Charles I de Créquy, duc de Lesdiguières and Maréchal de France (1578–1638), a French general, courtier, and ambassador to Rome from 1633 to 1634.[11] With its shuddering aversion to sexual violence and its indictment of pre-Christian Rome as an essentially criminal enterprise, the Louvre painting is easily enough imagined in the home of the young priest and legal scholar Omodei. Conversely, the Metropolitan Museum picture, which marshals violence to geometric order and stampeding bodies into an antique relief, reminds us that from the rape will arise Rome, from the crime, a civilization. What message could be more apposite for a collector who had made his career fighting in Louis XIII's army and dancing at his court?

Martial choreography

A time-honored subject in European art, the abduction of the Sabine women had grown particularly popular in the early seventeenth century, satisfying contemporary collectors' dual appetites for sex and violence. For a painter setting out to portray the subject in 1630s Rome, Pietro da Cortona's was the picture to beat (fig. 25). Commissioned by the Sacchetti family, this vast canvas—more than four meters wide—then hung in the very same room at their villa as a copy after Poussin's *Triumph of Venus* (known as the *Triumph of Flora*) (fig. 6).[12] Cortona had followed the compositional model of Polidoro da Caravaggio's mural on the facade of the Palazzo Milesi. Now badly damaged, the fresco was much admired and copied in early modern Rome (fig. 26).[13] Making changes to the composition as he painted (some still visible to the naked eye), Cortona condensed the story's action into three figural vignettes pressed up against the picture plane.[14] Roman soldiers at left and right hoist high their Sabine captives, who twist their necks and raise their arms in graceful distress. At center a third Roman drags his future bride across the ground.

Though he pursued a more methodical procedure, Poussin borrowed from Cortona (and Polidoro) the idea of three principal assaults set against a backdrop of condensed movement. We see this idea take shape in a second figure study (plate 27); here the motif of the soldier dragging his captive is worked out at right, with the more complex grouping of a young Sabine woman, an old Sabine man, and a Roman captor entangled at center. At left the artist explored a variant on the Hercules and Antaeus pair: a sinewy male nude steps forward with his right foot and grasps his captive under her arm, bearing the weight of her body on his chest and cheek. Again, she kicks her feet, extending a fluted arm as if to cry for help. The three groupings create a frieze of forceful gesture and dramatic wash, set against a backdrop of more schematic figures—flat in appearance, rendered only with pen—that evoke the chaos of a battle in progress.

This compositional idea—a sculptural frieze set against a dense fabric of smaller figures—forms the basis for the painting today in the Metropolitan Museum (plate 30). At right appears a variant on the Sabine-father-Roman trio from the figure study: a soldier in a golden cuirass towers above his prize, preparing to stab the old man. Beside this group, the more novel invention of a weeping Sabine wet nurse and two infants lends pathos to the scene and reminds us that issue itself—the bearing of children—is here at issue. Two variations on the Hercules and Antaeus pair complete the frieze at left, while above them on a columned porch stands Romulus, raising his cloak to signal the Roman attack.[15]

Only one vignette is repeated verbatim from the figure study: the woman in green and the soldier with a brazen helmet are posed in precisely the same configuration as the woman with a fluted arm and her abductor in the drawing. Poussin had obviously made wax models for these figures, which also appear, more schematically

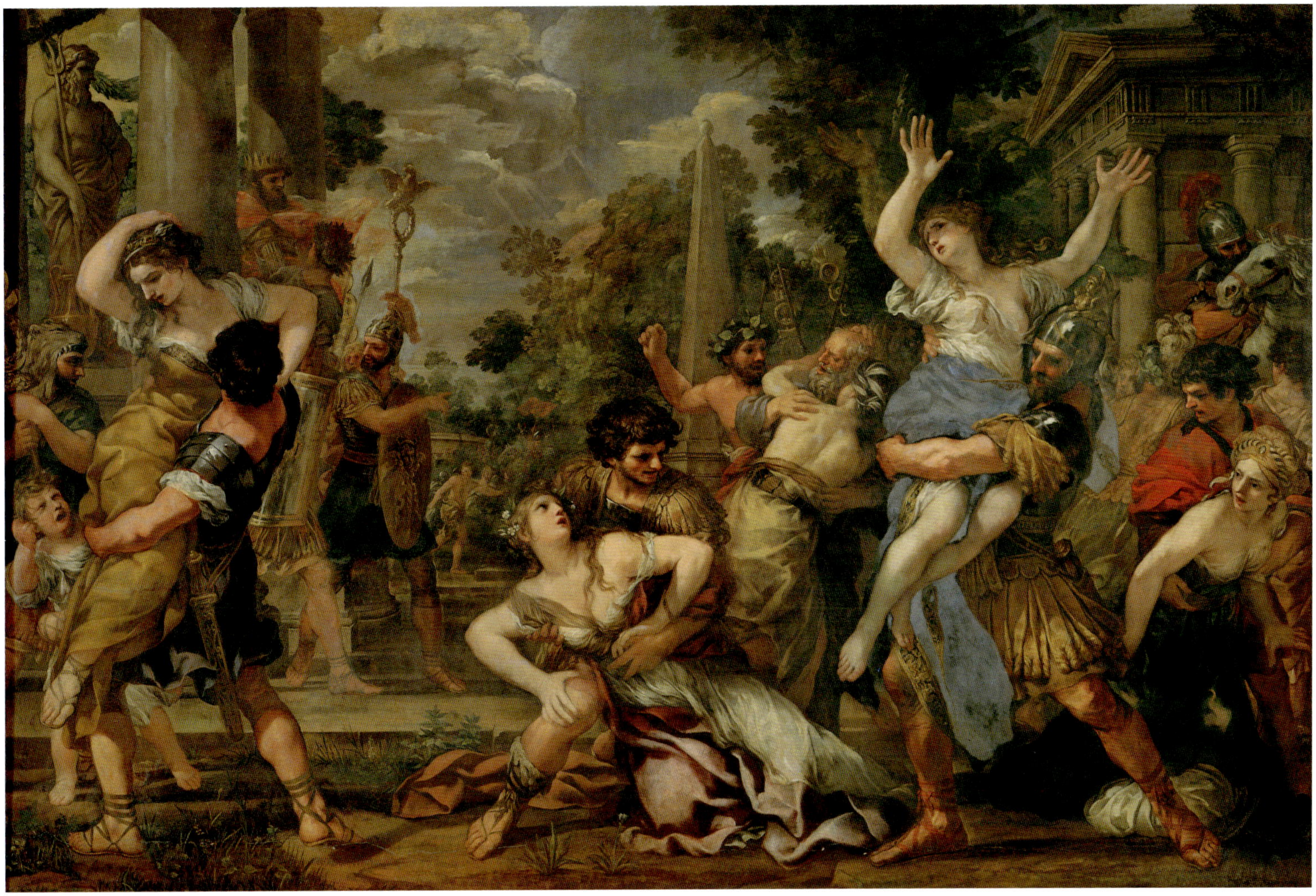

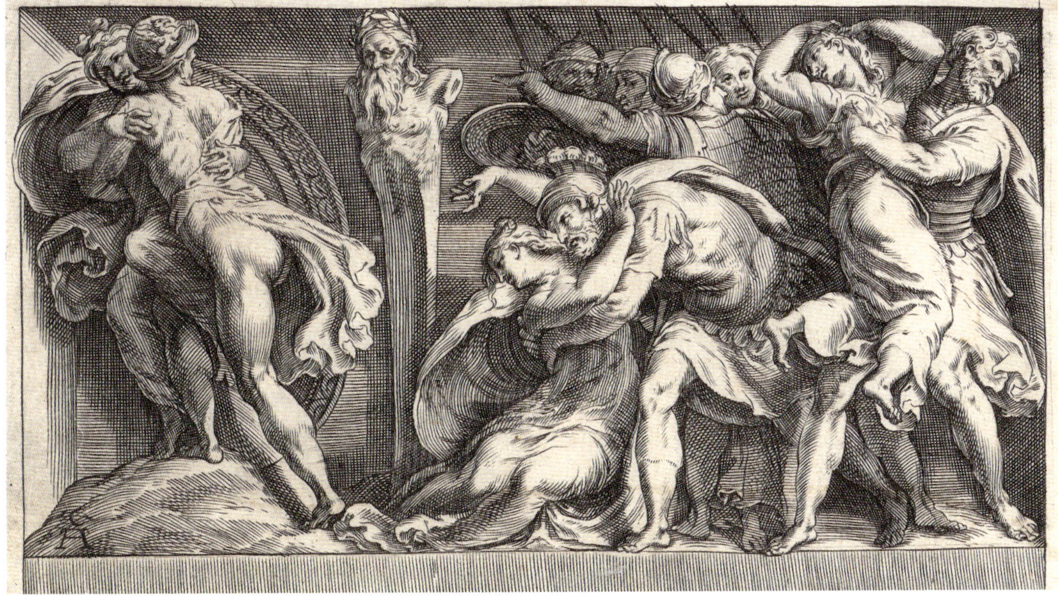

FIGURE 25
Pietro da Cortona (Italian, 1596–1669), *Abduction of the Sabine Women*, ca. 1630. Oil on canvas, 280.5 × 476 cm (110½ × 187⅜ in.). Rome, Pinacoteca Capitolina, inv. PC 137

FIGURE 26
Cherubino Alberti (1553–1615), *The Abduction of the Sabine Women*, after Polidoro da Caravaggio, late sixteenth or early seventeenth century. Engraving, 15.2 × 21.7 cm (6 × 8½ in.) (image). San Francisco, Fine Arts Museums, Achenbach Foundation, inv. 1963.30.37160

rendered, in the two surviving compositional studies (plates 28, 29). For two of the other vignettes in the Metropolitan Museum frieze, Poussin drew inspiration from immediately recognizable sculptures. To play the fearsome Roman in golden armor at right, the painter cast the Galatian Suicide (fig. 27), then displayed in the Ludovisi gardens, which was among the most celebrated archaeological finds of the seventeenth century.[16] The sculpture depicts a man clutching the body of a woman with one hand and preparing to plunge a dagger into his own breast with the other.[17] Poussin plainly relished the figure's defiant, emphatic pose, which he replicated faithfully in the Metropolitan Museum painting, merely reversing its orientation and adjusting the angle of the knife. This adjustment has narrative meaning, converting the figure from a suicide to an assailant, but it also lengthens the slashing diagonal of the soldier's body, answering the perpendicular gestures of two women carried off at left in the same painting.

One of these women marks the picture's other sculptural citation. With furrowed brow and parted lips, the captive in blue at left throws back her head and raises her arms. Poussin borrowed these features of her pose from Giambologna's 1581–82 *Abduction of a Sabine Woman* (fig. 28), displayed in the Loggia dei Lanzi in Florence: arguably the greatest achievement of late Renaissance sculpture in Italy.[18] There the composition involves two men, one crouching below as the other scoops up his quarry in a muscular corkscrew. Poussin adjusted the pose of the abductor, who in the painter's formulation grabs his future bride by the waist and under the seat, counterbalancing her weight by leaning backward and planting his right foot firmly before him.

These adjustments accommodate Giambologna's pair to the geometric regime of the Metropolitan Museum composition. Here, whether carrying off a bride or preparing to deliver a blow, Roman bodies, on the whole, sweep upward from right to left; and whether in grief, anger, or despair, Sabine bodies sweep upward from left to right.[19] In the background, for example, a Roman soldier and his charger rear up and to the left, while the woman in his arms reaches helplessly up and to the right; the three bodies (horse, soldier, Sabine) create a tight, insistent *X*. In the foreground, the two abducted women at left form elegant parallels, reaching over their lunging captors' heads. At right the crawling child, the young woman, and the old man form a line that slants from lower left to upper right. The gold-armored Roman slices through this diagonal in a savage, sweeping perpendicular.

Romulus, standing above the fray, barely lifts his cloak in a solemn, sovereign gesture that announces his exemption from the passions erupting at his command. His pose also seems to foreshadow the outcome of the violence below: while his scepter describes a diagonal from lower right to upper left, the hem of his cloak traces a perpendicular line. Here the vectors identified with Roman and Sabine movement converge: the chiastic structure of the whole composition is marshaled to order in and by the body of the king. By assigning pattern to the soldiers' and Sabines' thrashing limbs, Poussin here invites us to extract historical meaning from contingent horror. We witness this scene with the organizing vision of retrospect, aware of the order that will emerge from the chaos.

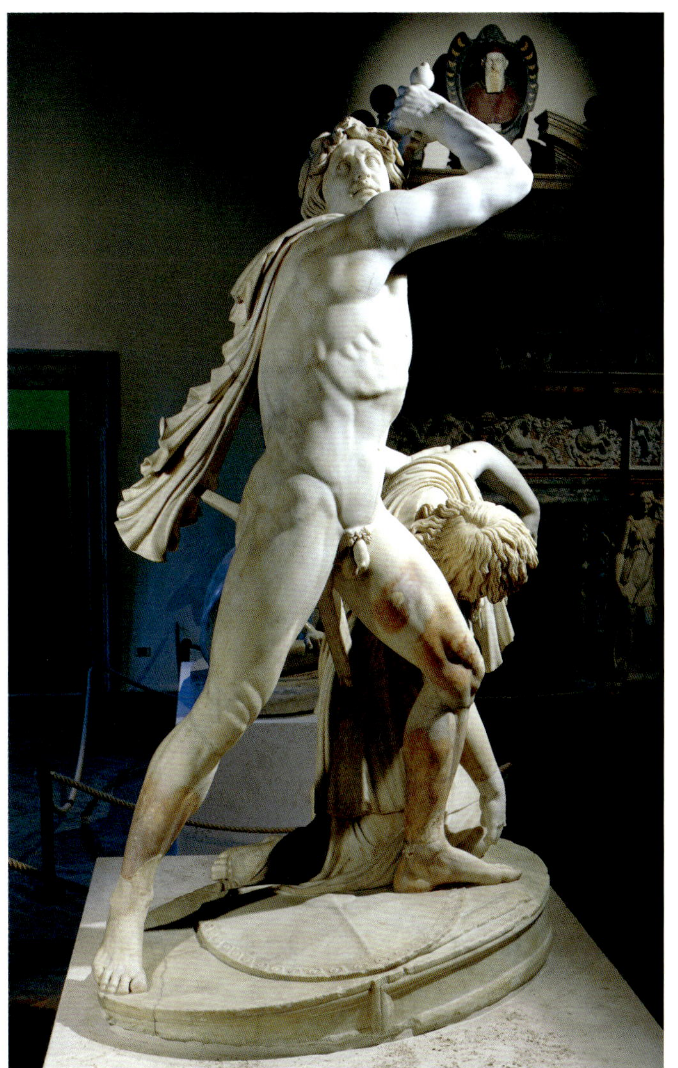 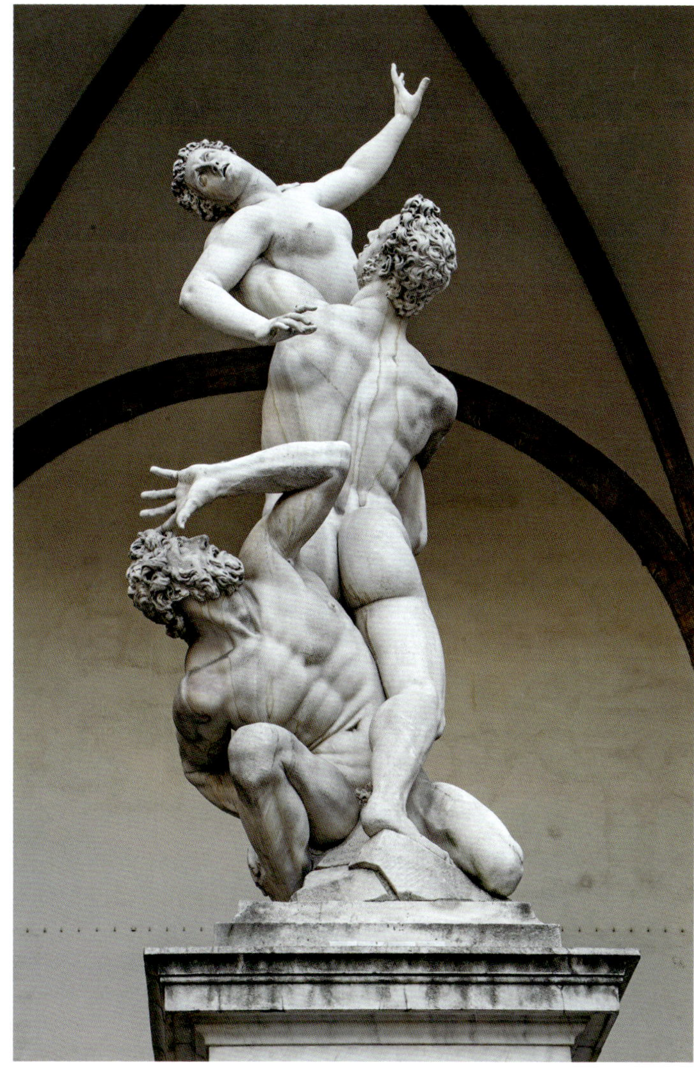

The Maréchal de Créquy

Both the Metropolitan Museum picture's martial geometry and its rather showy citation of two sculptures as famous as the Galatian Suicide and Giambologna's *Abduction of a Sabine Woman* would have flattered the tastes of its original owner. The Maréchal de Créquy was a member of the French *noblesse d'épée* decorated many times over.[20] He had fought with distinction at Montpellier and in the Piedmont. Named Maréchal de France in 1622, he also served, back in Paris, as Chief Gentleman of the King's Bedchamber. He was, in other words, among the first citizens of France, a man Richelieu himself described with grudging admiration.[21] Créquy's missions in Rome were to persuade the Holy See to join forces with France against Spain and to obtain the annulment of a secretly contracted marriage between the duc d'Orléans and Marguerite de Lorraine. In these endeavors he failed, but his secondary goal was to proclaim the splendor of his own nation, to demonstrate through lavish consumption France's superiority to her great rival, Spain. In this he succeeded quite handsomely.

FIGURE 27

The Galatian Suicide, also known as the Ludovisi Gaul, Roman, probably first century CE. Marble, 211 cm (83 in.). Rome, Palazzo Altemps, inv. 8608

FIGURE 28

Giambologna (Flemish, act. Italy, 1529–1608), *Abduction of a Sabine Woman*, 1582. Marble, 410 cm (161⅜ in.). Florence, Loggia dei Lanzi

Established at the Palazzo Orsini, Créquy lived on a grand scale, maintaining a suite of five hundred servants, retainers, and hangers-on, from poets and painters to the little person known as "Créquy's dwarf," whose portrait bust the ambassador commissioned from Poussin's friend Duquesnoy.[22] During the thirteen months of his embassy, Créquy amassed a formidable collection, comprising one hundred sixty-three oil paintings.[23] Though he bought masterpieces by Veronese and Caravaggio, he focused on the work of more recent Bolognese and Northern European painters active in Rome: Domenichino (1581–1641), Giovanni Lanfranco (1582–1647), Guido Reni (1575–1642), Poussin, Claude Lorrain (1604/5–1682), Jean Lemaire (1597–1659), and so on. Although he received several paintings as diplomatic gifts, he seems to have purchased most of them himself and commissioned a number—including Poussin's—directly from their makers.[24]

Described by his contemporaries as a learned soldier, Créquy was particularly interested in Roman history and versed, like Poussin, in the "language of the Caesars."[25] Reading Plutarch and Livy would have acquainted him with the abduction of the Sabines as a necessary evil, amply justified by the subsequent glory of Rome. Nor would the significance of Poussin's martial choreography have been lost on the general; for a man of his nationality and class, military and dance training went hand in hand. Ballet lessons, like instruction in fencing and dressage, played a central role in every French nobleman's education, subjecting the body to a discipline at once graceful and implicitly violent.[26]

Like other members of Louis XIII's court, Créquy took part in annual *ballets de cour*, strange and sumptuous amateur performances marking the winter Carnival season. His first recorded appearance in such an entertainment was in the 1623 *Ballet des bacchanales*, which took wine and love as its themes.[27] Fresh from battle in the Piedmont, he played the part of a "Desbauché de l'amour"—roughly, a love-drunk fool; such casting was a courtly joke, submitting a fearsome warrior to the pleasure of the crown. The following February he appeared in another Carnival entertainment, the *Ballet des volleurs*. This one followed a nocturnal theme, with entrances for Night, Serenaders, Thieves, and a chorus of Stars.[28] Louis XIII himself appeared as a Sea Captain and Créquy as a Pirate. Like other ballets of the 1620s, this one was full of sexual innuendo and mock violence, but resolved into order: grave geometric dances, pattern, coordination, the glory of France, and the triumph of civility.

One subject, two Modes?

Poussin seems to have reserved the Galatian Suicide citation for Créquy: it does not appear in either of his compositional drawings or in the painting at the Louvre, made for Omodei. But the Giambologna reference recurs in all three, migrating from the middle distance at left in the Uffizi drawing (plate 28), to the right foreground of the Chatsworth drawing (plate 29), and back to the left foreground of the Louvre painting (plate 31). This itinerary (fig. 29) offers a case in point for Poussin's use of the toy theater and schematic wash drawings to work through his compositions—their distribution of figures, their rhythm of light and shadow. But in the Louvre picture (plate 31) he also introduced an important change in the rendering of the vignette. Whereas in Créquy's

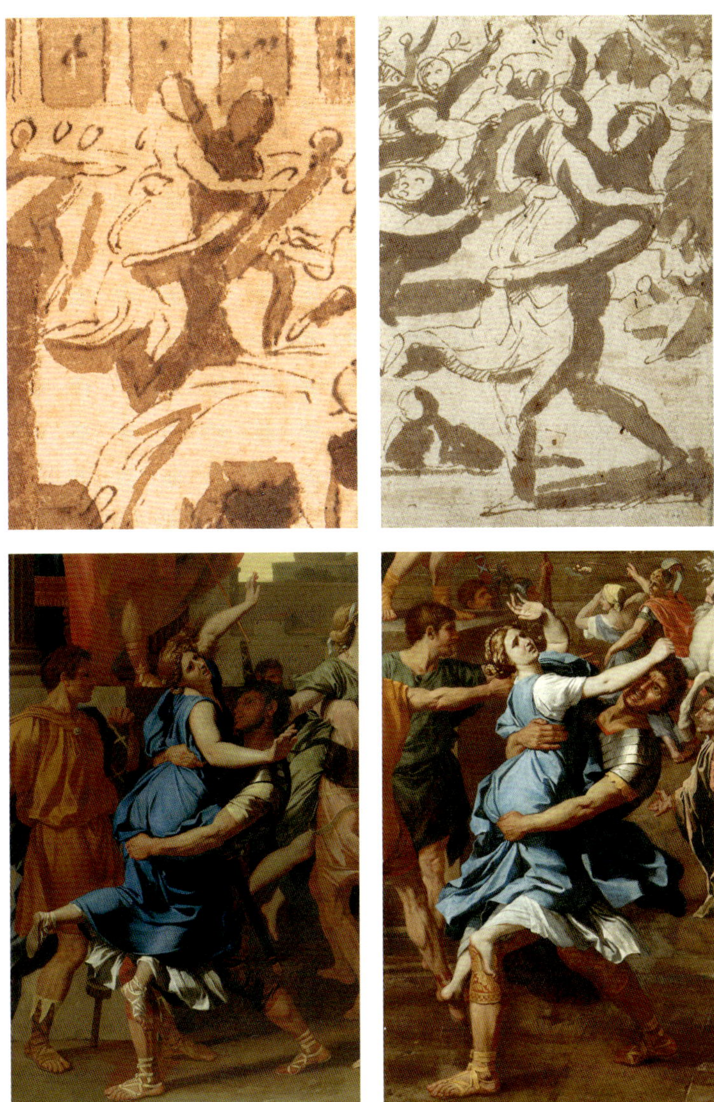

painting and in both compositional studies, the hoisted woman extends her arms before her in graceful counterpoise, in the picture painted for Omodei she grabs a fistful of her captor's hair. The gesture feels inelegant—and true. It is in keeping with the more visceral, chaotic realism of this version as a whole. Here Poussin gives us dirty paving stones and tear-stained cheeks, the toothless mouths of Sabine elders, the new Roman Forum still, it seems, a construction site. As in the compositional drawings, the Temple of Capitoline Jupiter looms in the left background, but the building at the right is under scaffolding.[29]

We recognize other figural vignettes from the compositional studies too, but the effect of crowding already present in those drawings is here taken a step farther. Bodies in the Louvre painting tumble together, forming a throng, not a frieze. Foreground and background merge into a continuous space through which the conflict spills up and across the canvas, onto the temple porch and away into the side streets. This configuration conveys a powerful sense of the abduction as it was surely lived: a scrum of lust and terror. In this context, the Giambolognesque captive holds new and

FIGURE 29
Details from the two studies for *The Abduction of the Sabine Women* (Uffizi, plate 28; and Chatsworth, plate 29) with details from the two paintings of *The Abduction of the Sabine Women* (Metropolitan Museum, plate 30; and Louvre, plate 31)

specific narrative meaning, for the tragedy of an individual family seems to frame the scene. Fleeing to the right, a Sabine father in a golden tunic turns back to look at the young woman borne off to the left: is she his daughter? As in a tragic play, the representation of these characters as individuals invites us to identify with the pain that they experience. The outcome of the struggle—the rise of Rome—now seems almost irrelevant. Romulus is literally upstaged; his violent gesture and parted lips match the terrible passion of his men.

As we have seen, Poussin's reasons for portraying the same event in two very different ways likely had something to do with the tastes of his patrons, but he was also increasingly interested in the artist's power to excite various emotional responses in the viewer. He would explain this power some years later, in 1647, using language borrowed from music theory to formulate the so-called Letter on the Modes, a note to a disgruntled client asserting that the painter must adapt his mode of depiction to suit the subject at hand.[30] Sweet, lighthearted subjects should be sweetly painted; somber ones, portrayed with gravity; and so on. While Leonardo, like other art theorists, had suggested in his *Trattato* that expressive gestures presented the artist with his primary means of transmitting emotion from an image to its observer,[31] Poussin's Letter on the Modes locates affective power in the rather more abstract formal properties of harmony, proportion, and composition.[32]

In the *Sabines* group, the artist's recycling of the same expressive gestures—his reuse of the very same wax figurines from drawing to drawing and picture to picture—seems to bear out this claim. The fungible meaning of the rape itself—variously framed by ancient writers as a triumphant moment in military history, an erotic anecdote, an original sin of Rome[33]—presented Poussin with an opportunity to experiment. Accordingly, despite their shared repertoire of gestures, Poussin's two finished paintings of this event achieve radically different emotional outcomes. The artist's power to excite a response here resides not only in his skill at representing the expressions of individual figures (the wailing captive in the postcard drawing) but also in his ability to orchestrate the movements and poses of multiple figures, combining these with other pictorial elements to create a compositional whole whose affective powers are greater than the sum of its parts. With different palettes, different degrees of naturalism, different proportions of figure to landscape, and above all, different stagings of movement in space, the two *Abduction*s demonstrate their author's power to conjure varied emotions in the viewer, wringing two meanings from a single story.[34]

Poussin and Degas

In Poussin's lifetime, the picture painted for Créquy was the more famous of the two. The Maréchal's embassy concluded in July 1634, and his paintings were sent back to Paris, where they would hang in a sumptuous residence on the rue de Cerisaie.[35] Open to visitors until Créquy's death in battle four years later, the collection presented a splendid, almost haphazard, display of the kind more commonly found in seicento Roman palaces than Parisian hôtels particuliers.[36] It was much admired by his countrymen, and the fact that Poussin had secured a place in it was essential to the artist's subsequent success in France, for *The Abduction of the Sabine Women* was the first work in Poussin's new classical manner to reach his native country.[37] With the cream of the collection, the picture was "purchased" (though never paid for) out of the ambassador's estate by Cardinal Richelieu, who displayed it in his palace opposite the Louvre.[38]

But in the end, Omodei's version would prove more consequential for Poussin's reception and legacy in France, for Créquy's picture passed upon the death of Richelieu to the cardinal's niece and from there to the collector Jean Néret de La Ravoye (1643–1701),[39] evading the grasp of Louis XIV, whose minister of finance and works, Jean-Baptiste Colbert (1619–1683), set out in the 1660s to amass for the crown the largest collection of Poussin's pictures in the world.[40] Unable to secure Créquy's *Abduction*, the crown acquired Omodei's, shipped to Paris from the Roman port of Civitavecchia in the spring of 1685.[41] So Poussin's tragic telling of the Sabine story, not his heroic-historical one, came to hang in the Grande Galerie of the Louvre, to be seen and studied by generations of French painters, especially after the transformation of the palace into a museum at the end of the eighteenth century.[42]

There, in late 1861 or early 1862, the young Edgar Degas (1834–1917) set up his easel. Recently returned from his own studies in Italy, he had not yet begun painting the ballet pictures that would make him famous as an Impressionist in the 1870s. He had come to copy Poussin's rape (plate 32). Preparing a canvas of almost identical dimensions with a reddish-brown ground, Degas incised into it the paving stones, the Temple of Jupiter, the structures of a Roman Forum still under construction. Though he was already beginning to work wet-into-wet in the modern style, here he matched Poussin figure for figure, color for color, stroke for stroke.[43] Like Poussin, he painted the background first, leaving the figures in reserve, to be added one by one. The copy took him months (one colleague claimed a year[44]), for, though he had made an assiduous study of many other old masters, this copy—in its ambition and scale, in its painstaking, almost slavish replication of the master's technical procedures—is quite unlike anything else in Degas's oeuvre.[45]

What drew him to Poussin's picture? Degas was then at work on his own "battle of the sexes"—an open-air confrontation between adolescent Spartans, male and female.[46] But surely he recognized something deeper in Poussin's orchestration of complex, colliding movement, already suspended between battle and ballet.[47] In its skillful deployment of tangled bodies, its making of meaning from frozen movement, the copy after Poussin seems to look ahead a decade in Degas's career to an obsession that would begin at the opera house in the rue Le Peletier. Making careful drawings—and, famously, wax models of his own—Degas would devote much of the rest of his life to scenes of dancers. But already here, in his faithful copy, action is arrested, dissected, and reconfigured, as the greatest modern painter of dance follows in the footsteps of Poussin.

NOTES

Translations of ancient texts refer to standard Loeb editions.

1   Poussin's drawings for the *Trattato* were commissioned by Cassiano dal Pozzo; this one illustrates a passage on the distribution of weight in motionless bodies. See Leonardo 1651, 75 (263). See also Barone 2009, Sparti 2003, and Rosenberg and Prat 1994, no. 129. On a similar reuse of figures in the *Trattato* and the *Saving of Pyrrhus* ([painting] Musée du Louvre, Paris; [drawing] Royal Collection, Windsor), see Rosenberg 2015, no. 11; Prat 2013, 33–34; and London et al. 1995–96, no. 31.

2   Livy, *History of Rome* 1.9:9–16; Plutarch, *Life of Romulus* 14.2–15.5; Virgil, *Aeneid* 8.635–38; and Ovid, *The Art of Love* 1.100–134; a glancing reference also appears in *Fasti* 3.

3   Each of the classical accounts rationalizes the rape differently (see Beard 1999). Livy (1.9:16, trans. B. O. Foster) details the divvying up of women according to their looks, assuring us that the Romans' subsequent wooing "excused their act on the score of passion and love." Plutarch (14.6, trans. Bernadette Perrin) suggests that the Romans scrupulously avoided married women, insisting, "they did not commit the rape out of wantonness." Ovid pairs his eroticized account with a recommendation of the theater as an assignation spot (since the rape took place during the Consualia games). Virgil's telling appears in the course of his description of the relief design on the shield of Aeneas. Here, though described as "lawless," the abduction is justified first as a historical inevitability and second as an object of aesthetic delight, represented in a work of art.

4   Brigstocke, for example, described the Metropolitan Museum painting as "a well-choreographed ballet" (Oxford 1990–91, no. 28). See also Unglaub 2006, 169; Fumaroli 1982, 41; Licht 1954, 120; George 1936, 9; and others. As several of these authors point out, Poussin's approach to the Sabines story owes a debt to Raphael's *Massacre of the Innocents*. On the choreography of that composition, famously recorded in a print by Marcantonio Raimondi (surely familiar to Poussin), see Powell 2012, 179–92.

5   Arasse 2000, 337. For discussions of Providence in Poussin's thought and work, see Paris 2015.

6   For a summary of dating debates between Blunt and Mahon—and, more recently, Boyer, Volf, Sparti et al.—see Rosenberg 2015, no. 10.

7   That is, during the Maréchal de Créquy's Roman embassy (discussed below).

8   A surviving receipt for Poussin's *Destruction of the Temple of Jerusalem* (Kunsthistorisches Museum, Vienna) is dated January 11, 1636; that painting bears a very close stylistic and compositional relationship to the Louvre *Abduction of the Sabine Women*, suggesting that both date to the middle 1630s. See Sparti 2004–5, 186–89.

9   A crucial discussion of the drawings' relationships appears in Prat 2013, 36. Prat's assertion that the Uffizi drawing (plate 28) postdates the Chatsworth drawing (plate 29), because Poussin enclosed the Uffizi composition with pen lines, seems to discount the possibility that the Chatsworth sheet might have been trimmed.

10 Bellori 1672, 449. On Omodei, see also Spiriti 1993 and 2013. His ownership is documented from 1655, when he tried to sell both the *Triumph of Venus* (known as the *Triumph of Flora*) (fig. 6) and the *Abduction of the Sabine Women* to Louis XIV's first minister of finance, Nicolas Fouquet; see Thuillier 1960, 103n2.

11 Félibien 1725, 4:24. Créquy's ownership is confirmed by his posthumous inventory; see Boyer and Volf 1988, 32, no. 130. On the role of Melchior de Gilliers (1589–1669) in Créquy's commission, see also Olson 2002, 68.

12 See Zirpolo 2005, 60–62; and the Sacchetti inventory of July 4, 1639 (Getty Provenance Index, no. I–344). Listed in that inventory as an original work, the Sacchetti *Triumph* was more likely the copy today attributed to Poussin's friend Jean Lemaire (Pinacoteca Capitolina, Rome); see Loire 2010 and Guarino and Masini 2006, no. 192.

13 On Poussin's interest in Polidoro, see Schütze 1996, 580; and Keazor 1994, 271–75.

14 See Rome 1997–98, no. 7 (Patrizia Masini).

15 A detail taken from Plutarch, *Life of Romulus*, 14.5. On the gesture, see also Bätschmann 1990, 122; Fumaroli 1982, 41; and Costello 1947, 203–4.

16 Apparently unearthed during the construction of the Villa Ludovisi in the early 1620s (see Venetucci et al. 1983, no. 64), the sculpture had already been cited by 1624 in Rubens's *Council of the Gods* (Musée du Louvre, Paris) at the Palais du Luxembourg. That picture was surely familiar to Poussin, who worked at the palace while Rubens's cycle was in progress (Félibien 1725, 4:315), and to the Maréchal de Créquy, a member of the French court.

17 See Marvin 2002. Assigned various titles in the seventeenth century, the sculpture was consistently interpreted as a suicide. It appears in the Ludovisi inventory of 1623 as a "certain Marius slaying his daughter and himself," (Haskell, Penny et al. 2021, no. 68), and François Perrier published it as a "Statue of Pyramus and Thisbe" (Perrier 1638, no. 32). Judith Bernstock (2000, 183) has read French nationalistic significance into Poussin's selection of a sculpture depicting a Gaul, but the sculpture was not thus identified in the seventeenth century.

18 The subject of Giambologna's work is intentionally vague; see M. Cole 2008.

19 Avigdor Arikha described the same phenomenon in terms of rhyme (Houston and Princeton 1983, 33).

20 On Créquy, see Humbert 1962; see also Chorier 1681.

21 *Le Rôle de Richelieu*, cited in Thuillier 1995, 155: "grand cœur, peu de conduite, sans secret, homme peu appliqué, paresseux, capable le cul sur la selle." ("A great heart, little in the way of conduct, without secrets, a man of little application, somewhat lazy, most competent with his backside in the saddle.")

22 Galleria Nazionale d'Arte Antica, Palazzo Barberini, Rome, inv. 2578. See Lavin 1970, 132–37.

23 On Créquy's collection, see Boyer and Volf 1988; and Schnapper 1988–94, 2:158–59.

24 Félibien 1725, 4:24.

25 Chorier 1681, 270. See also the dedication to Créquy in Conti 1627, n.p.

26 On the connection between ballet and military training, see Van Orden 2005, especially 90–95.

27 Bordier et al. 1623; see also Lacroix 1868–70, 2:327–45, especially 343–45. On Créquy's role in this ballet and its iconographic connections to Poussin's work, see Beeny 2016, 65, 128–29, 165, and 198n794.

28 Bordier et al. 1624; and Lacroix 1868–70, 3:1–17. See also Beeny 2016, 166.

29 On the architecture here, see Bayard 2011; Pinson 1997, 118; and Bätschmann 1990, 122–23.

30 Poussin to Chantelou, November 24, 1647. See Jouanny 1911, no. 156; and Poussin 2014, 135–36. For further discussion, see Jonathan Unglaub's essay "*A Dance to the Music of Time*: The Wellspring of the Modes" in this volume.

31 See Leonardo 1651, 12–13 (58). Leonardo's concept of expressive gesture is indebted to Leon Battista Alberti's 1435 treatise on painting, *Della pittura* (also admired by Poussin).

32 See Freedberg 1999.

33 See note 3 above.

34   From the late 1620s through the mid-1640s, Poussin painted a series of
     pairs, doubled treatments of the same subject: two *Abduction*s *of the
     Sabine Women*, two *Massacre*s *of the Innocents*, two *Nurture*s *of Jupiter*, two
     Arcadian Shepherds, two sets of The Seven Sacraments. See Brigstocke
     1996 and Green 2000.

35   On the posthumous inventory of the Hôtel de Créquy, taken in May 1638, see
     Boyer and Volf 1988.

36   See Cropper 1996, 264; and Schnapper 1988–94, 2:158–59.

37   See Bonfait 2015, 38–40; Boyer and Volf 1988, 25; and Wild 1980, 2:29.

38   According to a posthumous inventory taken in January 1643 (see Levi 1985,
     62, no. 1002bis). Richelieu's failure to pay is noted in Tallement des Réaux
     1834–35, 1:387.

39   On Néret de La Ravoye, see Bonfait 1988 and Schnapper 1988–94, 2:407–8.

40   Notably through the 1665 purchase of thirteen Poussins from the duc de
     Richelieu. On the place of Poussin in Louis XIV's collecting strategy, see
     Rosenberg 2015, 28–40; and Bonfait 2015, 106–17.

41   Purchased in February 1685, the picture was packed and shipped in April;
     see Gady 2002, 167–68. The state of the sky may reflect the hardships of this
     journey (Rosenberg 2015, no. 10).

42   On the historic installation of Poussin's paintings at the Louvre, see Laveis-
     sière 1993.

43   S. Campbell 2009, no. 1 (entry by Richard Kendall, with technical notes by
     Rosamond Westmoreland). See also David Hockney's discussion in Finkel
     2019, 44.

44   The writer and sometime artist George Moore, who knew Degas some
     twenty years later, claimed the copy had taken a year to paint (Moore 1891,
     321). It was, in any case, something of a legend among the artist's friends;
     see, for example, Edmond Duranty's fictionalized discussion in the 1872
     novella "Le peintre Louis Martin" (Duranty 1881, 335–37).

45   On Degas's copies, see Reff 1963, 1964, 1965, and 1971. Though the pace
     of Degas's copying generally slowed in the early 1860s, his interest in
     Poussin's work quickened; he produced pencil drawings after *The Plague
     at Ashdod* and after one of Poussin's studies for *Extreme Unction*, as well
     as an elaborate ink and wash drawing after *The Triumph of Venus* (known as
     The Triumph of Flora). These must be considered against the backdrop of
     a contemporary French Academy that beatified Poussin for reasons of its
     own; see Goldstein 1996.

46   *Young Spartans Exercising* (National Gallery, London, inv. NG3860).

47   See George 1936, 8–9.

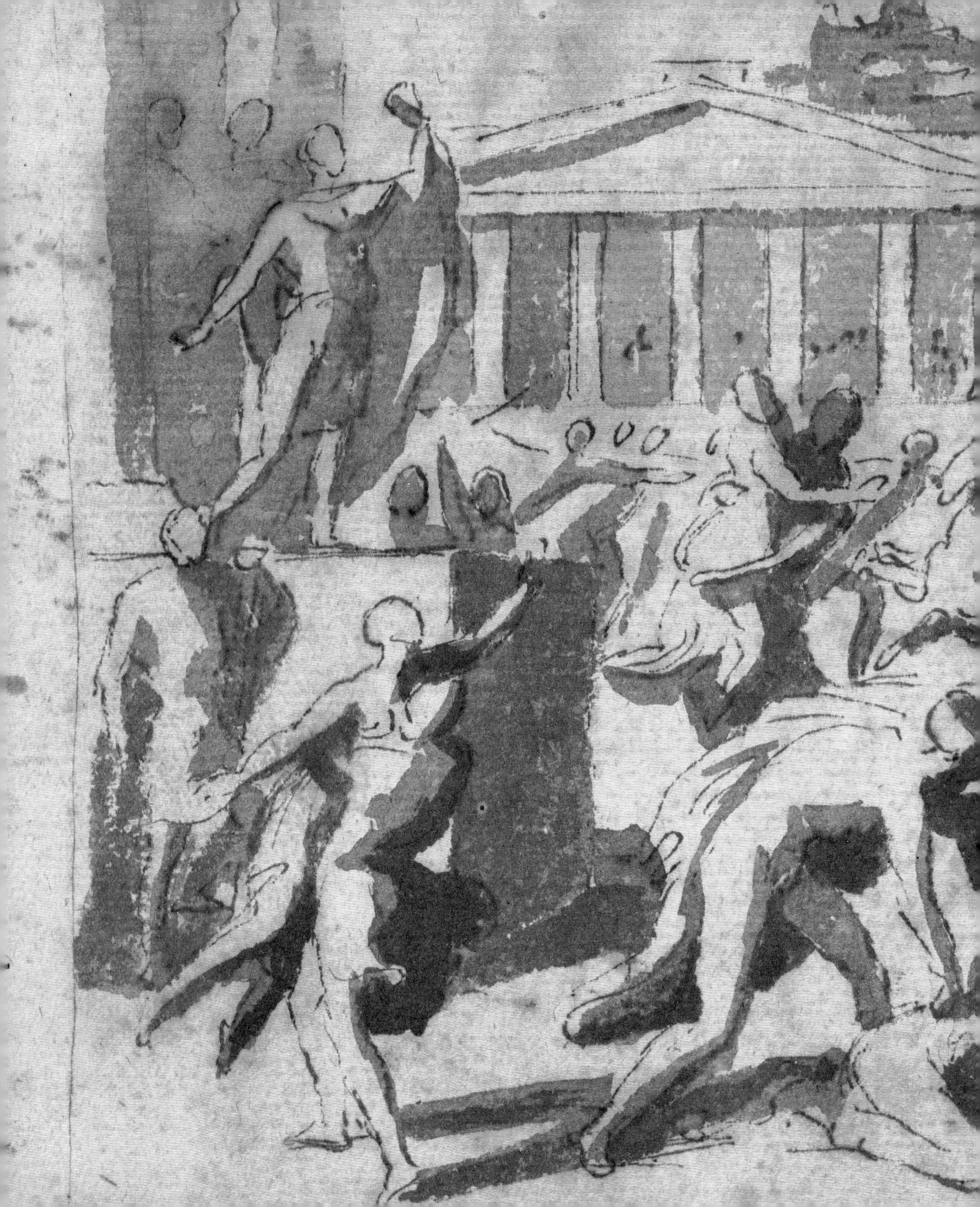

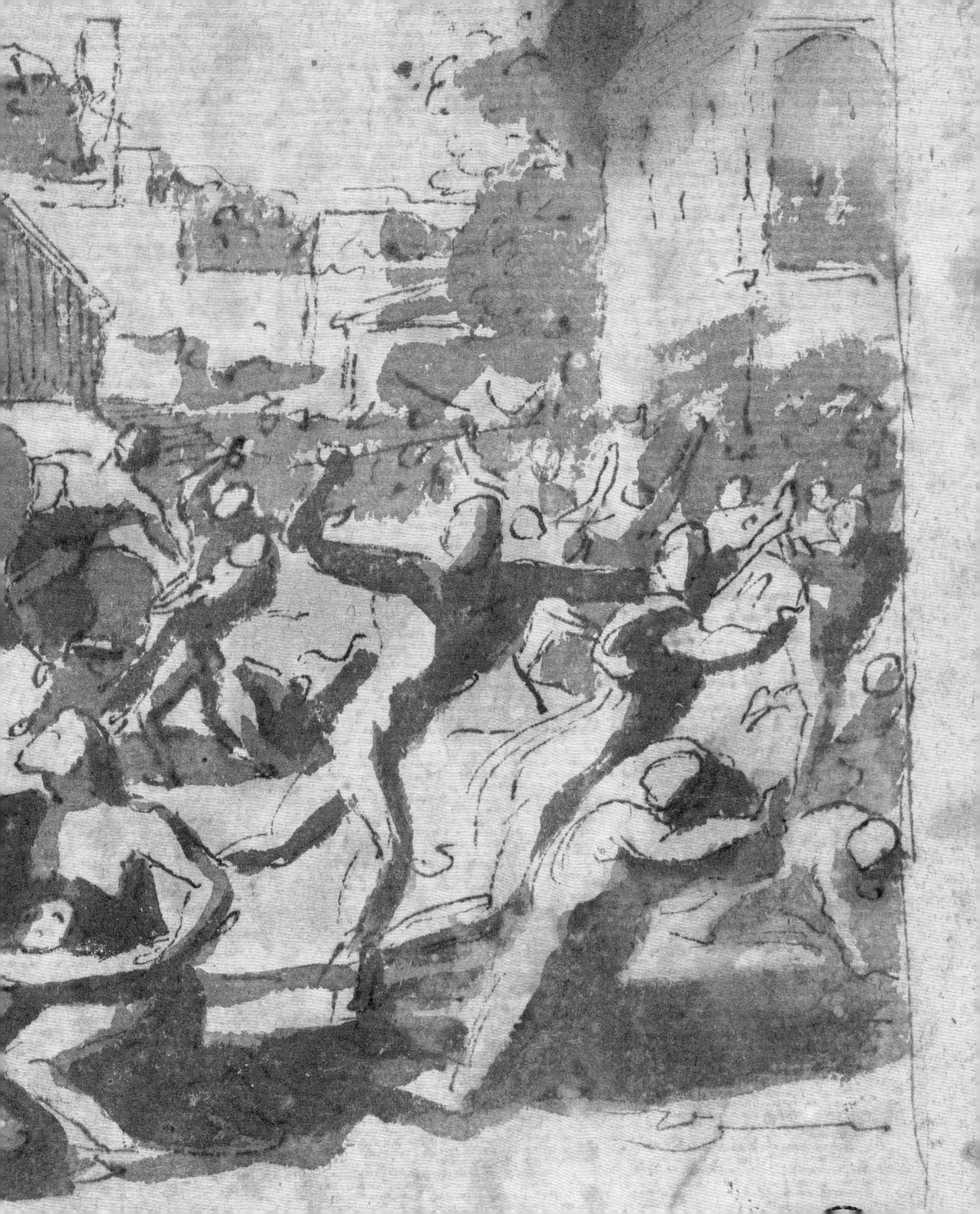

Nicolas Poussin

STUDY FOR THE ABDUCTION OF THE ABDUCTION OF THE SABINE WOMEN

ca. 1633
Pen and brown ink and brush and brown
wash over traces of black chalk on paper
11.6 × 8.1 cm (4½ × 3⅛ in.)
Windsor, Royal Collection/HM Queen
Elizabeth II, inv. RCIN 911904

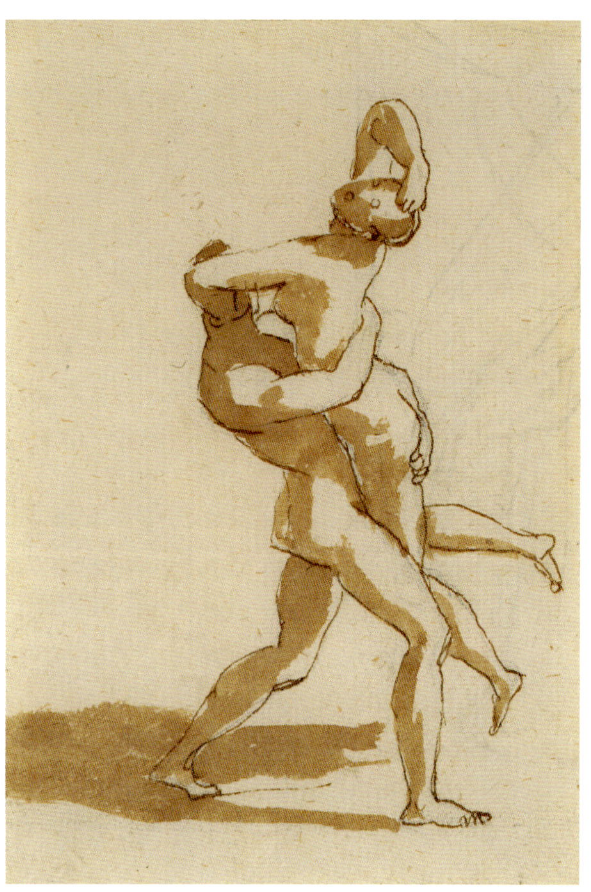

27

Nicolas Poussin

STUDY FOR THE ABDUCTION OF THE SABINE WOMEN

ca. 1633
Pen and brown ink and brush and brown
wash over traces of black chalk on paper
11.3 × 19.4 cm (4½ × 7⅝ in.)
Windsor, Royal Collection/HM Queen
Elizabeth II, inv. RCIN 911903

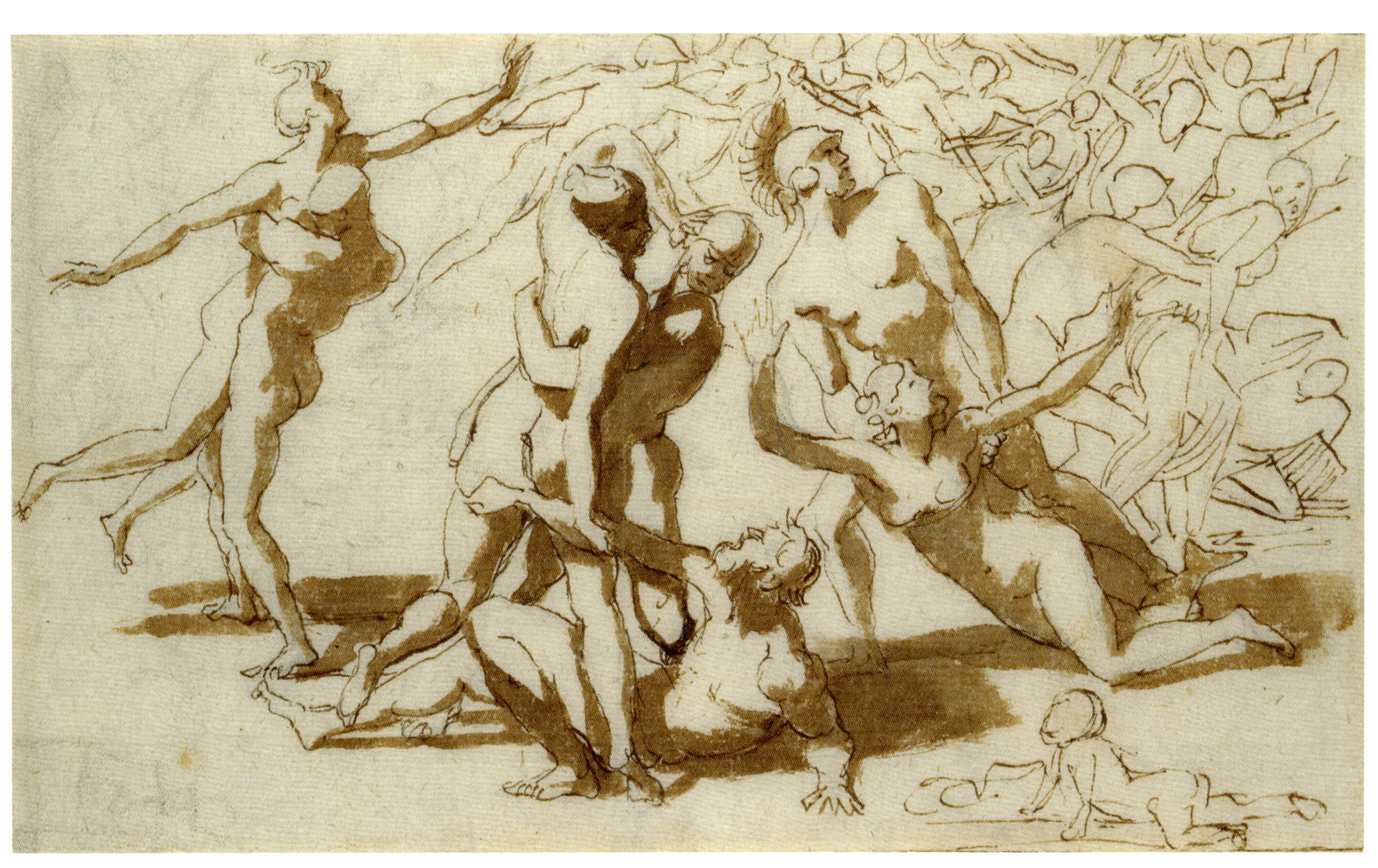

28

Nicolas Poussin

STUDY FOR THE ABDUCTION OF THE SABINE WOMEN

ca. 1633
Pen and brown ink and brush and brown
wash on paper
16.2 × 20.8 cm (6⅜ × 8¼ in.)
Florence, Gallerie degli Uffizi,
inv. GDS 900 E

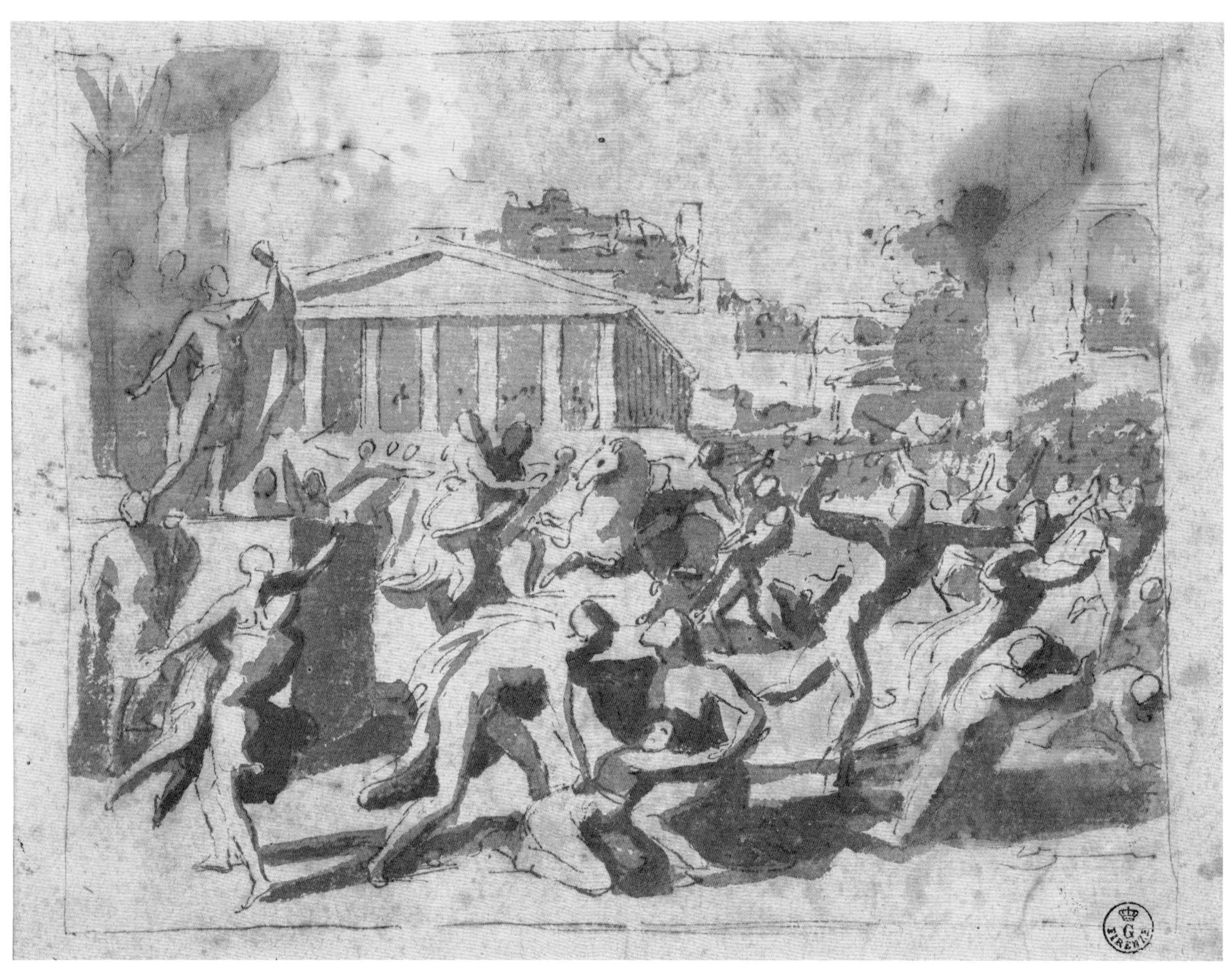

29

Nicolas Poussin

STUDY FOR THE ABDUCTION OF THE SABINE WOMEN

ca. 1633
Pen and brown ink and brush and brown
wash on paper
16.4 × 22.4 cm (6½ × 8⅞ in.)
Chatsworth, Collection of the Duke of
Devonshire, inv. 861

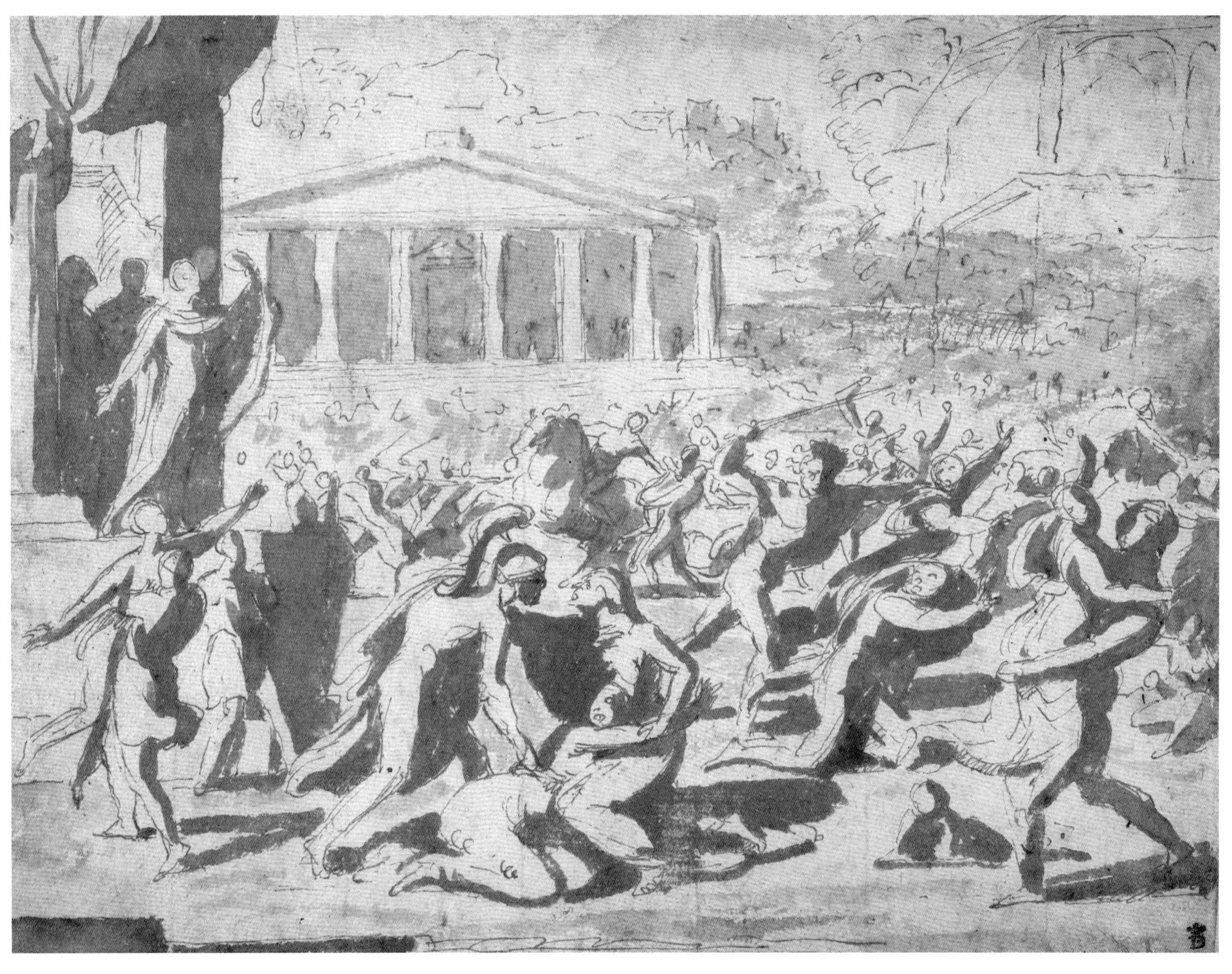

30

Nicolas Poussin

THE ABDUCTION OF
THE SABINE WOMEN

Probably 1633–34

Oil on canvas

154.6 × 209.9 cm (60⅞ × 82⅝ in.)

New York, The Metropolitan Museum

of Art, Harris Brisbane Dick Fund, 1946,

inv. 46.160

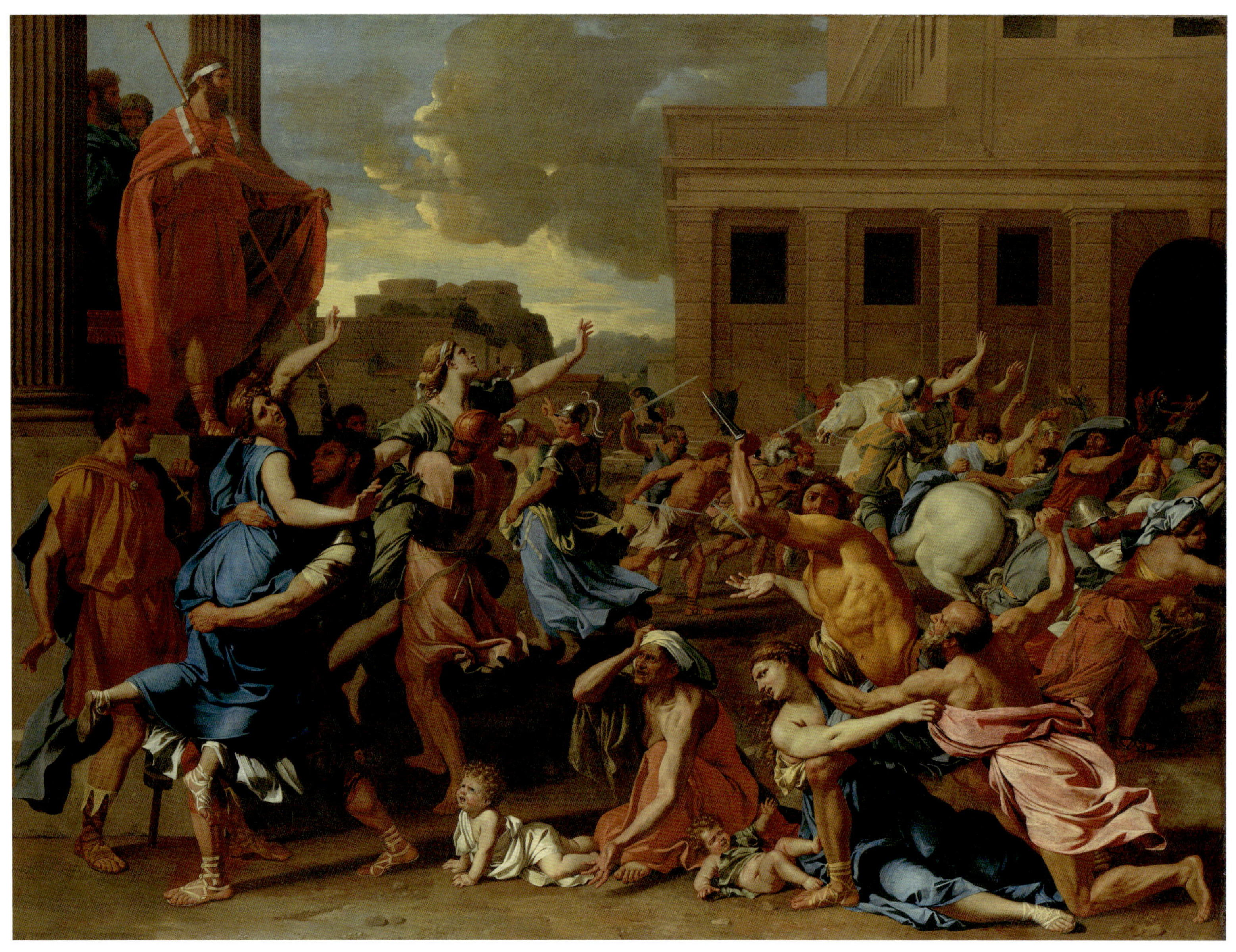

Nicolas Poussin
THE ABDUCTION OF THE SABINE WOMEN

ca. 1634–35
Oil on canvas
159 × 206 cm (62⅝ × 81⅛ in.)
Paris, Musée du Louvre, Département
des Peintures, inv. 7290

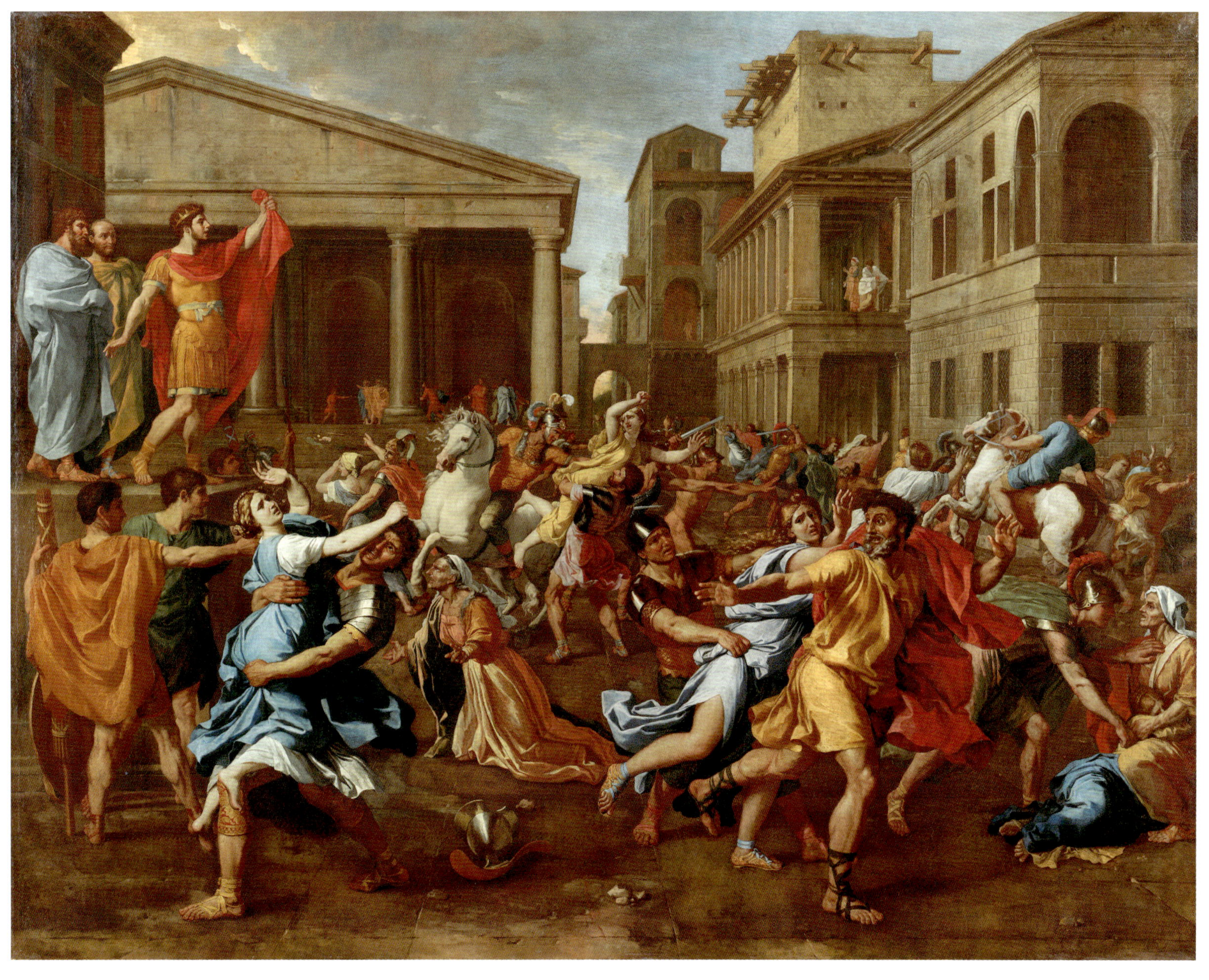

32

Edgar Degas
French, 1834–1917

THE ABDUCTION OF THE SABINE WOMEN (after Poussin)

ca. 1861–62
Oil on canvas
150.2 × 207 cm (59⅛ × 81½ in.)
Pasadena, The Norton Simon
Foundation, Gift of Mr. Norton Simon,
inv. F.1983.06.P

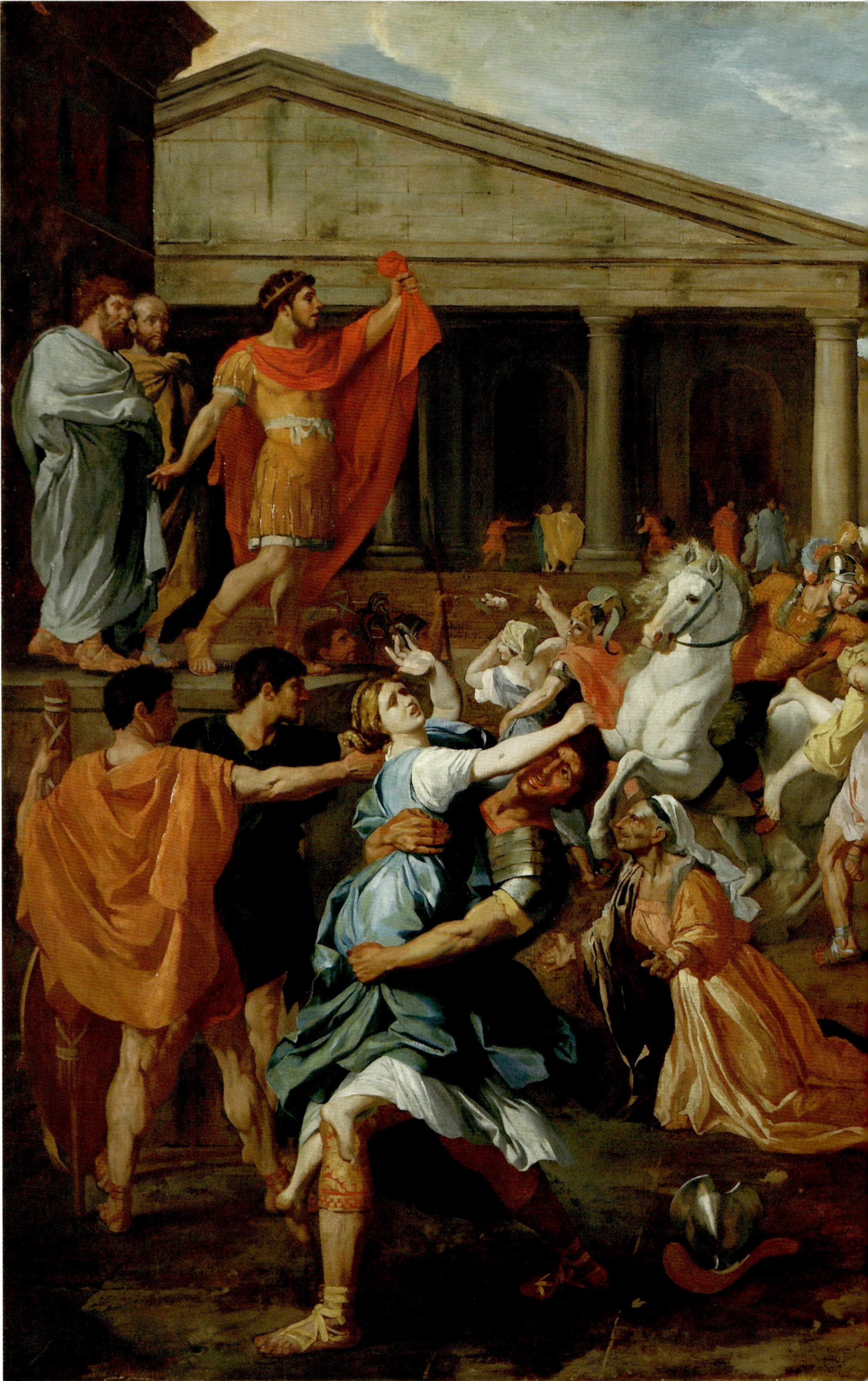

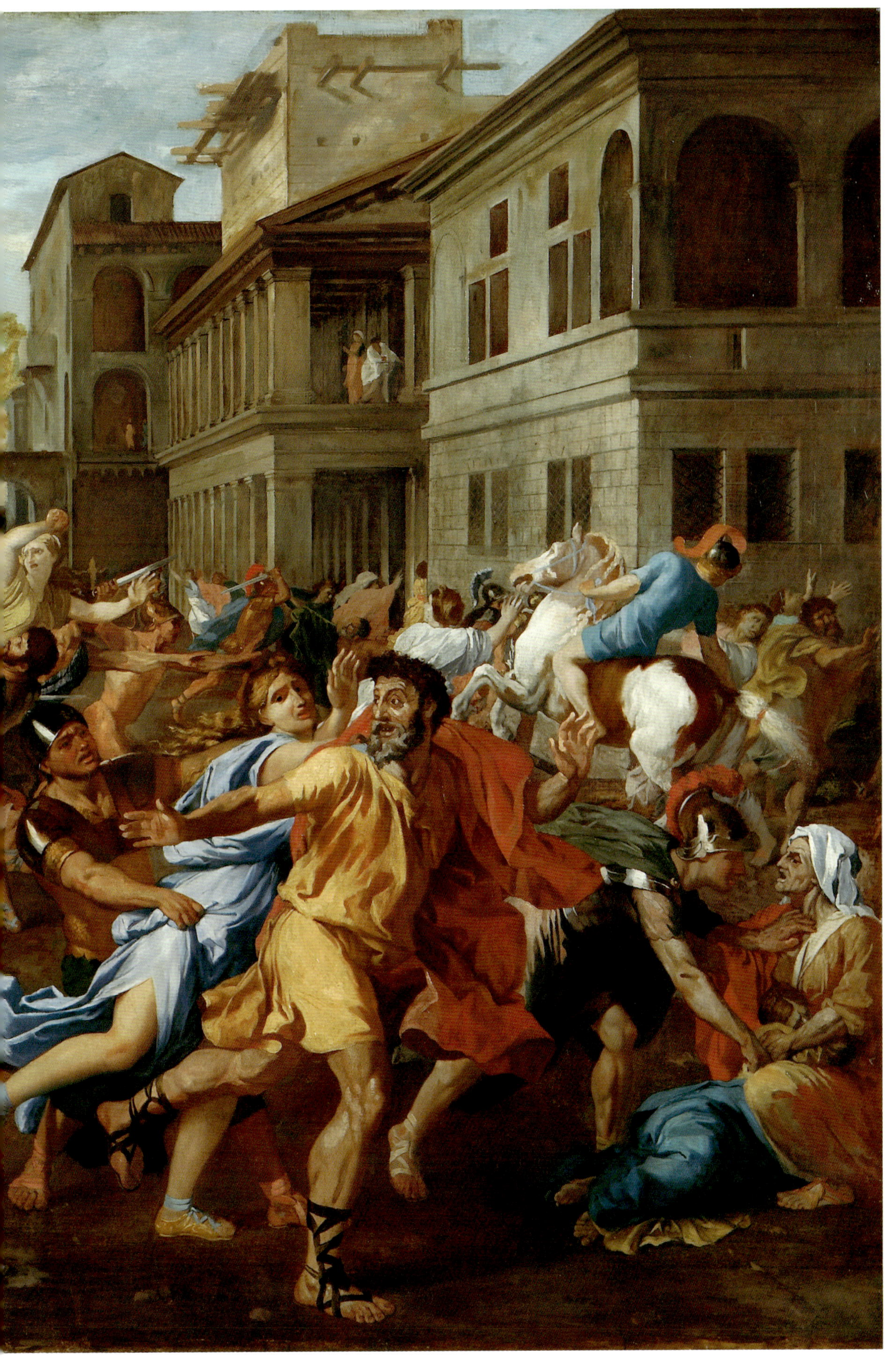

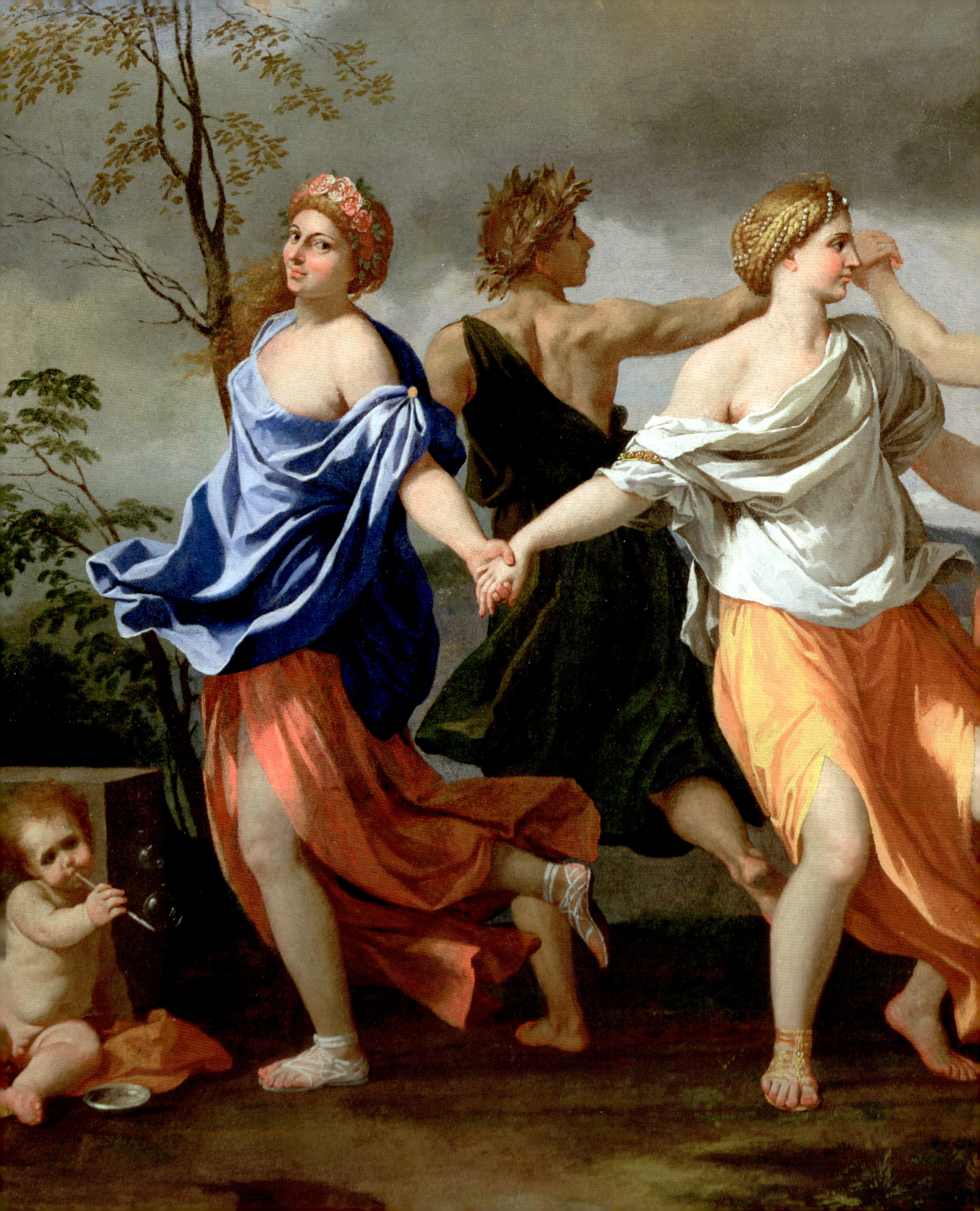

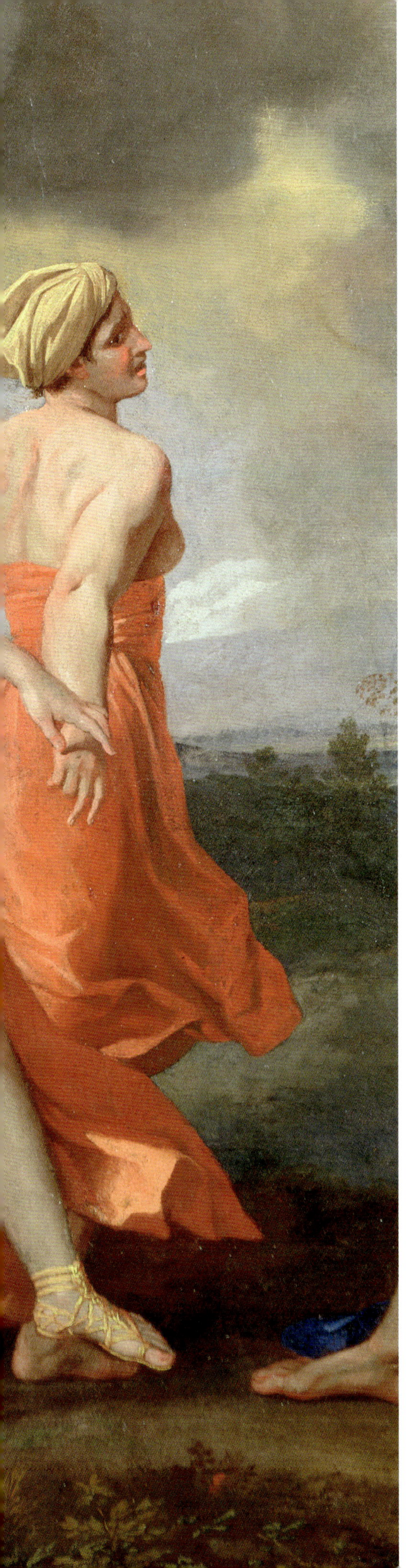

A DANCE TO THE MUSIC OF TIME
THE WELLSPRING OF THE MODES

JONATHAN UNGLAUB

The nighttime storm has passed and dawn awakens. The sky lightens to cerulean blue, as gray clouds tinged with amber, gold, and orange roll away. Below, the landscape unfolds through the mist to a nearby river. Despite the meteorological precision of the cloudscape, the auroral light derives not from the sun itself but from its mythological embodiment: Apollo, astride his chariot, is heralded by Dawn strewing flowers and accompanied by the dancing Hours. Below, the celestial apparition finds its equivalent in the quartet of dancers, whose flowing garments intensify the atmospheric hues of azure, tangerine, pale yellow, and rose. The elegantly coiffured pair in front wear resplendent tunics that slip from their shoulders: they clasp hands as their gracefully sandaled feet negotiate a slight jeté and landing. Seen from behind, another pair, a man and a woman in simpler garb, dance unshod. A stone plinth at right and a two-headed herm at left frame an improvised stage for the circle of dancers, who measure their steps in response to the chords of the winged old man plucking his lyre, Father Time himself. A seminude child reclining at Time's feet fixates on the granules passing through an hourglass, while his similarly pudgy companion inflates his cheeks to blow bubbles. These are as fleeting as the dance is perpetual, revolving for as long as Time keeps time. Here, in *A Dance to the Music of Time* (plate 33), Poussin achieved a supreme balance between visual enchantment and poetic sophistication. The painting is in many ways the apogee of the artist's dance compositions of the 1630s and their disposition of the balletic roundel.[1]

While the visual and chromatic splendor of *Dance* is Poussin's own, its subject results from an extraordinary intellectual collaboration. Poussin here served a patron who mastered the literary, musical, and choreographic components of contemporary spectacle: the poet and impresario Giulio Rospigliosi (1600–1669). This learned prelate, who held several important offices under Urban VIII and subsequent pontiffs (becoming Pope Clement IX himself in 1667), authored the libretti for pioneering opera productions—most featuring danced interludes—mounted regularly by the Barberini in their Roman palaces between 1632 and 1644.[2] Concurrently, Rospigliosi was among

Poussin's most frequent Italian patrons after Cassiano dal Pozzo, commissioning some half dozen works from the painter.[3] According to Bellori and Félibien, Rospigliosi devised the poetic conceits for three of Poussin's pictures: the *Arcadian Shepherds* (Musée du Louvre, Paris), *Time Saving Truth from Discord and Envy* (lost), and *A Dance to the Music of Time*. Together these works mark a rare foray by the artist into overt moralizing pictorial allegory.[4]

Based on the descriptions in Bellori and Félibien, one can readily decipher Rospigliosi's allegory. The protagonists are Poverty, the wreathed male figure seen from behind, who extends his hand to Labor, who wears unrefined attire and is, like Poverty, barefoot. Labor's tireless efforts lead to Wealth, with her pearled coiffure and gleaming garments, who lets her hand slip from the cause of her prosperity, pulled away by a voluptuous figure with a floral crown. This figure represents Pleasure—Bellori calls her Luxury—who will squander the riches and fall inevitably back into poverty. Father Time's musical accompaniment suggests that this cycle repeats itself indefinitely, while the putti blowing bubbles and holding an hourglass show the vanity of pursuing wealth and pleasure. The apparition of Apollo's chariot in the zodiac, led by Aurora and followed by the Hours, further reinforces the cyclical aspects of human labor, ambition, and decadence as measured through the sun's daily course. The two-headed herm represents Janus, Roman god of transitions and the New Year, whose presence signals an annual cycle.[5] Poussin's balletic ensemble draws upon the traditional themes of the wheel of fortune and the dance of the seasons. The contemporary treatise *Harmonie universelle* (1636) by Marin Mersenne investigated the harmonious synchrony of music and dance as reflecting the ordered cosmos, which is at some level the theme of Poussin's painting, as it aligns celestial and terrestrial choreographies.[6]

As with *A Bacchanalian Revel before a Term* (plates 12 and 13), a compositional drawing for the *Dance* survives (plate 34). Poussin reworked it in significant ways in the final painting. His bold, fluid sweeps of iron gall ink wash suggest a more intense chiaroscuro than the overall luminosity of the final painting. While most of the figural motifs are already present, the space is significantly more compressed, with Apollo's horses galloping immediately above the dancers, and a proportionally larger ring of the zodiac extending beyond the upper edge of the sheet. The two putti recline as attributes at the feet of Time, behind whom a palm tree partially conceals the cloud-borne Aurora. The dancers themselves are more lithe and livelier in the drawing. Their painted counterparts move with a heavier step in a slowing of tempo suited to a weightier exposition of the theme. Indeed, infrared imaging of the sheet (fig. 30) reveals the grid that Poussin used to transpose his design onto the canvas, effectively taming the frenzied, exuberant dance, much as his dynamic chiaroscuro wash gave way to a bright, balanced palette.[7] In the transfer, Poussin gave Poverty, initially female, a clearly masculine back and shoulders. The garment clinging seductively to Pleasure's torso in the drawing, still visible in X-ray analysis of the underpainting, evolves into windswept folds in the painting, where she gazes back alluringly over her shoulder toward Wealth and the beholder.[8]

In the final painting, Poussin incorporated artistic references to create a paragon of pictorial beauty and eloquence. The quartet of dancers recalls the ancient relief of

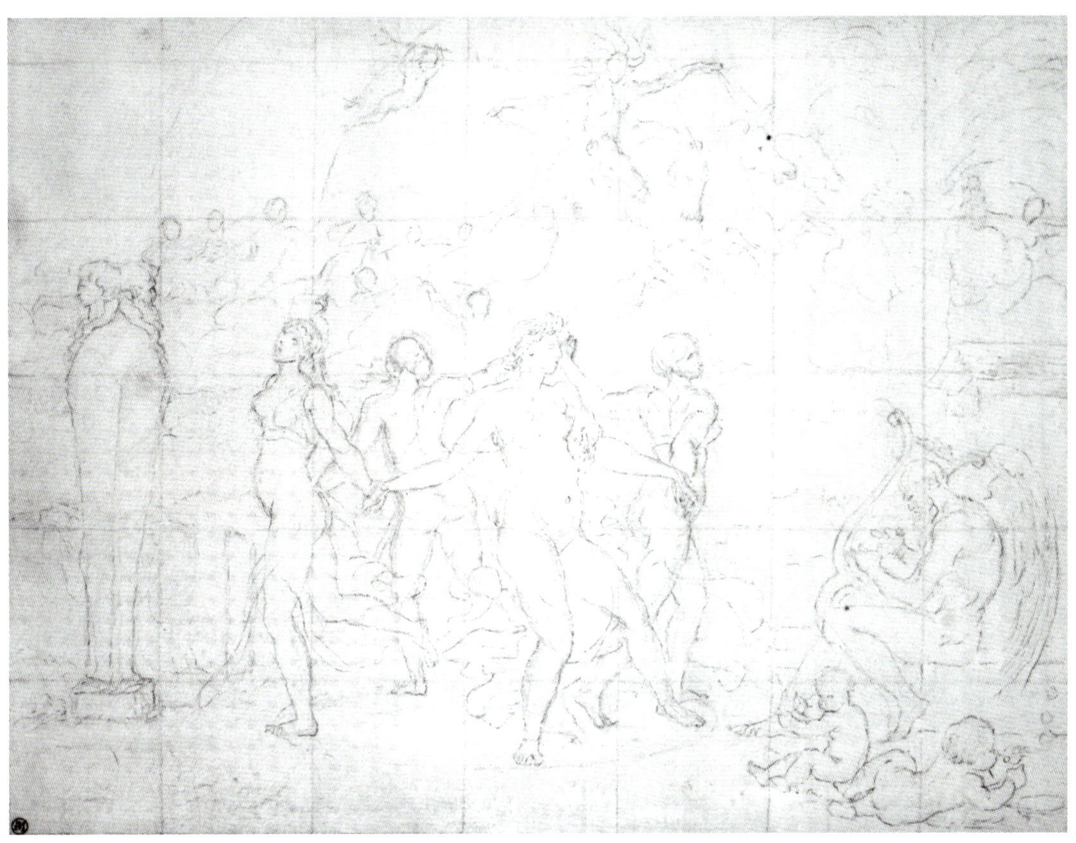

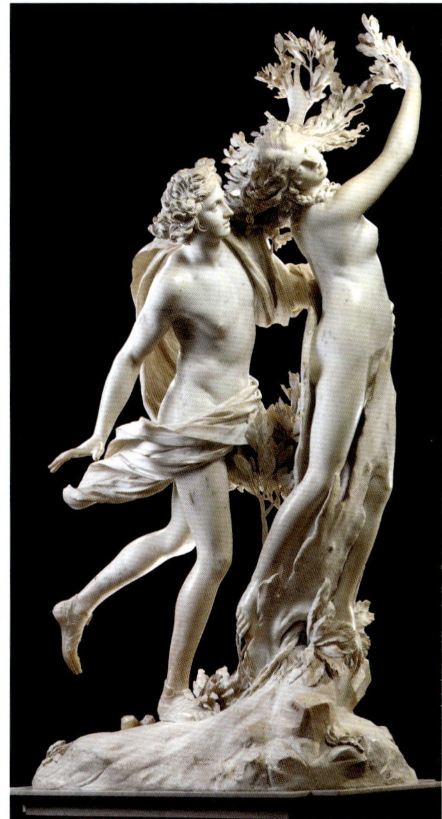

five conjoined dancers then displayed at the Villa Borghese (plate 11). This was the prototype for one of the most renowned works in Rome, Guido Reni's 1615 *Aurora* (Palazzo Pallavicini-Rospigliosi, Rome), whose dancing Hours and petal-sprinkling Dawn Poussin reprised in miniature. Apollo, his chariot, and the ring of the zodiac derive from Marcantonio Raimondi's engraving after Raphael's *Judgment of Paris*, whose protagonist likewise anticipates the pose and muscular physique of Time. His playing and the accompanying roundel reenvision Apollo serenading the dancing Muses in Mantegna's *Parnassus*. The reclining children conform to the contemporary putto type of the sculptor Duquesnoy.[9] The way Pleasure overlaps a pair of trees recalls Daphne's metamorphosis into a laurel, so memorably captured in Bernini's celebrated group (fig. 31); indeed, Pleasure's pose and gait conjure up his lustful Apollo. This sculpture bore a famous inscription by Urban VIII admonishing that those who pursue the "pleasure of fleeting forms" grasp but "sprays of leaves and bitter fruit," which accords poetically with Rospigliosi's conceit.[10] The putto's bubble—the ultimate fleeting form—complements the implicit arboreal elision, as Pleasure yields to Poverty's crown of desiccated foliage.[11]

Recent studies have anchored the painting in the cultural milieu of Rospigliosi and the operas he produced for the papal court, where allegory imbued the visual and musical splendor of the performances with deeper meaning.[12] The allegorical personifications that proliferate in Rospigliosi's libretti often performed dances, as recorded in the scenographic engravings accompanying the lavishly published scores

FIGURE 30
Infrared reflectograph of *Study for a Dance to the Music of Time* (plate 34), showing transfer grid

FIGURE 31
Gian Lorenzo Bernini (1598–1680), *Apollo and Daphne*, 1622–25. Carrara marble, 243 cm (95 11/16 in.). Rome, Galleria Borghese

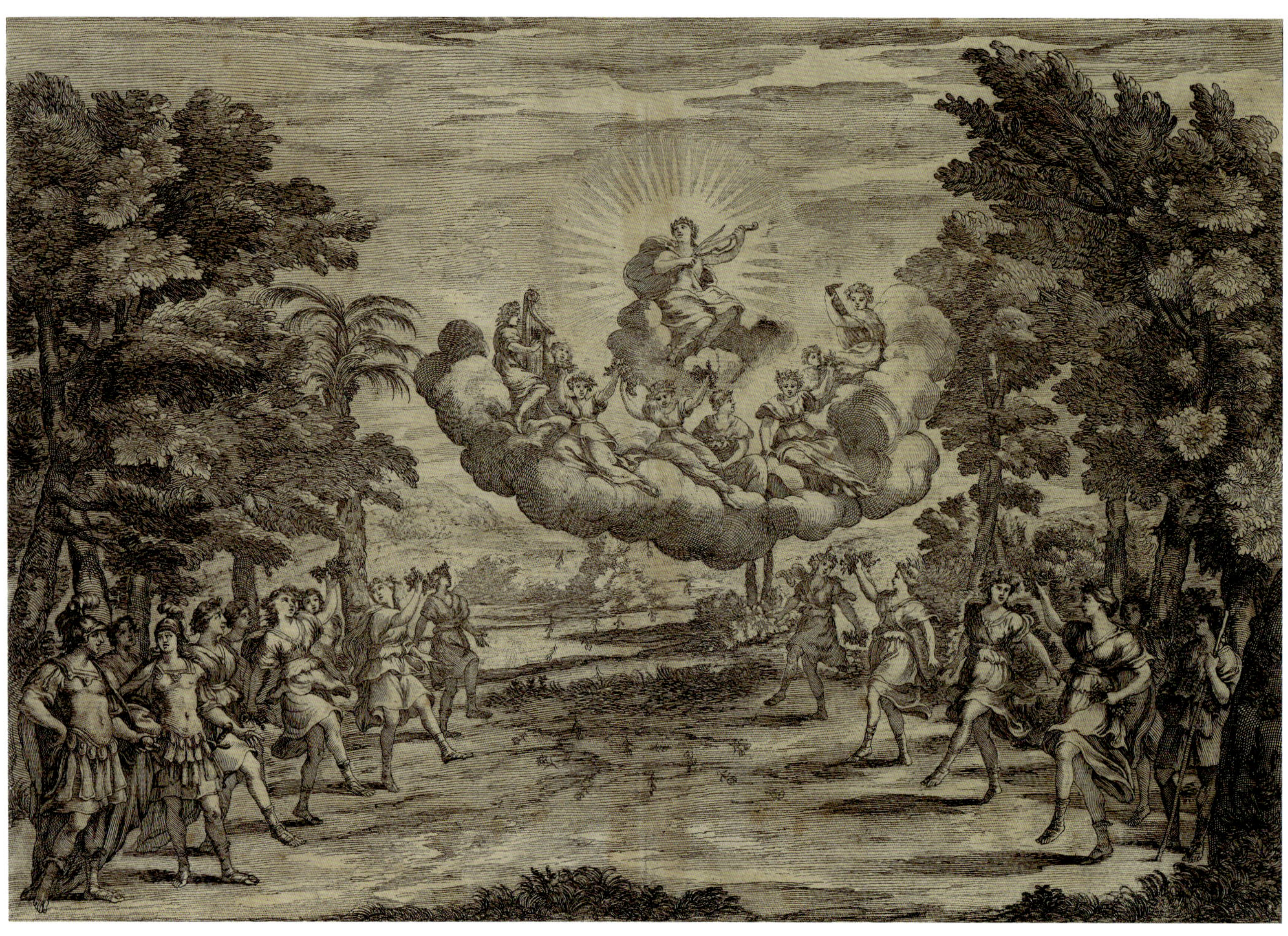

of *Il Sant'Alessio* (first performed 1632) and *Erminia sul Giordano* (first performed 1633). In the final scene of the former, Religion extols Alessio's steadfast commitment to impoverished piety, while Christian virtues dance to either side.[13] The *Erminia* shares both the riverbank pastoral setting of Poussin's painting and its celestial accompaniment, since in its final scene Zephyrs invoke Apollo: "O Sun, before the fiery chariot plunges into the wave, / turn your merry brow to these shores."[14] The god then descends to serenade a ballet of nymphs dressed in flowing tunics as they perform their steps, much like Poussin's dancers (fig. 32).

Rospigliosi's subsequent opera, *Santi Didimo e Teodora*, performed during Carnival at the Palazzo Barberini in 1635 and 1636, featured personifications and a ballet comparable to Poussin's painting.[15] The libretto recounts Didymus's conversion of the Egyptian princess Theodora, who resolves to maintain her chaste commitment to Christ despite the amorous advances of a wealthy pagan prince. In act 1, a quartet of vices, alarmed that a beautiful princess embraces death and suffering over embellishment and delight, plots to lure her back to status, luxury, and conjugal love. These include Piacere and Ricchezza, Pleasure and Wealth, who likewise appear in Poussin's *Dance*; in the opera, though, they are joined by Ozio and Vanità, Idleness and Vanity, creating a full circle of vices. Significantly, these allegorical figures appear in a lush garden of perpetual springtime, where a "balletto di ninfe" ensues to the musical accompaniment of Ricchezza, who sings the refrain: "with a charming foot upon the grass / already the breezes play, / and with placid harmonies / the riverbanks already resound."[16] Such parallels need not be illustrative, but they underscore how Poussin's imagery aligns with Rospigliosi's renowned creative output, patronized by the ruling papal family. The prelate must have viewed the painting as a distillation of ideas and motifs from his own operatic spectacles.

Beyond their allegorical collaboration, Rospigliosi shared Poussin's understanding of pictorial style and expression that would culminate in the painter's theory of the Modes. In a 1637 letter to his brother Camillo, Rospigliosi explained the differences between two frescoes in the Palazzo dei Conservatori by Giuseppe Cesari, known as the Cavaliere d'Arpino: *The Abduction of the Sabines*, fearsome in subject, and *The Discovery of the Infants Romulus and Remus*, a vivid pastoral landscape. Despite a composition that perfectly captured the chaos, Rospigliosi claimed that the unpleasing color scheme of the former "has been maintained washed out and pallid to express the pallor and whitening in the faces of these women, who see themselves being assaulted; and one can hardly doubt that in the midst of such fear they could be shown in any other mode and in order to represent this event with decorum, I do not believe that one could do otherwise. Nonetheless, it is seen that the same artist in the other picture of Romulus and Remus knew how to adopt a different manner."[17] Rospigliosi's observations find a striking parallel in a letter that Poussin seems to have written the same year, explaining a similar distinction between his *Abduction of Rinaldo* (Gemäldegalerie, Berlin) and *Camillus and the Schoolmaster of Falerii* (Musée du Louvre, Paris): "I have painted in the manner that you will see, in so much that the subject [the *Abduction of Rinaldo*] in itself is tender, in marked contrast to that of Monsieur La Vrillière [*Camillus*], which is of a much more severe manner, as is reasonable, considering that the subject is heroic."[18] Poussin here contrasted the pictorial manner best suited to a lyrical interlude from Torquato Tasso's epic *Jerusalem Delivered*, where an enamored sorceress disarms a Christian knight, with that appropriate for a violent episode from Roman history, where the general Camillus commands students to attack their abusive schoolmaster.

A decade later, in a letter to his foremost French patron, Paul Fréart de Chantelou, Poussin similarly differentiated between the august solemnity of apostolic succession in *The Sacrament of Ordination* (fig. 33), one of The Seven Sacraments series, and the delightful ensemble of beauties in *The Finding of Moses* (fig. 34), painted for a rival collector. In doing so, Poussin articulated a theory of form, style, and expression to his patron, famously invoking the ancient musical Modes. In reassuring Chantelou that his austere Sacrament did not betray any favoritism toward the patron of the enchanting Nile scene, Poussin echoed Rospigliosi's rationale for the discordances of the Cavaliere d'Arpino's Sabine picture: "Can you not see that it is the nature of the subject that has caused this effect and your disposition, and that the subjects that I have to represent for your pictures [that is, the Sacraments] require a different manner altogether. The whole art of painting lies in this."[19] Poussin then explained that subject matter, style, and calculated emotional effect must together conform to a particular Mode, based on ancient Greek musical theory as reformulated in Gioseffo Zarlino's

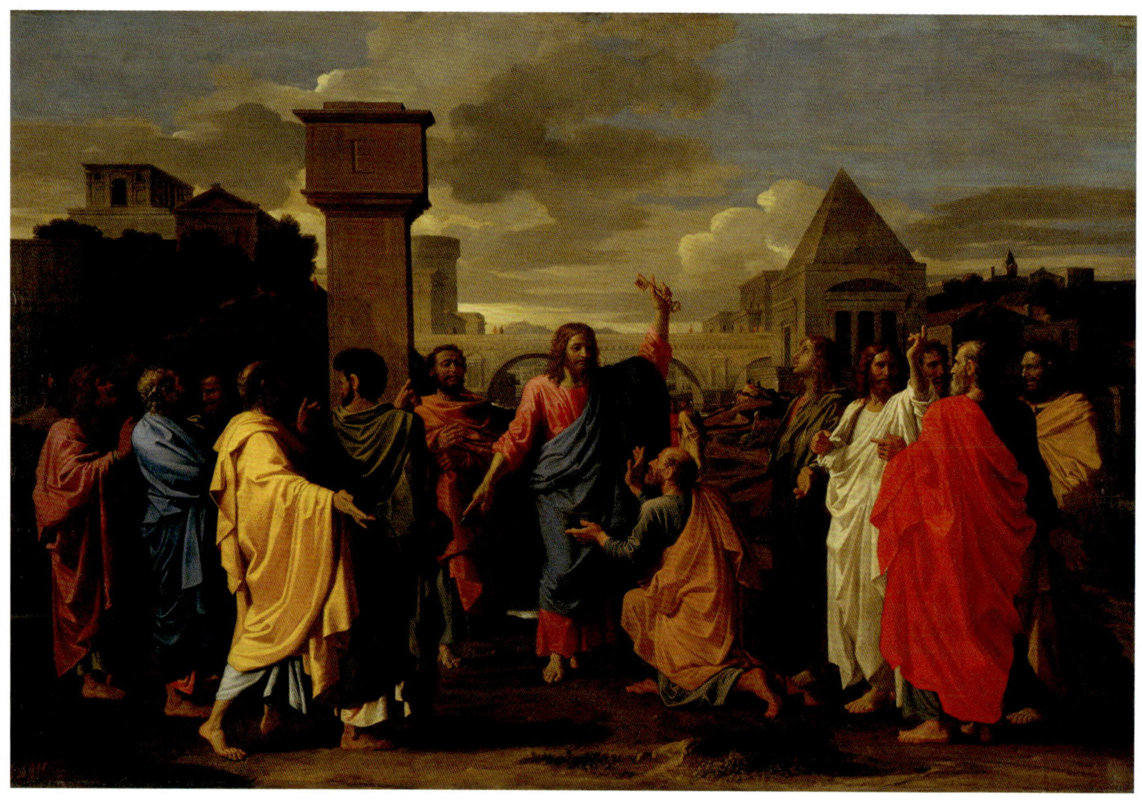

Istitutioni harmoniche of 1558, from which Poussin culled a series of unacknowledged paraphrases.[20] Within a particular Mode, "all the things that enter into the composition are placed together proportionally whence proceeds the power to induce the soul of the spectator to diverse passions." Poussin then defined the characteristics of each Mode, beginning with the one pertaining to *Ordination*: "The ancients would call Dorian that mode which was firm, grave, and severe and they applied it to subjects that were grave, severe, and full of wisdom." Though Poussin did not specify, *The Finding of Moses* embodies the Hypolydian Mode, which "contains in itself a certain suavity and sweetness that fill the soul of the spectator with joy."[21]

The important question is why Poussin would have referred to a treatise on the ancient musical Modes in order to enlighten Chantelou about the necessary harmony of style and subject. Here the artist's relationship with Rospigliosi is decisive, since he had applied comparable ideas to the evaluation of paintings. The comments on the Cavaliere d'Arpino's *Abduction of the Sabines* anticipated Poussin's definition of the Phrygian Mode, with its sharp, vehement, and "frightful" effects that "render the spectator stupefied."[22] Rospigliosi's observations conform with analyses of the Modes that liken them to *genere* (genres): basic parameters for the decorous rendition of different kinds of subjects.[23] Indeed, Zarlino maintains that the Mode was a "determined and proportioned order of rhythm and harmony, accommodated to the subject matter."[24] Yet Rospigliosi does not limit his observations to the consonance of martial subject and violent chaos depicted; he also notes how the pallid coloration might displease viewers affectively. Such observations seem to anticipate Poussin's understanding of

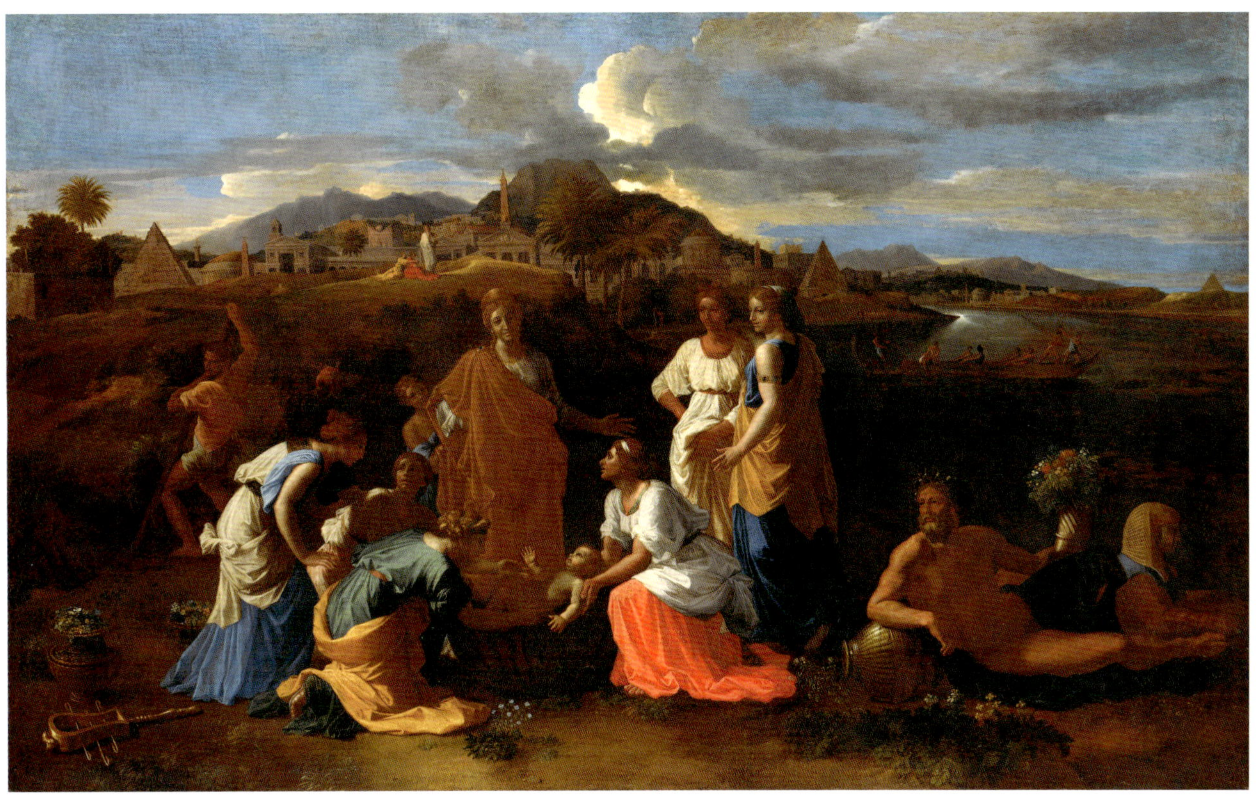

the Modes as a system governing the overall structural harmonies and visual effects that directly manipulate the spectator's perception.

The music of the ancients and its expressive power in relation to lyrics and dance were the subject of intense inquiry in the late sixteenth and early seventeenth centuries, of which one consequence was the development of opera itself.[25] Rospigliosi was Poussin's conduit to studies in the theory and performance of ancient music underway in the Barberini circle. The principal figure in these discussions was Giovanni Battista Doni (1595–1647), who aimed to revive the ancient genres of music in order to re-create the passions of classical tragedy with their reputed musical accompaniment.[26] Rospigliosi himself authored the prologue and choral intermezzi for Doni's staging of the *Troades* (*The Trojan Women*) by the first-century playwright Seneca, a production that showcased Doni's belief that ancient tragedy was partly sung and relied on a choreography of conventional gestures.[27]

In addition to his antiquarian research, Doni wrote a treatise on staged music, encompassing its composition, performance, scenography, and choreography: *Il Trattato della musica scenica* (ca. 1630s, published posthumously).[28] Here Doni applied the concept of the Modes more programmatically to various types of voices and characterizations, and specifically to allegorical personifications of virtues, vices, and other abstract entities:

One must note the correspondence these have with the four principal and equal tones, the Dorian, Phrygian, Lydian, and Mixolydian; and furthermore the analogy these have with the four humours, Seasons, and Elements. For example, the Dorian we assign to Melancholy, to Autumn, to the Earth, and to dryness. The Phrygian to the choleric temperament, Summer, Fire, and Heat. The Lydian to the sanguine temperament, to Spring, to Air, and to Humidity; and the Mixolydian to the phlegmatic temperament, to winter, to water, to cold . . . for the Ages and the Passions, infancy will be given the Mixolydian, Adolescence the Lydian, Youth the Phrygian, and Old Age the Dorian. To Love, Joy, and Delight, the Lydian: to Pain, Sadness and suffering, the Mixolydian: to Wrath and Fury, the Phrygian.[29]

This remarkable passage, in which Doni associated four Modes with the quartets of personified seasons, elements, temperaments, and ages, is significant for two reasons. First, it shows Doni discussing the Modes in a context that is quite different from the revival of ancient Greek music, applying their characteristics to dramatic representation, thus paving the way for Poussin's application of the Modes to narrative painting. Second, Doni recommended that allegorical ensembles of contrasting and complementary ideas should be differentiated according to Mode in their realization on stage.[30] Though he did not specify Modal equivalents, Doni included among his many examples of personifications Ricchezza, Povertà, Felicità, and Servitù, who correspond to the protagonists of Poussin's *Dance*.

Doni's alignment of the Modes with the proper characterization of allegorical quartets opens the possibility that Poussin's *Dance to the Music of Time* is in essence a Modal exercise. Going back to the discourses of the French Academy, commentators have analyzed the chromatic, compositional, and expressive unity of several of Poussin's paintings in terms of Mode.[31] But since Rospigliosi's picture uniquely features distinct allegorical personifications who are also dancers in a musical performance, the possibility that we may be witnessing a moralizing cycle expressed through Modal specimens is worth investigating. Poussin paints the destitute figure of Poverty in dark, lugubrious tones, suggesting Mixolydian mournfulness. Labor careens forcefully out and back, her agitated expression evoking simmering Phrygian ire. The poised elegance and regal detachment of Wealth capture Dorian grandeur. Pleasure skips jauntily and gazes coquettishly with Lydian joyfulness. Proceeding in reverse order, the dancers' coloration corresponds to the seasonal counterparts of the Modes: the floral crown and rich hues of Pleasure evoke Lydian spring, Wealth's golden tones the autumnal Dorian, Labor's fiery orange and yellows the Phrygian summer, and the brittle foliage and cool shades of Poverty the wintry Mixolydian. The senescent figure of Time and the babes holding emblems of evanescence, not to mention the course of Apollo's chariot and the Janus herm marking daily and annual cycles, inject the various foursomes of time—the Ages, the Seasons—into the circular perpetuity of the *Dance*. Poussin and Rospigliosi's collaboration on *A Dance to the Music of Time* and their mutual exposure to Doni's precepts thus not only produced one of Poussin's most poised and elegant compositions but also served as the wellspring for developing the painter's most innovative and musically informed theoretical approach to pictorial expression: the Modes.

NOTES

1   For comprehensive accounts, see Beresford 1995 and Alsdorf 2008.

2   On Rospigliosi's clerical and literary career, see Romei 2005 and Meloncelli 1982. For operatic productions, see Murata 1981, 1–67 and 221–347; and Hammond 1994, 199–254.

3   On Rospigliosi's patronage, which also includes a late private altarpiece depicting Saint Francesca Romana (Musée du Louvre, Paris), see Beresford 1995, 15–31; Fumaroli 2001, 9–80; and Negro 2007, 24–51. Long believed to have been among Rospigliosi's commissions, the *Arcadian Shepherds* is first recorded in the Parisian collection of Henry Avice (1615–1680); see Batalla-Lagleyre 2016 and Rosenberg 2015, 150–59, no. 15.

4   Bellori 1672, 447–48; and Félibien 1725, 86–87.

5   On the iconography, for which Poussin selectively consulted Cesare Ripa's *Iconologia* (1603), see Beresford 1995, 24–31, building on Bellori 1672, 447–48; and Félibien 1725, 86–87.

6   On these interpretations, see Beresford 1995, 24–31; Panofsky 1936, 241–43; and more extensively in Beeny 2016, 36 and 230–31.

7   The author and the exhibition curators wish to thank Aidan Weston-Lewis, Graeme Gollan, and Frances Fowle of the National Galleries of Scotland for generously sharing this infrared image.

8   On the design evolution, see Beresford 1995, 33–39; Alsdorf 2008, 204–5; and Rosenberg and Prat 1994, 1:278–79, no. 144.

9   On visual sources, see Beresford 1995, 41–45.

10   Baldinucci 1682, 9; on the Barberini distich's context, see Montanari 2016, 3–47.

11   On Poverty wearing a laurel crown as a reference to the artist—Apollo made his transformed beloved sacred to art—see Alsdorf 2008, 207.

12   Beresford 1995, 28-29; Fumaroli 2001, 71–81; and Alsdorf 2008, 205–6.

13   Landi 1634. On *Sant'Alessio*, performed at the Palazzo Barberini in 1632 and 1634, see Hammond 1994, 199–204, 208–14; and Murata 1981, 19–23, 221–48.

14   Rossi 1637. Quotation from act 3, scene 10, in Rospigliosi 1998, 50. On the 1633 performances, see Hammond 1994, 204–8; and Murata 1981, 23–27, 249–52.

15   On the *Santi Didimo e Teodora* and contemporary responses, see Hammond 1994, 224–26; and Murata 1981, 28–31, 253–57.

16   Rospigliosi, *Santi Didimo e Teodora*, 1.6.45–48, in Rospigliosi 1999, 24–27. These correspondences are a key touchpoint for dating the painting, which has been placed between 1634–5 and 1638–40. See Beresford 1995, 13; and Thuillier 1994a, 256, no. 141.

17   Biblioteca Apostolica Vaticana, Vaticanus Latinus 13362 (September 12, 1637), 305r–v. Transcribed in Roberto 2004, 380-81. For other artistic issues broached in this letter addressing copies of famous paintings sent back to Pistoia, see Unglaub 2011.

18   Poussin to Jacques Stella [ca. 1637]. Jouanny 1911, 4, no. 2; and Poussin 2014, 37.

19   Poussin to Chantelou, November 24, 1647. Jouanny 1911, 372, no. 156; and Poussin 2014, 134–35. For a translation of the Modes letter from November 24, 1647, from which I deviate slightly, see Blunt 1967, 367–70.

20   Zarlino 1558. On Poussin and Zarlino, see Blunt 1967, 225–27, 367–70; and Hammond 1996.

21   Poussin to Chantelou, November 24, 1647. Jouanny 1911, 372–74, no. 156; and Poussin 2014, 135–36.

22   Poussin to Chantelou, November 24, 1647. Jouanny 1911, 374, no. 156; and Poussin 2014, 136.

23   Sohm 2001, 116–30. For a less rhetorical approach, emphasizing the direct physiological response, see Freedberg 1996.

24   Zarlino 1558, 364. For a modern translation, see Zarlino 1983, 10.

25   For general background, see Bianconi 1987; Pirrotta et al. 1982; and Murata 1984.

26   See in particular the *Compendio del trattato de' generi e de' modi della musica* (1635). On theorists in the Barberini circle, see Hammond 1994, 99–102; and Fumaroli 1989, 75–87. On Doni and the Modes, see Palisca 1997.

27   Hammond 1994, 240–41; and Murata 1984, 132–33.

28   Giovanni Battista Doni, *Trattato della musica scenica*, in Doni 1763, 2:1–144.

29   "Capitolo XXX: Delle Virtù, e Vizj, e simili Personaggi ideali," in Doni 1763, 88–89.

30   Doni's understanding of affective types and allegories in relation to Poussin's Modes is considered in N. J. Barker 2000, 13–19.

31   Montagu 1992. For a literal comparison of Mode intervals to ratios in Poussin's compositional matrices and color schemes, see N. J. Barker 2000.

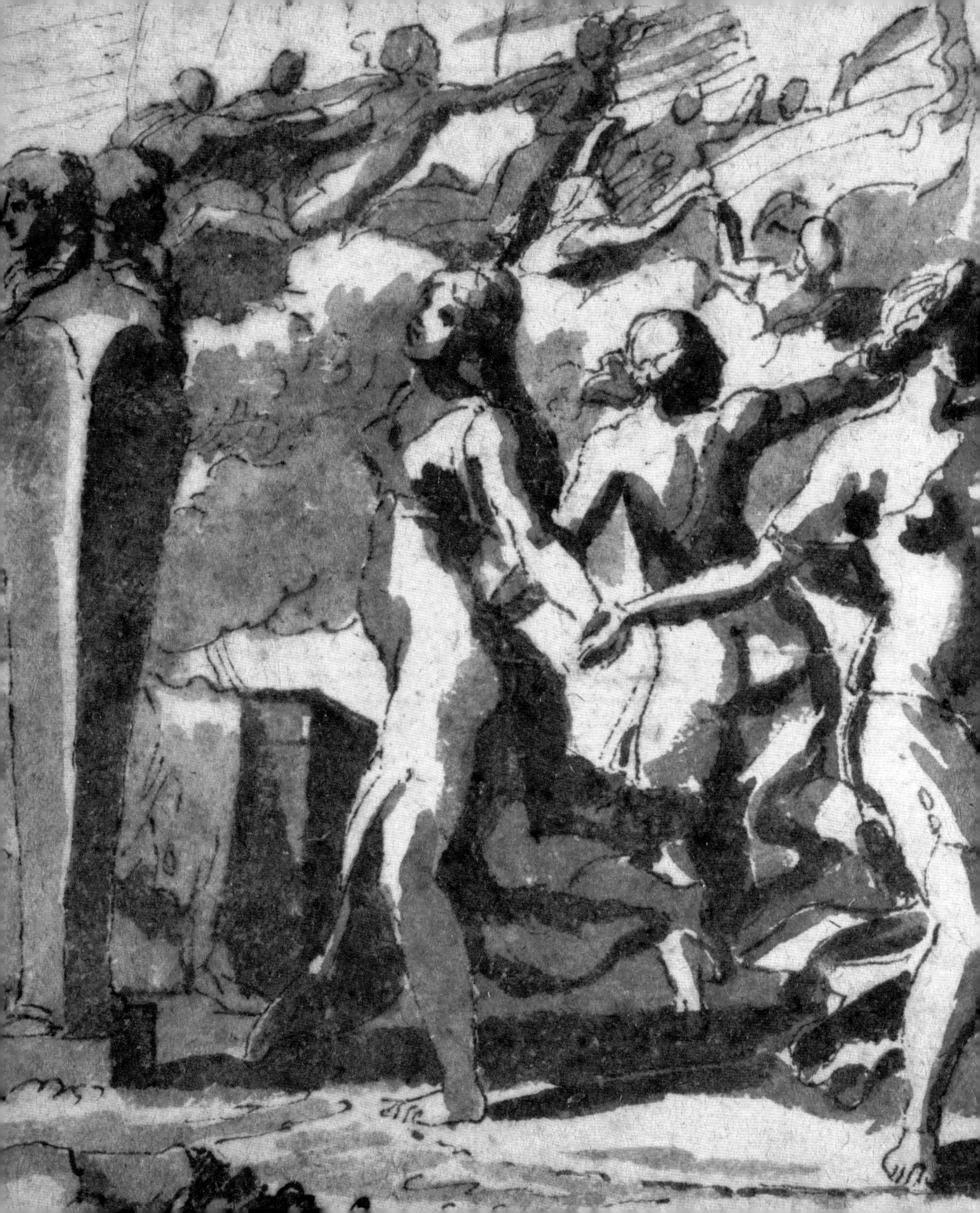

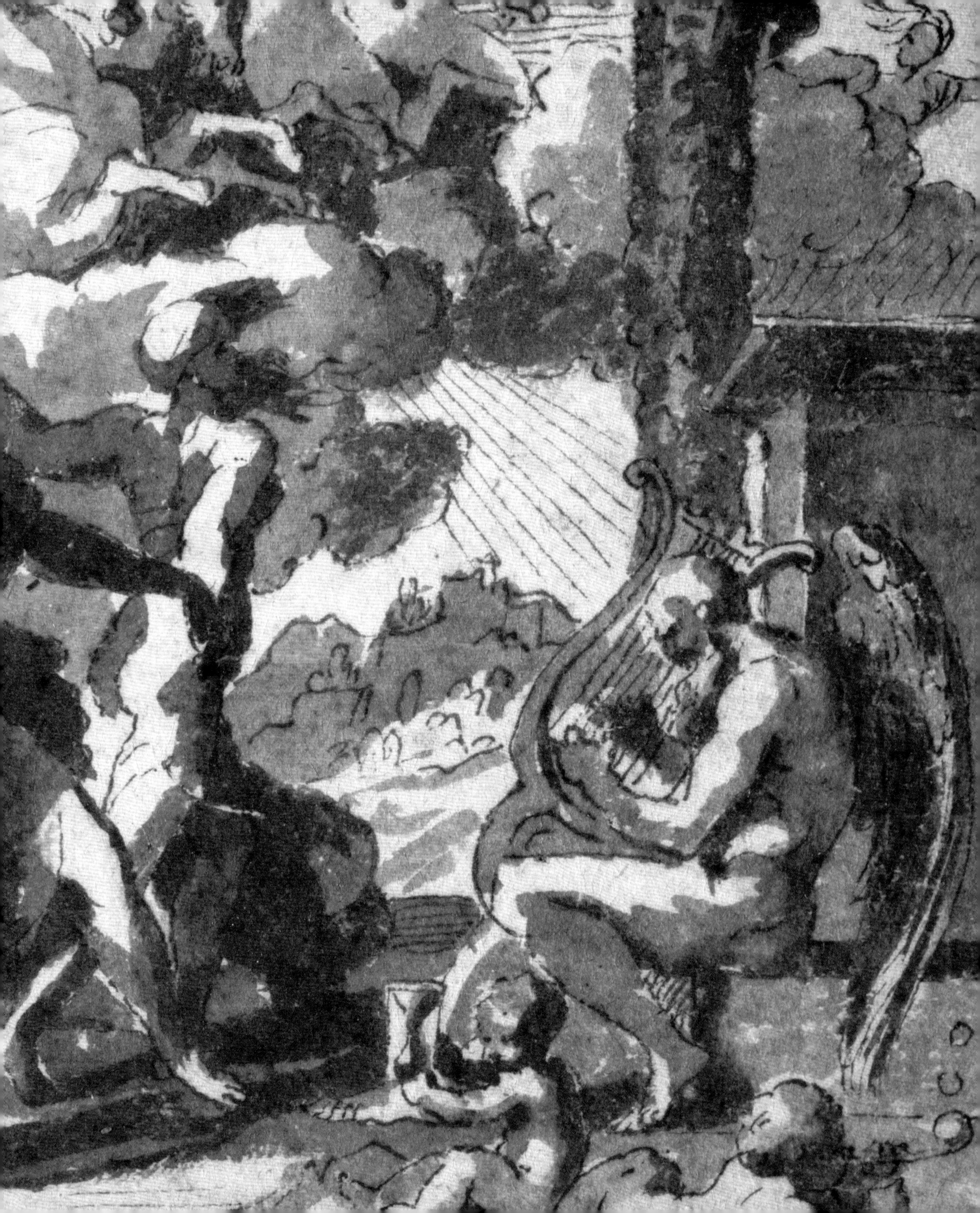

Nicolas Poussin

A DANCE TO THE
MUSIC OF TIME

ca. 1634
Oil on canvas
82.5 × 104 cm (32½ × 41 in.)
London, The Wallace Collection,
inv. P108

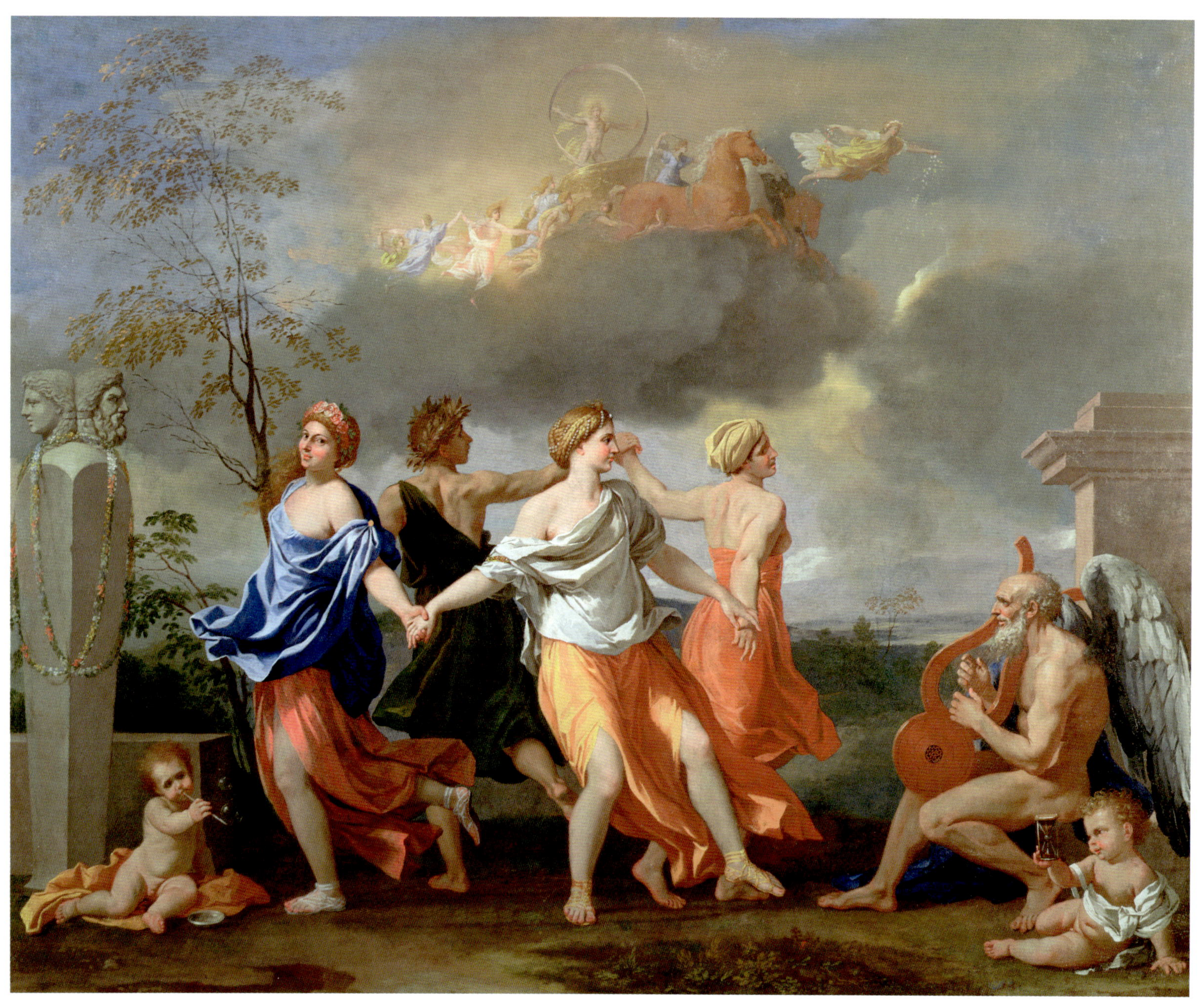

34

Nicolas Poussin

STUDY FOR A DANCE TO THE MUSIC OF TIME

ca. 1634
Pen and brown ink and brush and brown wash over traces of black chalk on paper
14.8 × 19.9 cm (5⅞ × 7⅞ in.)
Edinburgh, National Galleries of Scotland, Purchased by Private Treaty, with the aid of the Art Fund (Scottish Fund), the Pilgrim Trust, the Edith M. Ferguson Bequest, and Contributions from two private donors, 1984, inv. D 5127

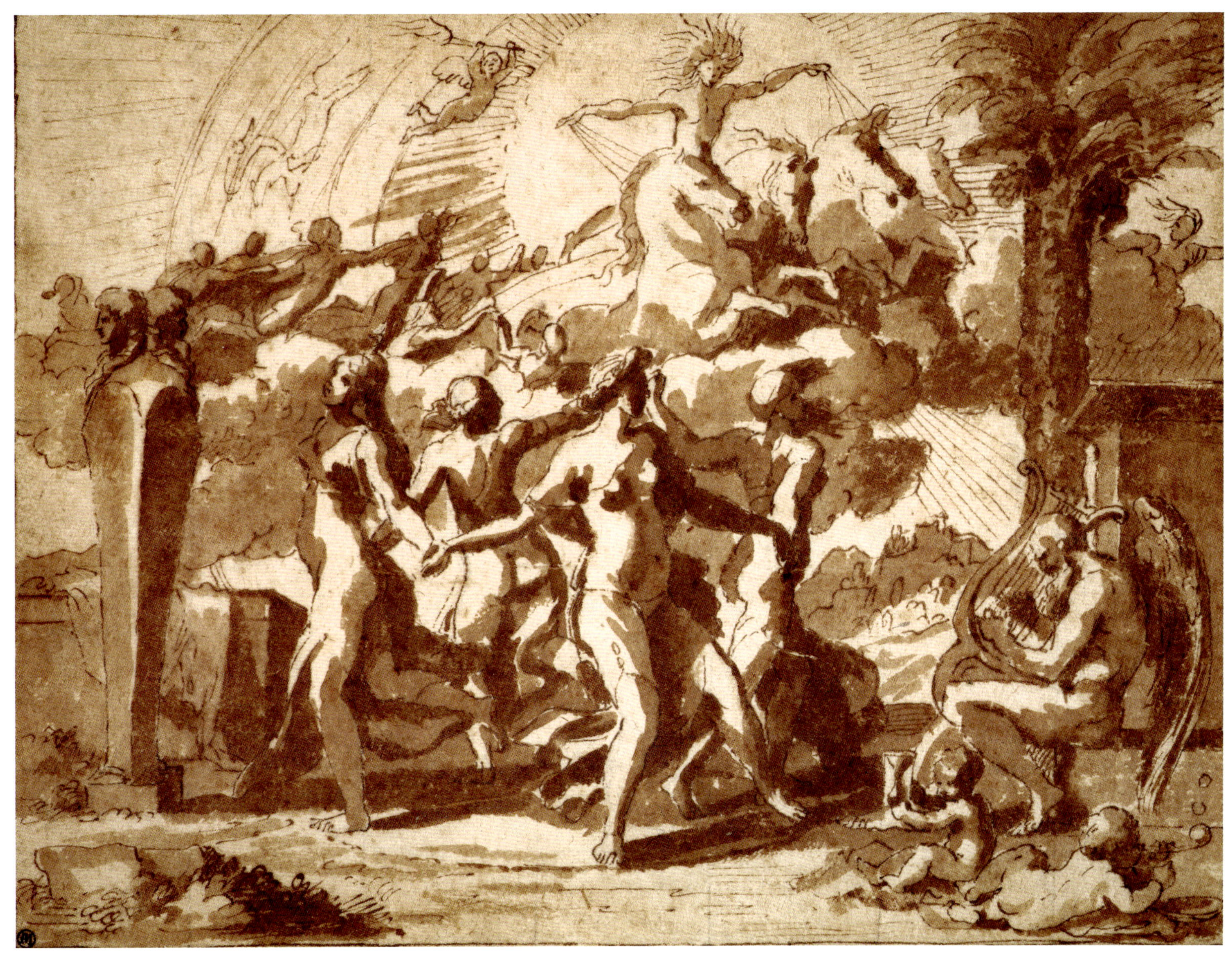

CHECKLIST OF THE EXHIBITION

For works by Poussin, references are to major catalogues raisonnés and to monographic exhibition or collection catalogues containing further bibliography, provenance, and exhibition history. For antiquities, references are to studies containing further information on the objects' early modern reception.

Abbreviations

FB = Friedlaender and Blunt 1939–74 (with volume number)
RP = Rosenberg and Prat 1994 (all works listed appear in volume I)
L = Lugt 1921–56

Where the verso of a drawing is not described, it is either blank or laid down.

INVITATION TO THE DANCE

1
Nicolas Poussin
Bacchus and Ariadne
ca. 1625–26
Oil on canvas
122 × 169 cm (48 × 66½ in.)
Madrid, Museo Nacional del Prado, inv. P002312

References: Grautoff 1914 no. 49; Blunt 1966 no. R 66 (rejected); Rome and Dusseldorf 1977–78 no. 1 (Rosenberg); Thuillier 1994a no. 24; Rome 1998–99 no. 9 (Mahon); Rosenberg 2022.

2
Nicolas Poussin
The Triumph of Bacchus and Ariadne
ca. 1627
Pen and gray-brown ink and brush and pale gray-brown wash over red chalk on pale buff paper
12.6 × 41.4 cm (5 × 16¼ in.)
Stamped, lower right: L.1200
Windsor, Royal Collection/HM Queen Elizabeth II, inv. RCIN 911990

References: FB III no. 183; RP no. 61; London et al. 1995–96 no. 21.

3
Salpion of Athens
Krater decorated with Hermes Confiding the Infant Dionysos to the Nymphs of Nysa, and with Dancing Satyrs and Maenads
First century BCE
Parian marble
131 × 98 × 98 cm (51⅝ × 38⅝ × 38⅝ in.)
Naples, Museo Archeologico Nazionale, inv. 6673

References: Ferraro 1903, 144–46, 219; Grassinger 1991 no. 19.

4
Nicolas Poussin
Dancing Votary of Bacchus
ca. 1635
Pen and brown ink and brush and brown wash over traces of black chalk on paper
15.7 × 13.5 cm (6³⁄₁₆ × 5⁵⁄₁₆ in.)
Inscribed in pen, upper right *109*; inscribed in pen, on verso *GFM* (L.3343, unidentified)
Verso (not exhibited): fragmentary figure (?) sketch in black chalk
Los Angeles, J. Paul Getty Museum, inv. 86.GG.469

References: Blunt 1974, 243–44; Blunt 1979b, 139–40; RP no. 163.

5
Nicolas Poussin
Dancing Votary of Bacchus
ca. 1635
Pen and brown ink and brush and brown wash over traces of black chalk on paper
15.5 × 13.5 cm (6⅛ × 5⅜ in.)
Inscribed in pen, upper right *93*; inscribed in pen, on verso *GFM* (L.3343, unidentified)
Switzerland, Fondation Jan Krugier, inv. FJK100

References: Blunt 1979b, 139–40; RP no. 164.

6
Nicolas Poussin
Satyrs Dancing on a Wineskin
ca. 1636
Pen and brown ink and brush and brown wash over graphite on paper
24.8 × 31.8 cm (9¾ × 12½ in.)
Inscribed in pen, lower right *111*; stamped, lower right: L.1200
Windsor, Royal Collection/HM Queen Elizabeth II, inv. RCIN 911992

References: FB III no. A68 (as probably a copy); RP no. 208; London et al. 1995–96 no. 72.

7
Nicolas Poussin
Study for the Realm of Flora
ca. 1627
Pen and brown ink and brush and brown wash over red chalk on pale buff paper
21.1 × 29.1 cm (8¼ × 11½ in.)
Stamped, lower left: L.1200
Verso (not exhibited): faint red chalk variant of the same composition
Windsor, Royal Collection/HM Queen Elizabeth II, inv. RCIN 911983

References: FB III no. 214; RP no. 30; London et al. 1995–96 no. 20; Prat 2013 no. 22.

8
Nicolas Poussin
Bacchanal with a Guitar Player
ca. 1627
Oil on canvas
121 × 175 cm (47⅝ × 68⅞ in.)
Paris, Musée du Louvre, Département des Peintures, inv. 7296

[Los Angeles only]

References: Grautoff 1914 no. 41; Blunt 1966 no. 139; Thuillier 1994a no. 55; Rosenberg 2015 no. 4; Rosenberg 2022.

9
Nicolas Poussin
The Realm of Flora
1630–31
Oil on canvas
131 × 181 cm (51⅝ × 71¼ in.)
Dresden, Gemäldegalerie Alte Meister, Staatliche Kunstsammlungen, inv. 719

References: Grautoff 1914 no. 82; Blunt 1966 no. 155; Thuillier 1994a no. 84; Paris 1994–95 no. 44 (Rosenberg); Rosenberg 2022.

10
Nicolas Poussin
A Ritual Dance before a Temple
ca. 1635–40
Pen and brown ink and brush and brown wash over traces of black chalk on paper
20.8 × 31.4 cm (8⅛ × 12⅜ in.)
Stamped, lower left: L.1200
Windsor, Royal Collection/HM Queen Elizabeth II, inv. RCIN 911910

[Not exhibited]

References: FB III no. 194; RP no. 96; Paris 1994–95 no. 61 (Rosenberg); London et al. 1995–96 no. 38.

ANIMATING THE FRIEZE

11
Roman
Relief of Five Dancers before a Portico, known as the Borghese Dancers
Second century CE
Marble
72 × 187 × 14 cm (28¼ × 73⅝ × 5½ in.)
Paris, Musée du Louvre, Département des Antiquités Grecques, Étrusques et Romaines, inv. MA 1612

References: Bober and Rubinstein 1986 no. 59a; Rome 2000a no. 14; Rome 2011–12 no. 7; Haskell, Penny et al. 2021 no. 29.

12
Nicolas Poussin
Dance before a Herm of Pan
ca. 1628–30
Pen and brown ink and brush and brown wash over
traces of graphite on paper
20.6 × 32.7 cm (8⅛ × 12⅞ in.)
Stamped, lower right: L.1200
Verso (not exhibited): faint red chalk sketch for a
Holy Family
Windsor, Royal Collection/HM Queen Elizabeth II,
inv. RCIN 911979

References: FB III no. 196; RP no. 57; London et al.
1995–96 no. 25; Bilbao and New York 2007–8 no. 24
(Rosenberg).

13
Nicolas Poussin
A Bacchanalian Revel before a Term
ca. 1632–33
Oil on canvas
98 × 142.8 cm (38⅝ × 56¼ in.)
London, National Gallery, Bought, 1826, inv. NG62

References: Grautoff 1914 no. 83; Blunt 1966 no. 141;
Thuillier 1994a no. 87; Paris 1994–95 no. 47 (Rosenberg); Wine 2001 no. NG62; Rosenberg 2022.

14
Nicolas Poussin
Bacchanal around a Herm
ca. 1635–36
Brush and brown wash over black chalk on paper
18.1 × 25.9 cm (7⅛ × 10¼ in.)
Stamped, at lower right: L.1955; stamped, at lower
left: L.1886a
Paris, Musée du Louvre, Département des Arts
Graphiques, inv. MI 1103

[Los Angeles only]

References: FB III no. 199; RP no. 98; Paris 1994–95
no. 62 (Rosenberg).

15
Nicolas Poussin
The Adoration of the Golden Calf
ca. 1633–34
Oil on canvas
153.4 × 211.8 cm (60⅜ × 83⅜ in.)
London, National Gallery, Bought with a contribution
from the Art Fund, 1945, inv. NG5597

References: Grautoff 1914 no. 88; Blunt 1966 no.
22; Thuillier 1994a no. 100; Wine 2001 no. NG5597;
Rosenberg 2022.

16
Nicolas Poussin
*Hymenaeus Disguised as a Woman during an
Offering to Priapus*
ca. 1634–38
Oil on canvas
166.5 × 373 cm (65½ × 146⅞ in.)
São Paulo, Collection Museu de Arte de São Paulo
Assis Chateaubriand, Purchase, 1958, inv. MASP.
00046

References: Grautoff 1914 no. 72; Blunt 1966 no. 176;
Thuillier 1994a no. 116; Curie 2009 (in its entirety);
Rosenberg 2022.

DANCES FOR RICHELIEU

17
Nicolas Poussin
The Triumph of Pan
1636
Oil on canvas
135.9 × 146 cm (53½ × 57½ in.)
London, National Gallery, Bought with contributions
from the National Heritage Fund and the Art Fund,
1982, inv. NG6477

References: Grautoff 1914 no. 85; Blunt 1966 no.
136; Thuillier 1994a no. 112; Wine 2001 no. NG6477;
Rosenberg 2022.

18
Nicolas Poussin
The Triumph of Bacchus
1635–36
Oil on canvas
128 × 151.8 cm (50⅜ × 59¾ in.)
Kansas City, The Nelson-Atkins Museum of Art,
Purchase: William Rockhill Nelson Trust, inv. 31–94

References: Grautoff 1914 no. 86; Blunt 1966, no. 137
(as a copy); Thuillier 1994a under no. 113 (as probably
a copy); DeGalan 2021; Rosenberg 2022.

19A, 19B
Nicolas Poussin
Study for the Triumph of Pan (recto); *Studies for the
Triumph of Pan and the Triumph of Bacchus* (verso)
ca. 1635
Pen and brown ink over black chalk on paper (recto);
pen and ink and brush and pale gray-brown wash
on paper (verso)
12.9 × 20.7 cm (5⅛ × 8⅛ in.)
Stamped, lower right: L.930
Florence, Gallerie Uffizi, inv. GDS 905 E

[London only]

References: FB III no. 193; RP no. 86; Paris 1994–95
no. 56 (Rosenberg); Prat 2013 no. 43.

20A, 20B
Nicolas Poussin
Study for the Triumph of Bacchus (recto); *Study for
the Triumph of Pan* (verso)
ca. 1635
Pen and brown ink on paper (recto); pen and brown
ink over traces of black chalk on paper (verso)
20.2 × 31.4 cm (8 × 12⅜ in.)
Stamped, lower right: L.1200
Windsor, Royal Collection/HM Queen Elizabeth II,
inv. RCIN 911905

[London only]

References: FB III no. 185 (recto) and no. 189 (verso);
RP no. 83; Paris 1994–95 no. 55 (Rosenberg); London et al. 1995–96 no. 36; Prat 2013 no. 41 (recto),
no. 42 (verso).

21
Nicolas Poussin
Bacchanal
ca. 1635
Pen and brown ink and brush and brown wash over
traces of black chalk on paper
13.3 × 20.6 cm (5¼ × 8⅛ in.)
New York, The Metropolitan Museum of Art, Purchase, David T. Schiff Gift, 1998, inv. 1998.225

[London only]

References: FB IV no. 438; RP no. 93.

22
Nicolas Poussin
The Triumph of Pan
ca. 1635–36
Pen and brown ink and brush and brown wash over
traces of black chalk and stylus on paper
22.8 × 33.8 cm (9 × 13¼ in.)
Stamped, lower right: L.1200
Windsor, Royal Collection/HM Queen Elizabeth II,
inv. RCIN 911995

References: FB III no. 192; RP no. 94; London et al.
1995–96 no. 37.

23
Attic workshop
**Krater decorated with a Procession of Dionysos,
known as the Borghese Vase**
First century BCE
Marble
172 × 135 × 135 cm (67¾ × 53⅛ × 53⅛ in.)
Paris, Musée du Louvre, Département des Antiquités
Grecques, Étrusques et Romaines, inv. MR 985

References: Rome 2011–12 no. 3; Haskell, Penny
et al. 2021 no. 81.

24
Nicolas Poussin
The Triumph of Silenus
ca. 1636
Oil on canvas
142.9 × 120.5 cm (56¼ × 47½ in.)
London, National Gallery, Bought, 1824, inv. NG42

References: Grautoff 1914 no. 50; Blunt 1966 under
no. 138 (as a copy); Thuillier 1994a under no. 111 (as
a copy); Wine 2001 no. NG42 (as probably a copy);
Rosenberg 2022.

25
Nicolas Poussin
The Birth of Venus, also known as *The Triumph of
Neptune and Amphitrite*
ca. 1634–35
Oil on canvas
97.2 × 108 cm (38¼ × 42½ in.)
Philadelphia Museum of Art, The George W. Elkins
Collection, 1932, inv. E1932-1-1

[Los Angeles only]

References: Grautoff 1914 no. 87; Blunt 1966 no. 167;
Thuillier 1994a no. 110; Paris 1994–95 no. 54 (Rosenberg); Rosenberg 2022.

CHOREOGRAPHING VIOLENCE

26
Nicolas Poussin
Study for the Abduction of the Sabine Women
ca. 1633
Pen and brown ink and brush and brown wash over
traces of black chalk on paper
11.6 × 8.1 cm (4½ × 3⅛ in.)
Verso (not exhibited): black chalk fragmentary
figure study
Windsor, Royal Collection/HM Queen Elizabeth II,
inv. RCIN 911904

References: FB II no. 116; RP no. 79; Paris 1994–95
no. 75 (Rosenberg); London et al. 1995–96 no. 30;
Prat 2013 no. 39.

27
Nicolas Poussin
Study for the Abduction of the Sabine Women
ca. 1633
Pen and brown ink and brush and brown wash over
traces of black chalk on paper
11.3 × 19.4 cm (4½ × 7⅝ in.)
Verso (not exhibited): faint black chalk sketch for
The Adoration of the Shepherds (National Gallery,
London)
Windsor, Royal Collection/HM Queen Elizabeth II,
inv. RCIN 911903

References: FB II no. 117; RP no. 80; Paris 1994–95
no. 76 (Rosenberg); London et al. 1995–96 no. 29;
Prat 2013 no. 40.

28
Nicolas Poussin
Study for the Abduction of the Sabine Women
ca. 1633
Pen and brown ink and brush and brown wash
on paper
16.2 × 20.8 cm (6⅜ × 8¼ in.)
Stamped, lower right: L.930; inscribed on verso *900.
esp/ N. Poussin/ 900 esp*
Florence, Gallerie Uffizi, inv. GDS 900 E

[Los Angeles only]

References: FB II no. 115; RP no. 78; Paris 1994–95
no. 74 (Rosenberg); Prat 2013 no. 38.

29
Nicolas Poussin
Study for the Abduction of the Sabine Women
ca. 1633
Pen and brown ink and brush and brown wash
on paper
16.4 × 22.4 cm (6½ × 8⅞ in.)
Stamped, lower right: L.718
Chatsworth, Collection of the Duke of Devonshire,
inv. 861

[Not exhibited]

References: FB II no. 114; RP no. 77; Paris 1994–95
no. 73 (Rosenberg); Prat 2013 no. 37.

30
Nicolas Poussin
The Abduction of the Sabine Women
Probably 1633–34
Oil on canvas
154.6 × 209.9 cm (60⅞ × 82⅝ in.)
New York, The Metropolitan Museum of Art,
Harris Brisbane Dick Fund, 1946, inv. 46.160

[Los Angeles only]

References: Grautoff 1914 no. 71; Blunt 1966 no. 180;
Thuillier 1994a no. 103; Rosenberg 2022.

31
Nicolas Poussin
The Abduction of the Sabine Women
ca. 1634–35
Oil on canvas
159 × 206 cm (62⅝ × 81⅛ in.)
Paris, Musée du Louvre, Département des Peintures,
inv. 7290

[Not exhibited]

References: Grautoff 1914 no. 70; Blunt 1966 no. 179;
Houston and Princeton 1983 (in its entirety); Thuillier
1994a no. 131; Paris 1994–95 no. 72 (Rosenberg);
Rosenberg 2015 no. 10; Rosenberg 2022.

32
Edgar Degas
French, 1834–1917
The Abduction of the Sabine Women (after Poussin)
ca. 1861–62
Oil on canvas
150.2 × 207 cm (59⅛ × 81½ in.)
Pasadena, The Norton Simon Foundation, Gift of
Mr. Norton Simon, inv. F.1983.06.P

[Los Angeles only]

References:
Lemoisne 1946 II no. 273; Reff 1963, 246; S. Campbell 2009 no. 1 (Kendall).

A DANCE TO THE MUSIC OF TIME

33
Nicolas Poussin
A Dance to the Music of Time
ca. 1634
Oil on canvas
82.5 × 104 cm (32½ × 41 in.)
London, The Wallace Collection, inv. P108

[London only]

References: Grautoff 1914 no. 73; Blunt 1966 no.
121; Thuillier 1994a no. 141; Beresford 1995 (in its
entirety); Rosenberg 2022.

34
Nicolas Poussin
Study for a Dance to the Music of Time
ca. 1634
Pen and brown ink and brush and brown wash over
traces of black chalk on paper
14.8 × 19.9 cm (5⅞ × 7⅞ in.)
Stamped, lower left: L.1852; inscribed on verso of
mount *Marriets Coll/ Calonnes d[itt]o*
Edinburgh, National Galleries of Scotland, Purchased by Private Treaty, with the aid of the Art Fund
(Scottish Fund), the Pilgrim Trust, the Edith M. Ferguson Bequest, and Contributions from two private
donors, 1984, inv. D 5127

References: FB II no. 149; RP no. 144; Paris 1994–95
no. 90 (Rosenberg); London and Edinburgh 2010–11
no. 49; Prat 2013 no. 104.

REFERENCES CITED

Alsdorf 2008
Alsdorf, Bridget. "Pleasure's Poise: Classicism and Baroque Allegory in Poussin's 'Dance to the Music of Time.'" *Seventeenth Century* 23 (2008): 198–224.

Anguillara 1584
Anguillara, Giovanni Andrea dell'. *Le metamorfosi di Ovidio* (1561). Venice: B. Giunti, 1584.

Arasse 2000
Arasse, Daniel. "Rome, Poussin et les Sabines." In *L'Europa e l'arte italiana, per i cento anni dalla fondazione del Kunsthistorisches Institut in Florenz*, edited by Max Seidel, 337–51. Venice: Marsilio, 2000.

Arikha 1994–95
Arikha, Avigdor. "De la boîte, des figurines et du mannequin." In Paris 1994–95, 44–47.

Baldinucci 1682
Baldinucci, Filippo. *Vita del Cavaliere Gio. Lorenzo Bernino*. Florence: Vincenzio Vangelisti, 1682.

N. J. Barker 2000
Barker, Naomi Joy. "'Diverse Passions': Mode, Interval and Affect in Poussin's Paintings." *Music in Art* 25, no. 1/2 (Spring–Fall 2000): 5–24.

S. Barker 2004
Barker, Sheila. "Poussin, Plague, and Early Modern Medicine." *Art Bulletin* 86, no. 4 (December 2004): 659–89.

Barone 2009
Barone, Juliana. "Poussin as Engineer of the Human Figure: The Illustrations for Leonardo's Trattato." In *Re-Reading Leonardo: The Treatise on Painting across Europe, 1550–1900*, edited by Claire Farago, 197–236. Farnham, UK, and Burlington, VT: Ashgate, 2009.

Bassani Pacht and Kerspern 2011
Bassani Pacht, Paola, and Sylvain Kerspern. "Le décor peint à Richelieu: L'action, la gloire et le pinceau." In Orléans and Tours 2011, 115–28.

Bastet 2006
Bastet, Delphine. "Étude iconographique des *Bacchanales Richelieu* de Nicolas Poussin." *Studiolo: Revue d'histoire de l'art de l'Académie de France à Rome* 4 (2006): 167–86.

Batalla-Lagleyre 2016
Batalla-Lagleyre, Gabriel. "Henry Avice, un collectionneur du Grand Siècle: 'Les Bergers d'Arcadie' de Nicolas Poussin en leur milieu." *Revue de l'Art* 192, no. 2 (2016): 31–40.

Bätschmann 1990
Bätschmann, Oskar. *Nicolas Poussin: Dialectics of Painting*. London: Reaktion, 1990. First published as *Dialektik der Malerei*, Munich: Prestel, 1982.

Bayard 2011
Bayard, Marc. "Poussin scénographe ou dramaturge? Quelques précisions sur Poussin et l'antique." In *Poussin et la construction de l'Antique (Actes de colloque, Villa Médicis, Rome, Nov. 13–14, 2009)*. Edited by Marc Bayard and Elena Fumagalli, 407–31. Rome: Académie de France à Rome, 2011.

Beard 1999
Beard, Mary. "The Erotics of Rape: Livy, Ovid, and the Sabine Women." In *Female Networks and the Public Sphere in Roman Society*, edited by Päivi Setälä and Liisa Savunen, 1–10. Rome: Institutum Romanum Finlandiae, 1999.

Beeny 2016
Beeny, Emily A. "Poussin, Ballet, and the Birth of French Classicism." PhD diss., Columbia University, 2016.

Beeny 2019a
Beeny, Emily A. "Jeunes filles en vert: Une relecture du 'Triomphe de Flore' de Nicolas Poussin." *La Revue du Louvre et des musées de France* 4 (2019): 30–44.

Beeny 2019b
Beeny, Emily A. "Poussin's Idolatrous Dances." In *Tributes to David Freedberg: Image and Insight*, edited by Claudia Swan, 27–44. Turnhout: Brepols, 2019.

Beeny 2020
Beeny, Emily A. "*Le Raphaël des français*: Nicolas Poussin and the Legacy of Raphael." In *Raphael: The Power of Renaissance Images; The Dresden Tapestries and Their Impact*. Dresden, Staatliche Kunstsammlungen, Gemäldegalerie Alte Meister, June 6–August 30, 2020. Catalogue edited by Stephan Koja and Larissa Mohr, 241–57. Dresden: Sandstein Verlag, 2020.

Bellori 1672
Bellori, Giovanni Pietro. *Le vite dei' pittori, scultori et architetti moderni*. Rome: Mascardi, 1672.

Beresford 1995
Beresford, Richard. *A Dance to the Music of Time by Nicolas Poussin*. London: Trustees of the Wallace Collection, 1995.

Berger 2007
Berger, Robert W. "Poussin's Source(s) for his Marine Painting in Philadelphia: A *Triumph of Venus* after Apuleius." *Zeitschrift für Kunstgeschichte* 70, no. 3 (2007): 433–39.

Bernstock 2000
Bernstock, Judith. *Poussin and French Dynastic Ideology*. New York: Peter Lang, 2000.

Bianconi 1987
Bianconi, Lorenzo. *Music in the Seventeenth Century*. Cambridge: Cambridge University Press, 1987.

Bilbao and New York 2007–8
Poussin and Nature: Arcadian Visions. Bilbao, Museo de Bellas Artes, October 8, 2007–January 13, 2008; New York, Metropolitan Museum of Art, February 12–May 11, 2008. Catalogue edited by Pierre Rosenberg. New York: Metropolitan Museum of Art; New Haven, CT: Yale University Press, 2008.

Blunt 1951
Blunt, Anthony. *The 'Golden Calf' in the National Gallery, London*. London: P. L. Humphries, 1951.

Blunt 1953
Blunt, Anthony. *Art and Architecture in France, 1500–1700*. London: Penguin, 1953.

Blunt 1966
Blunt, Anthony. *The Paintings of Poussin: A Critical Catalogue*. 2 vols. London: Phaidon, 1966.

Blunt 1967
Blunt, Anthony. *Nicolas Poussin: The A. W. Mellon Lectures in the Fine Arts, 1958; National Gallery of Art, Washington, DC*. 2 vols. London: Phaidon, 1967.

Blunt 1974
Blunt, Anthony. "Newly Identified Drawings by Poussin and His Followers." *Master Drawings* 12, no. 3 (Autumn 1974): 239–48, 295–319.

Blunt 1979a
Blunt, Anthony. *The Drawings of Poussin*. New Haven, CT: Yale University Press, 1979.

Blunt 1979b
Blunt, Anthony. "Further Newly Identified Drawings by Poussin and His Followers." *Master Drawings* 17, no. 2 (Summer 1979): 119–46.

Blunt 1999
Blunt, Anthony. *Art and Architecture in France 1500–1700*. Revised and edited by Richard Beresford. New Haven, CT, and London: Yale University Press, 1999.

Bober and Rubinstein 1986
Bober, Phyllis, and Ruth Rubinstein. *Renaissance Artists and Antique Sculpture: A Handbook of Sources*. London: Harvey Miller; New York: Oxford University Press, 1986.

Bonfait 1988
Bonfait, Olivier. "The Second Generation of Collectors of Poussin: Jean Neyret de la Ravoye." *Burlington Magazine* 130, no. 1023 (June 1988): 459–64.

Bonfait 1996
Bonfait, Olivier, ed. *Poussin et Rome: Actes du colloque à l'Académie de France à Rome et à la Bibliotheca Hertziana, 16–18 novembre 1994*. Paris: Réunion des Musées Nationaux, 1996.

Bonfait 2015
Bonfait, Olivier. *Poussin et Louis XIV: Peinture et monarchie dans la France du grand siècle*. Paris: Hazan, 2015.

Bordier et al. 1623
Bordier, René, et al. *Vers pour le ballet du Roy représentant les Bacchanales, dansé par Sa Majesté au mois de février 1623*. Paris: Jean Sara, 1623.

Bordier et al. 1624
Bordier, René, et al. *Vers pour le Ballet des Volleurs, dansé par le Roy en la grande salle du Louvre, au mois de février 1624*. Paris: Jean Sara, 1624.

Boyer and Volf 1988
Boyer, Jean-Claude, and Isabelle Volf. "Rome à Paris: Les tableaux de Maréchal de Créquy (1638)." *Revue de l'Art* 79 (1988): 22–41.

Boyer et al. 2009
Boyer, Jean-Claude, Barbara Gaehtgens, and Bénédicte Gady, eds. *Richelieu, patron des arts*. Paris: Éditions de la Maison des Sciences de l'Homme, 2009.

Brigstocke 1996
Brigstocke, Hugh. "Variantes, copies et imitations. Quelques réflexions sur les méthodes de travail de Poussin." In Mérot 1996, 1:201–28.

Bull 1995
Bull, Malcolm. "Poussin's Bacchanals for Cardinal Richelieu." *Burlington Magazine* 137, no. 1102 (January 1995): 5–11.

Bull 1998
Bull, Malcolm. "Poussin and Nonnos." *Burlington Magazine* 140, no. 1148 (November 1998): 724–38.

Bull 2001
Bull, Malcolm. "Poussin's Loves of the Goddesses." *Gazette des Beaux-Arts*, 6th ser., vol. 137 (2001): 61–70.

Cambridge and Paris 2014–15
Silent Partners: Artist and Mannequin from Function to Fetish. Cambridge, The Fitzwilliam Museum, October 14, 2014–January 25, 2015; Paris, Musée Bourdelle, March 31–July 12, 2015. Catalogue by Jane Munro. Cambridge: The Fitzwilliam Museum, 2014.

S. Campbell 2009
Campbell, Sara, ed. *Degas in the Norton Simon Museum*. Vol. 2 of *Nineteenth-Century Art in the Norton Simon Museum*. New Haven, CT: Yale University Press; Pasadena: Norton Simon Museum, 2006–9.

S. J. Campbell 2004
Campbell, Stephen J. *The Cabinet of Eros: Renaissance Mythological Painting and the Studiolo of Isabella d'Este*. New Haven, CT, and London: Yale University Press, 2004.

Carrella et al. 2008
Carella, Anna, et al. *Marmora pompeiana nel Museo archeologico nazionale di Napoli: Gli arredi scultorei delle case pompeiane*. Naples: Electa, 2008.

Cartari 1571
Cartari, Vincenzo. *Le Imagini de i dei de gli antichi, nelle quali si contengono gl'idoli, riti, ceremonie, & altre cose appartenenti alla religione de gli antichi* (1556). Venice: G. Ziletti, 1571.

Cavazzini 2008
Cavazzini, Patrizia. *Painting as Business in Early Seventeenth-Century Rome*. University Park: Pennsylvania State University Press, 2008.

Cavazzini 2013
Cavazzini, Patrizia. "Nicolas Poussin, Cassiano dal Pozzo and the Roman Art Market in the 1620s." *Burlington Magazine* 155, no. 1329 (December 2013): 808–14.

Chantilly 1994–95
Nicolas Poussin 1594–1665. La collection du musée Condé à Chantilly. Chantilly, Musée Condé, September 27, 1994–January 6, 1995. Catalogue by Pierre Rosenberg, Louis-Antoine Prat, and Véronique Damian. Paris: Réunion des Musées Nationaux, 1994.

Chantilly 2017–18
Nicolas Poussin. Chantilly, Musée Condé, September 11, 2017–January 7, 2018. Catalogue by Pierre Rosenberg and Nicole Garnier-Pelle. Dijon: Éditions Faton; Chantilly: Domaine de Chantilly, 2017.

Chastel 1960
Chastel, André, ed. *Nicolas Poussin: Actes du colloque international, Paris, 19–21 septembre 1958*. 2 vols. Paris: Centre National de la Recherche Scientifique, 1960.

Chorier 1681
Chorier, Nicolas. *Histoire de la Vie de Charles de Créquy de Blanchefort, duc de Lesdiguières*. Grenoble: L. Nicolas, 1681.

Claridge and Clayton 1996–
Claridge, Amanda, and Martin Clayton, general eds. *The Paper Museum of Cassiano dal Pozzo, a Catalogue Raisonné: Drawings and Prints in the Royal Library at Windsor Castle, the British Library, the British Museum, the Institut de France and Other Collections*. 32+ vols. London: Royal Collection, British Museum, and Warburg Institute, 1996–.

Colantuono 1989
Colantuono, Anthony. "Titian's Tender Infants: On the Imitation of Venetian Painting in Baroque Rome," *I Tatti Studies in the Italian Renaissance* 3 (1989): 207–34.

B. Cole 2008
Cole, Brendan. "The Mask of Dionysus? Notes towards a re-examination of Poussin's 'Triumph of Pan.'" *Eton Collections Review* 3 (December 2008): 66–103.

B. Cole 2012
Cole, Brendan. "The Mask of Dionysus: A Reinterpretation of Poussin's 'Triumph of Pan.'" *Artibus et Historiae* 33, no. 65 (2012): 231–74.

M. Cole 2008
Cole, Michael. "Giambologna and the Sculpture with No Name." *Oxford Art Journal* 31, no. 3 (2008): 339–59.

Conti 1627
Conti, Natale. *Mythologie ou explication des fables*. Translated by Jean Baudouin. Paris: P. Chevalier and S. Thibout, 1627.

Costello 1947
Costello, Jane. "The Rape of the Sabine Women by Nicolas Poussin." *Metropolitan Museum of Art Bulletin*, n.s., 5, no. 8 (April 1947): 197–204.

Costello 1950
Costello, Jane. "The Twelve Pictures 'Ordered by Velasquez' and the Trial of Valguarnera." *Journal of the Warburg and Courtauld Institutes* 13, no 3/4 (1950): 237–84.

Coural 1960
Coural, Jean. "Les termes de Poussin à Versailles." *La Revue des Arts* 10 (1960): 67–74.

Cropper 1996
Cropper, Elizabeth. "Ritorno al crocevia." In Bonfait 1996, 257–70.

Cropper and Dempsey 1996
Cropper, Elizabeth, and Charles Dempsey. *Nicolas Poussin: Friendship and the Love of Painting*. Princeton, NJ: Princeton University Press, 1996.

Curie 2009
Curie, Pierre, ed. *Poussin Restauração: Hymeneus travestido assistindo a uma dança em honra a Príapo*. São Paulo: ITC-Instituto Totem Cultural, Imprensa Oficial, 2009.

Davies 1957
Davies, Martin. *The French School*. London: National Gallery, 1957.

DeGalan 2020
DeGalan, Aimee Marcereau, ed. *French Paintings and Pastels, 1600–1945: The Collections of the Nelson-Atkins Museum of Art*. Kansas City, MO: Nelson-Atkins Museum of Art, 2020. https://nelson-atkins.org/publications/french-paintings-catalogue/doi: 10.37764.78973

DeGalan 2021
DeGalan, Aimee Marcereau. "Nicolas Poussin, *The Triumph of Bacchus*, 1635–1636." Catalogue entry (February 2021) in DeGalan 2020.

DeGrazia and Steele 1999
DeGrazia, Diane, and Marcia Steele. "The Grande Machine." *Cleveland Studies in the History of Art* 4 (1999): 64–75.

Delisle 1858
Delisle, Léopold. "Dessins, estampes et statues de la succession de Nicolas Poussin (1678)." *Archives de l'art français* 6 (1858–60): 246–54.

Dempsey 1963
Dempsey, Charles. "Poussin and Egypt." *Art Bulletin* 45, no. 2 (June 1963): 109–19.

Dempsey 1965
Dempsey, Charles. "Poussin's 'Marine Venus' at Philadelphia: A Re-Identification Accepted." *Journal of the Warburg and Courtauld Institutes* 28 (1965): 338–43.

Dempsey 1966a
Dempsey, Charles. "The Classical Perception of Nature in Poussin's Earlier Works." *Journal of the Warburg and Courtauld Institutes* 29 (1966): 219–49.

Dempsey 1966b
Dempsey, Charles. "The Textual Sources of Poussin's 'Marine Venus' in Philadelphia." *Journal of the Warburg and Courtauld Institutes* 29 (1966): 438–42.

Dempsey 2010
Dempsey, Charles. "Nicolas Poussin et l'invention de l'idylle mythologique." In *Daniel Arasse, historien de l'art: Actes de colloque, Institut National d'Histoire de l'Art, 8–10 juin, 2006*, edited by Frédéric Cousinié, 121–32. Paris: Institut National d'Histoire de l'Art, 2010.

Di Penta 2016
Di Penta, Miriam. *Andrea De Leone (Napoli 1610–1685): Dipinti e disegni*. Rome: De Luca, 2016.

Doni 1635
Doni, Giovanni Battista. *Compendio del trattato de' generi e de' modi della musica*. Rome: Andrea Fei, 1635.

Doni 1763
Doni, Giovanni Battista. *Trattato della musica scenica*. In *De' trattati di musica di Gio. Battista Doni*, vol. 2 of *Lyra Barberina*. Edited by Antonio Francio Giori and Giovanni Battista Passeri. Florence: Stamperia Imperiale, 1763.

Duranty 1881
Duranty, Edmond. "Le peintre Louis Martin" (1872). In *Le pays des arts* (Paris: Charpentier, 1881), 313–50.

Edinburgh 1981
Sacraments and Bacchanals: Paintings and Drawings on Sacred and Profane Themes by Nicolas Poussin 1594–1665. Edinburgh, National Gallery of Scotland, October 16–December 13, 1981. Catalogue by Hugh Brigstocke et al. Edinburgh: Trustees of the National Galleries of Scotland, 1981.

Erdmann et al. 2013
Erdmann, Robert G., et al. "Reuniting Poussin's Bacchanals Painted for Cardinal Richelieu through Quantitative Canvas Weave Analysis." *Journal of the American Institute for Conservation* 52 (2013): 1–21.

Félibien 1725
Félibien, André. *Entretiens sur les vies et sur les ouvrages des plus excellens peintres anciens et modernes* (1685). 6 vols. Paris: Imprimerie S.A.S., 1725.

Ferraro 1903
Ferraro, Salvatore. *Memorie religiose e civili della città di Gaeta*. Naples: F. Giannini, 1903.

Finkel 2019
Finkel, Jori. *It Speaks to Me: Art that Inspires Artists*. Munich and New York: DelMonico Books and Prestel, 2019.

Flemming 1996
Flemming, Victoria von. "Le Neptune et Vénus de Poussin: L'intertextualité comme chance de la démarche interprétative." In Bonfait 1996, 309–27.

Fort Worth 1988
Poussin: The Early Years in Rome. Fort Worth, Kimbell Art Museum, September 24–November 27, 1988. Catalogue by Conrad Oberhuber. New York: Hudson Hills Press; Fort Worth: Kimbell Art Museum, 1988.

Freedberg 1999
Freedberg, David. "De l'effet de la musique aux effets de l'image; ou pourquoi les modes ne sont pas les *affetti*." In *La Jérusalem délivrée du Tasse: Poésie, peinture, musique, ballet, actes de colloque, Musée du Louvre 13–14 novembre 1996*, edited by Giovanni Careri, 311–38. Paris: Klincksieck and Musée du Louvre, 1999.

Freedberg 2002
Freedberg, David. *Eye of the Lynx: Galileo, His Friends, and the Beginnings of Modern Natural History*. Chicago and London: University of Chicago Press, 2002.

Friedlaender 1961
Friedlaender, Walter. "Hymenaea." In *De Artibus Opuscula XL: Essays in Honor of Erwin Panofsky*, edited by Millard Meiss, 153–56. New York: New York University Press, 1961.

Friedlaender and Blunt 1939–74
Friedlaender, Walter, and Anthony Blunt. *The Drawings of Nicolas Poussin: Catalogue Raisonné*. 5 vols. London: Warburg Institute, 1939–74.

Fumagalli 1994–95
Fumagalli, Elena. "Poussin et les collectionneurs romains au XVIIe siècle." In Paris 1994–95, 48–57.

Fumaroli 1982
Fumaroli, Marc. "Muta Eloquentia: La représentation de l'éloquence dans l'œuvre de Poussin." *Bulletin de la Société de l'histoire de l'art français* (1982): 29–48.

Fumaroli 1989
Fumaroli, Marc. *L'Inspiration du Poète de Poussin, essai sur l'allégorie du Parnasse*. Paris: Rèunion des Musèes Nationaux, 1989.

Fumaroli 2001
Fumaroli, Marc. *Nicolas Poussin: "Sainte Françoise Romaine annonçant à Rome la fin de la peste."* Paris: Musée du Louvre, 2001.

Gady 2002
Gady, Bénédicte. "L'Étrange Monsieur de La Teulière." In *L'Idéale classique. Les échanges artistiques entre Rome et Paris au temps de Bellori (1640–1700), actes de colloque de l'Académie de France à Rome*, 7–9 juin 2000, edited by Oliver Bonfait and Anne-Lise Desmas, 161–85. Paris: Somogy, 2002.

Galassi 1996
Galassi, Susan Grace. *Picasso's Variations on the Masters: Confrontations with the Past*. New York: Harry N. Abrams, 1996.

George 1936
George, Waldemar. "Sur quelques copies de Degas." *La Renaissance de l'art français et des industries de luxe* (January–February 1936): 5–8.

Glanville 2016
Glanville, Helen. "Aspect and Prospect—Poussin's 'Triumph of Silenus'." *Artibus et Historiae* 37, no. 74 (2016): 241–54.

Goldner and Hendrix 1992
Goldner, George, and Lee Hendrix. *European Drawings 2, Catalogue of the Collections*. Malibu: J. Paul Getty Museum, 1992.

Goldstein 1996
Goldstein, Carl. "Poussin et les Académies au XIX siècle." In Mérot 1996, 2:887–905.

Graham-Dixon 2003
Graham-Dixon, Andrew. *In the Picture: The Year through Art*. London: Allen Lane, 2003.

Grassinger 1991
Grassinger, Dagmar. *Römische Marmorkratere*. Mainz: P. von Zabern, 1991.

Grautoff 1914
Grautoff, Otto. *Nicolas Poussin: Sein Werk und sein Leben: Katalog der Gemälde*. 2 vols. Munich and Leipzig: Georg Müller, 1914.

Green 2000
Green, Tony. *Nicolas Poussin Paints The Seven Sacraments Twice*. Watchet, UK: Paravail, 2000.

Guarino and Masini 2006
Guarino, Sergio, and Patrizia Masini. *Pinacoteca Capitolina. Catalogo generale*. Milan: Mondadori Electa, 2006.

Hammond 1994
Hammond, Frederick. *Music & Spectacle in Baroque Rome: Barberini Patronage under Urban VIII*. New Haven, CT: Yale University Press, 1994.

Hammond 1996
Hammond, Frederick. "Poussin et les modes: Le point de vue d'un musicien." In Bonfait 1996, 75–91.

Haskell 1963
Haskell, Francis. *Patrons and Painters: A Study in the Relations between Italian Art and Society in the Age of the Baroque*. New York: Knopf, 1963.

Haskell, Penny et al. 2021
Haskell, Francis, Nicholas Penny, Adriano Aymonino, and Eloisa Dodero. *Taste and the Antique: The Lure of Classical Sculpture 1500–1900: A Revised, Updated and Extended Edition*. Turnhout: Harvey Miller Publishers, 2020.

Houston and Princeton 1983
Nicolas Poussin: The Rape of the Sabines (The Louvre Version). Houston, Museum of Fine Arts, January 21–March 20, 1983; Princeton University Art Museum, April 3–May 29, 1983. Catalogue by Avigdor Arikha. Houston: Museum of Fine Arts, 1983.

Humbert 1962
Humbert, Jacques. *Le Maréchal de Créquy, gendre de Lesdiguières (1573–1638)*. Paris: Hachette, 1962.

Jouanny 1911
Jouanny, Charles. "Correspondance de Nicolas Poussin." *Archives de l'art français* 5 (1911).

Keazor 1994
Keazor, Henry. "Zu zwei Zeichnungen Nicolas Poussins." *Zeitschrift für Kunstgeschichte* 57, no. 2 (1994): 268–75.

Keazor 1995
Keazor, Henry. "Nicolas Poussin." *Kunstchronik* 48 (1995): 337–59.

Kerspern 1996
Kerspern, Sylvain. "De Vaux-le-Vicomte à Versailles: Les termes de Poussin." In Mérot 1996, 1:271–84.

Kurita 1999
Kurita, Hidenori. "Poussin and Raphael: Secrets behind the Borrowing and the Creation." In *Poussin and Raphael: Exhibition Realized by the Special Cooperation of Bibliothèque Nationale de France*. Nagoya, Aichi Prefectural Museum of Art, March 5–April 11, 1999; Ashikaga Museum of Art, April 24–May 30, 1999. Catalogue edited by Hidenori Kurita, 163–74. Nagoya: Aichi Prefectural Museum of Art, 1999.

Lacroix 1868–70
Lacroix, Paul. *Ballets et mascarades de cour de Henri III à Louis XIV 1581–1652*. 6 vols. (1868–70). Geneva: Slatkine, 1868.

Landi 1634
Landi, Stefano. *Il S. Alessio. Dramma musicale . . . Dall'Eminentissimo, et Reverndissimo Signore Card. Barberino fatto rappresentare*. Rome: P. Masotti, 1634.

Langmuir 2004
Langmuir, Erika. *The National Gallery: Companion Guide*. Rev. ed. London: National Gallery, 2004.

Laveissière 1993
Laveissière, Sylvain. "Où sont les Poussin?" *Revue du Louvre. La revue des musées de France* 5/6 (December 1993): 133–39.

Lavin 1970
Lavin, Irving, and Marilyn Aronberg Lavin. "Duquesnoy's 'Nano di Créqui' and Two Busts by Francesco Mochi." *Art Bulletin* 52, no. 2 (June 1970): 132–49.

Le Blond de Latour 1669
Le Blond de Latour, Antoine. *Lettre du sieur Le Blond de Latour à un de ses amis, contenant quelques instructions touchant la peinture*. Bordeaux: Pierre du Coq, 1669.

Lemoisne 1946
Lemoisne, Paul-André. *Degas et son œuvre*. 4 vols. Paris: Paul Brame et C. M. de Hauke, Arts et Métiers Graphiques, 1946–49.

Leonardo 1651
Leonardo da Vinci. *Trattato della pittura di Lionardo da Vinci, novamente dato in luce, con la vita dell'istesso autore, scritta da Rafaelle du Fresne*. Paris: G. Langlois, 1651.

Levey 1963
Levey, Michael. "Poussin's 'Neptune and Amphitrite,' at Philadelphia; a Re-Identification Rejected." *Journal of the Warburg and Courtauld Institutes* 26, no 3/4 (1963): 359–60.

Levi 1985
Levi, Honor. "L'Inventaire après décès du cardinal de Richelieu." *Archives de l'art français*, n.s., 27 (1985): 9–83.

Licht 1954
Licht, Fred Stephen. "Die Entwicklung der Landschaft in den Werken von Nicolas Poussin." PhD diss., Universität Basel, 1954.

Lingo 2007
Lingo, Estelle Cecile. *François Duquesnoy and the Greek Ideal*. New Haven, CT: Yale University Press, 2007.

Loh 2007
Loh, Maria H. *Titian Remade: Repetition and the Transformation of Early Modern Italian Art*. Los Angeles: Getty Research Institute, 2007.

Loire 2010
Loire, Stéphane. "Deux tableaux retrouvés au Louvre: 'Le Triomphe de Bacchus' de Pierre de Cortone et 'Le Passage de la Mer Rouge' de Giovanni Francesco Romanelli." *Bollettino d'Arte* 7, no. 4 (2010): 85–102.

London 1995
Nicolas Poussin: 1594–1665. London, Royal Academy of Arts, January 19–April 9, 1995. Catalogue by Richard Verdi, with an essay by Pierre Rosenberg. London: Zwemmer in association with the Royal Academy of Arts, 1995.

London et al. 1995–96
Poussin: Works on Paper; Drawings from the Collection of Her Majesty Queen Elizabeth II. London, Dulwich Picture Gallery, February 16–April 30, 1995; Houston, Museum of Fine Arts, August 27–November 12, 1995; Cleveland Museum of Art, November 22, 1995–January 24, 1996; New York, Metropolitan Museum of Art, February 6–March 31, 1996. Catalogue by Martin Clayton. London: Merrell Holberton, 1995.

London and Edinburgh 2010–11
Poussin to Seurat: French Drawings from the National Gallery of Scotland. London, The Wallace Collection, September 23, 2010–January 3, 2011; Edinburgh, National Gallery Complex, February 5–May 1, 2011. Catalogue by Michael Clarke. Edinburgh: Trustees of the National Galleries of Scotland, 2010.

Lugt 1921–56
Lugt, Frits. *Les marques de collections de dessins & d'estampes*. The Hague: Nijhoff, 1921–56; revised, expanded, and made available online by the Fondation Custodia (consulted in 2020). http://www .marquesdecollections.fr.

Madrid 2005
El Palacio del Rey Planeta: Felipe IV y el Buen Retiro. Madrid, Museo Nacional del Prado, July 6–November 27, 2005. Catalogue edited by Andrés Úbeda de los Cobos. Madrid: Museo Nacional del Prado, 2005.

Maffei 1707–9
Maffei, Paolo Alessandro. *Gemme antiche figurate*. Rome: F. Gonzaga, 1707–9.

Magne 1914
Magne, Émile. *Nicolas Poussin, Premier Peintre du Roi (1594–1665): Suivi d'un catalogue raisonné . . .* Brussels and Paris: G. van Oest, 1914.

Mahon 1960
Mahon, Denis. "Poussin's Early Development: An Alternative Hypothesis." *Burlington Magazine* 102, no. 688 (July 1960): 288–306.

Marucchi 1956-57
Marucchi, Adriana, ed. *Considerazioni sulla Pittura / Giulio Mancini*. 2 vols. Rome: Accademia Nazionale dei Lincei, 1956–57.

Marvin 2002
Marvin, Miranda. "The Ludovisi Barbarians: The Grand Manner." *Memoirs of the American Academy in Rome. Supplementary Volumes* 1 (2002): 205–23.

Melbourne 2014
Italian Masterpieces from Spain's Royal Court. Melbourne, National Gallery of Victoria, May 16–August 31, 2014. Catalogue by Andrés Úbeda de los Cobos. Melbourne: National Gallery of Victoria, 2014.

Meloncelli 1982
Meloncelli, R. "Clemente IX." In *Dizionario biografico degli Italiani*. 26 vols. Rome: Istituto dell'Enciclopedia italiana, 1960–. Vol. 26 (1982): 282–93.

Mérot 1996
Mérot, Alain, ed. *Nicolas Poussin (1594–1665): Actes du colloque organisé au musée du Louvre par le Service culturel, du 19 au 21 octobre 1994*, 2 vols. Paris: Documentation française, 1996.

Montagu 1992
Montagu, Jennifer. "The Theory of the Musical Modes in the Académie Royale de Peinture et de Sculpture." *Journal of the Warburg and Courtauld Institutes* 55 (1992): 233–48.

Montanari 2016
Montanari, Tomaso. *La libertà di Bernini: La sovranità dell'artista e le regole del potere*. Turin: Giulio Einaudi, 2016.

Montreal and Cologne 2002-3
Richelieu: Art and Power. Montreal, Musée des Beaux-Arts, September 18, 2002–January 5, 2003; Cologne, Wallraf-Richartz-Museum, January 31–April 20, 2003. Catalogue edited by Hilliard Goldfarb. Montreal: Musée des Beaux-Arts; Cologne: Wallraf-Richartz; Ghent: Snoeck-Ducaju & Zoon, 2002.

Moore 1891
Moore, George. *Impressions and Opinions*. London: David Nutt, 1891.

Murata 1981
Murata, Margaret. *Operas for the Papal Court 1631–1668*. Ann Arbor, MI: UMI Research Press, 1981.

Murata 1984
Murata, Margaret. "Classical Tragedy in the History of Early Opera in Rome." *Early Music History* 4 (1984): 101–34.

Negro 2007
Negro, Angela. *La collezione Rospigliosi: La quadreria e la committenza artistica di una famiglia patrizia a Roma nel Sei e Settecento*. Rome: Campisano, 2007.

Oberhuber 1996
Oberhuber, Konrad. "Raphael et Poussin." In Bonfait 1996, 67–74.

Olson 2002
Olson, Todd. *Poussin and France: Painting, Humanism, and the Politics of Style*. New Haven, CT: Yale University Press, 2002.

Olson 2010
Olson, Todd P. "Trophies: Poussin, Richelieu and the Transmission of Antiquity." In *Rome–Paris 1640: Transferts culturels et renaissance d'un centre artistique*, edited by Marc Bayard, 331–45. Rome: Académie de France à Rome; Paris: Somogy, 2010.

Orléans and Tours 2011
Richelieu à Richelieu: Architecture et décors d'un château disparu. Musée des Beaux-Arts d'Orléans and Musée des Beaux-Arts de Tours, March 12–June 13, 2011. Catalogue by Stijn Alsteens et al. Milan: Silvana, 2011.

Oxford 1990–91
A Loan Exhibition of Drawings by Nicolas Poussin from British Collections. Oxford, Ashmolean Museum, December 4, 1990–February 17, 1991. Catalogue by Hugh Brigstocke. London: Sotheby's, 1990.

Palisca 1997
Palisca, Claude. "Giovanni Battista Doni's Interpretation of the Greek Modal System." *Journal of Musicology* 15 (1997): 3–18.

Panofsky 1936
Panofsky, Erwin. "Et in Arcadia Ego: On the Concept of Transience in Poussin and Watteau." In *Philosophy and History: Essays Presented to Ernst Cassirer*, edited by Raymond Klibansky and H. J. Paton, 223–54. Oxford: Clarendon Press, 1936.

Panofsky 1950
Panofsky, Erwin. "Poussin's Apollo and Daphne in the Louvre." *Bulletin de la Société Poussin*, 3 (May 1950): 27–41.

Paris 1953–54
Chefs-d'œuvre du Musée d'art de São-Paulo. Paris, Musée de l'Orangerie, October 1953–January 1954. Paris: Musées Nationaux, 1953.

Paris 1985
Richelieu et le monde de l'esprit. Paris, Sorbonne, November 1985. Catalogue edited by the Chancellerie des Universités de Paris and Académie Française. Paris: Centre National de la Recherche Scientifique, 1985.

Paris 1994–95
Nicolas Poussin: 1594–1665. Paris, Galeries Nationales du Grand Palais, September 27, 1994–January 2, 1995. Catalogue by Pierre Rosenberg et al. Paris: Réunion des Musées Nationaux, 1994.

Paris 2015
Poussin et Dieu. Paris, Musée du Louvre, March 30–June 29, 2015. Catalogue edited by Nicolas Milovanovic and Mickaël Szanto. Paris: Hazan and Musée du Louvre, 2015.

Paris, New York, and Chicago 1982
France in the Golden Age: Seventeenth-Century French Paintings in American Collections. Paris, Galleries Nationales du Grand Palais, January 29–April 26, 1982; New York, Metropolitan Museum of Art, May 26–August 22, 1982; Chicago, The Art Institute of Chicago, September 18–November 28, 1982. Catalogue by Pierre Rosenberg. New York: Metropolitan Museum of Art, 1982.

Passeri 1772
Passeri, Giovanni Battista. *Vite de' pittori, scultori, ed architetti, che anno lavorato in Roma, morti dal 1641 fino al 1673*. Rome: G. Settari, 1772.

Perrier 1638
Perrier, François. *Segmenta nobilium signora et statuarum quae temporis dentem invidium evasure Urbis aeternae ruinis erepta*. Rome, 1638.

Perrier 1645
Perrier, François. *Icones et segmenta nobelium signorum et statuarum quae Romae adhunc extant*. Rome, 1645.

Pierguidi 2011
Pierguidi, Stefano. "Confronto e simmetria: Dai dipinti degli studioli di Isabella e Alfonso d'Este ai pendants di Nicolas Poussin." *Civiltà Mantovana* 3, no. 46 (2011): 54–86.

Pierguidi 2012
Pierguidi, Stefano. "Note sui dipinti di Poussin (e Vouet?) di provenienza Roccatagliata e dal Pozzo." *Studi Piemontesi* 41, no. 1 (2012): 113–23.

Pilon 1911
Pilon, Edmond. "La Danse dans l'œuvre de Poussin, de Watteau et de Corot." *La Revue bleue* 49, no. 2 (July 1911): 78–83.

Pinson 1997
Pinson, Yona. "Un langage muet: Métaphore et morale dans les éléments architecturaux et scénographiques de Nicolas Poussin." *Artibus et Historiae* 18, no. 36 (1997): 109–27.

Pintard 1960
Pintard, René. "Rencontres avec Poussin." In Chastel 1960, 1:31–46.

Pirrotta et al. 1982
Pirrotta, Nino, Elena Povoledo, and Karen Eales. *Music and Theatre from Poliziano to Monteverdi*. Cambridge: Cambridge University Press, 1982.

Poussin 2014
Poussin, Nicolas. *Lettres et propos sur l'art*. Edited by Anthony Blunt (1964), 3rd ed. Paris: Hermann, 2014.

Powell 2012
Powell, Olivia. "The Choreographic Imagination in Renaissance Art." PhD diss., Columbia University, 2012.

Prat 2013
Prat, Louis-Antoine. "Nicolas Poussin (1594–1665)." In Prat, *Le dessin au XVIIe siècle*, 14–88. Paris: Éditions du Louvre and Somogy, 2013.

Ravaud 2009
Ravaud, Elisabeth. "Hymeneus travestido assistindo a uma dança: Estudo cientifico." In Curie 2009, 81–92.

Reff 1963
Reff, Theodore. "Degas's Copies of Older Art." *Burlington Magazine* 105, no. 723 (June 1963): 238–51.

Reff 1964
Reff, Theodore. "New Light on Degas's Copies." *Burlington Magazine* 106, no. 735 (June 1964): 248–59.

Reff 1965
Reff, Theodore. "Addenda on Degas's Copies." *Burlington Magazine* 107, no. 747 (June 1965): 320–23.

Reff 1971
Reff, Theodore. "Further Thoughts on Degas's Copies." *Burlington Magazine* 113, no. 822 (September 1971): 534–43.

Roberto 2004
Roberto, Sebastiano. *Gianlorenzo Bernini e Clemente IX Rospigliosi: Arte e architettura a Roma e in Toscana nel Seicento*. Rome: Gangemi, 2004.

Robin 1998
Robin, Delphine. "Étude iconographique des Bacchanales Richelieu de Nicolas Poussin." PhD diss., Université de Paris IV, 1998.

Rome 1997–98
Pietro da Cortona, il meccanismo della forma: Ricerche sulla tecnica pittorica. Rome, Pinacoteca capitolina, November 14, 1997–February 8, 1998. Catalogue edited by Sergio Guarino. Milan: Electa, 1997.

Rome 1998–99
Poussin: Works from His First Years in Rome. Rome, Palazzo delle Esposizioni, November 26, 1998–March 1, 1999. Catalogue by Denis Mahon. Jerusalem: Israel Museum, 1999.

Rome 2000a
L'idea del bello: Viaggio per Roma nel Seicento con Giovan Pietro Bellori. Rome, Palazzo delle esposizioni, March 29–June 26, 2000. Catalogue edited by Evelina Borea and Carlo Gasparri. Rome: De Luca, 2000.

Rome 2000b
I segreti di un collezionista: Le straordinarie raccolte di Cassiano dal Pozzo 1588–1657. Rome, Galleria Nazionale di Arte Antica, Palazzo Barberini, September 29–November 26, 2000. Catalogue edited by Francesco Solinas. Rome: De Luca, 2000.

Rome 2011–12
I Borghese e l'antico. Rome, Galleria Borghese, December 7, 2011–April 9, 2012. Catalogue edited by Anna Coliva. Milan: Skira, 2011.

Rome and Dusseldorf 1977–78
Nicolas Poussin: 1594–1665. Rome, Académie de France, November 1977–January 1978; Düsseldorf, Städtische Kunsthalle, January–March 1978. Catalogue by Pierre Rosenberg. Rome: Edizioni d'elefante; Düsseldorf: Städtische Kunsthalle, 1977–78.

Romei 2005
Romei, Danilo, ed. *Lo Spettacolo del sacro, la morale del profano. Su Giulio Rospigliosi (Papa Clemente IX) Atti del Convengo Internazionale, Pistoia, 22–23 settembre 2000*. Florence: Polistampa, 2005.

Rosenberg 2009
Rosenberg, Pierre. "A obra: Hymeneus travestido assistindo a uma dança em honra a Príapo." In Curie 2009, 44–63.

Rosenberg 2011
Rosenberg, Pierre. "Les Bacchanales Richelieu: Ce que l'on sait et ce que l'on ne sait pas (encore)." In Orléans and Tours 2011: 129–35.

Rosenberg 2015
Rosenberg, Pierre. *Nicolas Poussin: Les tableaux du Louvre*. Paris: Louvre Éditions, 2015.

Rosenberg 2022
Rosenberg, Pierre. *Nicolas Poussin, 1594–1665: Catalogue raisonné des peintures*. Forthcoming in 2022.

Rosenberg and Prat 1994
Rosenberg, Pierre, and Louis-Antoine Prat. *Nicolas Poussin, 1594–1665: Catalogue raisonné des dessins*. 2 vols. Milan: Leonardo Editore, 1994.

Rosenberg and Stewart 1987
Rosenberg, Pierre, and Marion C. Stewart. *French Paintings 1500–1825: The Fine Arts Museums of San Francisco*. San Francisco: Fine Arts Museums, 1987.

Rospigliosi 1998
Rospigliosi, Giulio. *Melodrammi profani*. Edited by Danilo Romei. Florence: Studio editoriale fiorentino, 1998.

Rospigliosi 1999
Rospigliosi, Giulio. *Melodrammi sacri*. Edited by Danilo Romei. Florence: Studio editoriale fiorentino, 1999.

Rossi 1637
Rossi, Michelangelo. *Erminia sul Giordano. Dramma musicale rappresentato nel Palazzo dell'Illustrissimo, et Eccellentissimo Signore D. Taddeo Barberino*. Rome: P. Masotti, 1637.

Sandrart 1675
Sandrart, Joachim von. *Teutschen Academie: Zweyter Theil*. Nuremberg: Miltenberger, 1675.

Schnapper 1988–94
Schnapper, Antoine. *Curieux du grand siècle: Collections et collectionneurs dans la France du XVIIe siècle*. 2 vols. Paris: Centre National du Livre, 1988–94.

Schütze 1996
Schütze, Sebastian. "Aristide de Thèbes, Raphaël et Poussin: La représentation des *affetti* dans les grands tableaux d'histoire de Poussin des années 1620–1630." In Mérot 1996, 2:571–602.

Scott 2008
Scott, Deborah Emont, ed. *The Nelson-Atkins Museum of Art: A Handbook of the Collection*. 7th ed. Kansas City: Nelson-Atkins Museum of Art, 2008.

Sohm 2001
Sohm, Philip. *Style in the Art Theory of Early Modern Italy*. Cambridge: Cambridge University Press, 2001.

Solinas 1989
Solinas, Francesco, ed. *Cassiano dal Pozzo: Atti del seminario internazionale di studi, Università di Roma La Sapienza, 18 e 19 dicembre 1987*. Rome: De Luca, 1989.

Sommer 1961
Sommer, Frank. "Poussin's 'Triumph of Neptune and Amphitrite': A Re-Identification." *Journal of the Warburg and Courtauld Institutes* 24, no. 3/4 (July–December 1961): 323–27.

Sparti 1992
Sparti, Donatella Livia. *Le collezioni Dal Pozzo: Storia di una famiglia e del suo museo nella Roma seicentesca*. Modena: F. C. Panini, 1992.

Sparti 1993–94
Sparti, Donatella Livia. "Appunti sulle finanze di Nicolas Poussin." *Storia dell'Arte* 79 (1993–94): 341–50.

Sparti 2003
Sparti, Donatella Livia. "Cassiano Dal Pozzo, Poussin and the Making and Publication of Leonardo's 'Trattato.'" *Journal of the Warburg and Courtauld Institutes* 66 (2003): 143–88.

Sparti 2004–5
Sparti, Donatella Livia. "Poussin's Two Versions of *The Destruction of the Temple of Jerusalem* and Other Early Paintings." *Jahrbuch des Kunsthistorischen Museums Wien* 6/7 (2004–5): 181–203.

Spiriti 1993
Spiriti, Andrea. "Il cardinale Luigi Alessandro Omodei e la sua famiglia: Documenti e considerazioni." *Archivio storico lombardo* 119 (1993): 107–28.

Spiriti 2013
Spiriti, Andrea. "Luigi Alessandro Omodei e la sua famiglia: Una collezione cardinalizia fra Roma e Milano." In *Lo spazio del collezionismo nello Stato di Milano (secoli XVII–XVIII)*, edited by Andrea Spiriti, 205–46. Rome: Viello, 2013.

Standring 1988
Standring, Timothy J. "Some Pictures by Poussin in the Dal Pozzo Collection: Three New Inventories." *Burlington Magazine* 130, no. 1025 (August 1988): 608–26.

Standring 2009
Standring, Timothy J. "Poussin's Erotica." *Apollo* 169, no. 563 (March 2009): 82–88.

Standring 2017
Standring, Timothy J. "Poussin's Other Version of 'King Midas Turns an Oak Branch to Gold.'" *Yale University Art Gallery Bulletin Recent Acquisitions* (2017): 69–77.

Stefanoni 1627
Stefanoni, Pietro. *Gemmae antiquitus sculptae a Petro Stephanio*. Rome: M. Bolzettam de Cadorinis, 1627.

Tallement des Réaux 1834–35
Tallement des Réaux, Gédéon. *Les Historiettes de Tallemant des Réaux: Mémoires pour servir à l'histoire du XVIIe siècle* (ca. 1657–92). Edited by Louis Jean Nicolas Monmerqué, Hippolyte de Châteaugiron, and Jules-Antoine Taschereau. 6 vols. Paris: A. Levasseur, 1834–35.

Thuillier 1960
Thuillier, Jacques. "Pour un Corpus Pussinianum." In Chastel 1960, 2:49–238.

Thuillier 1994a
Thuillier, Jacques. *Nicolas Poussin*. Paris: Flammarion, 1994.

Thuillier 1994b
Thuillier, Jacques. "Poussin et le laboratoire." *Techne* 1 (1994): 13–20.

Thuillier 1995
Thuillier, Jacques. *Poussin before Rome, 1594–1624*. Translated by Christopher Allen. New York: Richard L. Feigen, 1995.

Twilley et al. 2015
Twilley, John, Nicole Myers, and Mary Schafer. "Poussin's Materials and Techniques for the Triumph of Bacchus at the Nelson-Atkins Museum of Art." In *Nicolas Poussin: Technique, Practice, Conservation,* 71–83. Special issue of *Kermes: La Rivista del Restauro* 27, no. 94/95, 2015.

Úbeda 2005
Úbeda de los Cobos, Andrés. "El ciclo de la Historia de Roma Antigua." In Madrid 2005, 168–89.

Unglaub 2004
Unglaub, Jonathan. "Poussin's Reflection." *Art Bulletin* 86, no. 3 (September 2004): 505–28.

Unglaub 2006
Unglaub, Jonathan. *Poussin and the Poetics of Painting: Pictorial Narrative and the Legacy of Tasso.* Cambridge: Cambridge University Press, 2006.

Unglaub 2011
Unglaub, Jonathan. "Poussin and Rospigliosi: Novità, Copies, and Modes." In *Novità. Neuheitskonzepte in den Bildkünsten um 1600,* edited by Ulrich Pfisterer and Gabriele Wimböck, 447–70. Berlin: Diaphanes, 2011.

Van den Berg 1942
Van den Berg, H. M. "Willem Schellinks en Lambert Doomer in Frankrijk." *Oudheidkundig Jaerboek* 11 (1942): 1–31.

Van Orden 2005
Van Orden, Kate. *Music, Discipline, and Arms in Early Modern France.* Chicago and London: University of Chicago Press, 2005.

Venice and Washington 2018–19
Tintoretto, 1519–1594. Venice, Palazzo ducale, September 7, 2018–January 6, 2019; and Washington, DC, National Gallery of Art, March 10–July 7, 2019. Catalogue edited by Robert Echols and Frederick Ilchman. Venice: Marsilio; New Haven, CT: Yale University Press; Washington, DC: National Gallery of Art, 2018.

Venetucci et al. 1983
Venetucci, Beatrice Palma, et al. *Museo Nazionale Romano: Le Sculture.* Vol. 1, *I Marmi Ludovisi.* Rome: De Luca, 1983.

Verdi 2019
Verdi, Richard. *Poussin as a Painter: From Classicism to Abstraction.* London: Reaktion, 2019.

Vermeule 1960
Vermeule, Cornelius C. "The Dal Pozzo-Albani Drawings of Classical Antiquities in the British Museum." *Transactions of the American Philosophical Society,* n.s., 50, part 5 (May 1960) [complete issue].

Vigenère 1614
Vigenère, Blaise de. *Les images ou tableaux de platte peinture des deux Philostrates sophistes grecs et les Statues de Callistrate* (1578). Paris, 1614.

Vignier 1676
Vignier, Benjamin. *Le Chasteau de Richelieu ou l'histoire des héros de l'antiquité avec des réfléxions morales par M. Vignier.* Saumur: Desbordes, 1676.

Weir 1998
Weir, Susan A. "Poussin's Marine Painting in Philadelphia Reconsidered." *Notes in the History of Art* 17, no. 2 (Winter 1998): 33–37.

Whitlum-Cooper 2021
Whitlum-Cooper, Francesca. "'The Triumph of Silenus' Reconsidered." *Burlington Magazine* 163, no. 1418 (May 2021).

Wilberding 2000
Wilberding, Erick. "Poussin's Illness in 1629." *Burlington Magazine* 142, no. 1170 (September 2000): 561.

Wild 1980
Wild, Doris. *Nicolas Poussin.* 2 vols. Zurich: Orell Füssli, 1980.

Wildenstein 1958
Wildenstein, Georges. "Les graveurs de Poussin au XVIIe siècle." *Gazette des Beaux-Arts* 46, nos. 1040–43 (September–December 1955), published in 1958.

Wine 2001
Wine, Humphrey. *The Seventeenth-Century French Paintings.* London: National Gallery Company, 2001.

Wittkower 1963
Wittkower, Rudolf. "The Role of Classical Models in Bernini's and Poussin's Preparatory Work." *Studies in Western Art: III, Latin American Art, and the Baroque Period in Europe (Acts of the 20th International Congress of the History of Art).* Princeton, NJ: Princeton University Press, 1963: 41–50.

Worthen 1979
Worthen, Thomas. "Poussin's Paintings of Flora." *Art Bulletin* 61, no. 4 (December 1979): 575–88.

Zarlino 1558
Zarlino, Gioseffo. *Le Istitutioni harmoniche.* Venice, 1558.

Zarlino 1983
Zarlino, Gioseffo. *On the Modes: Part Four of Le Istitutioni harmoniche 1558.* Translated by Vered Cohen; edited by Claude V. Palisca. New Haven, CT: Yale University Press, 1983.

Zirpolo 2005
Zirpolo, Lilian H. *Ave Papa, Ave Papabile: The Sacchetti Family, Their Art Patronage, and Political Aspirations.* Toronto: Centre for Reformation and Renaissance Studies, 2005.

ILLUSTRATION CREDITS

Fig. 1: © The Trustees of the British Museum

Fig. 2: Museo Archeologico Nazionale, Naples, Campania, Italy. Photo © Raffaello Bencini / Bridgeman Images

Figs. 3, 20; plates 2, 6, 7, 10, 12, 20a, 20b, 22, 26, 27; pp. 16–17, 42–43, 66–67: Royal Collection Trust / © Her Majesty Queen Elizabeth II 2020

Fig. 4: Palazzo Farnese, Rome, Italy. Photo © Fine Art Images / Bridgeman Images

Figs. 5, 10: Image © Museo Nacional del Prado / Art Resource, NY

Figs. 6, 29d; plate 31: © RMN-Grand Palais / Art Resource, NY. Photo: Tony Querrec

Figs. 7, 13, 26: Fine Arts Museums of San Francisco

Fig. 8: © RMN-Grand Palais / Art Resource, NY. Photo: Michel Urtado

Fig. 9: Los Angeles, Getty Research Institute (1364-278)

Fig. 11: British Library, London, UK © British Library Board. All rights reserved / Bridgeman Images

Fig. 12: Photo © Vatican Museums. All rights reserved

Fig. 14: © Museo Nacional del Prado

Figs. 15, 21; plates 11, 23; pp. 28–29: © RMN-Grand Palais / Art Resource, NY. Photo: Hervé Lewandowski

Figs. 16, 29c; plates 21, 30; pp. 78–79: www.metmuseum.org, CC0

Figs. 17–19: © RMN-Grand Palais / Art Resource, NY. Photo: René-Gabriel Ojéda

Fig. 22; plates 13, 24; p. 34: © The National Gallery, London

Fig. 23: Image courtesy of The Nelson-Atkins Museum of Art, Media Services / Photo: Robert Newcombe

Fig. 24: © Veneranda Biblioteca Ambrosiana / Mondadori Portfolio Fotoriproduzione

Fig. 25: Photo: Erich Lessing / Art Resource, NY

Fig. 27: Palazzo Altemps, Rome, Lazio, Italy. G. Dagli Orti / De Agostini Picture Library / Bridgeman Images

Fig. 28: Photo: Scala / Art Resource, NY

Fig. 29a; plates 19a, 19b, 28; pp. 92–93: Gabinetto Fotografico delle Gallerie degli Uffizi

Fig. 29b; plate 29: © The Devonshire Collections, Chatsworth. Collection of the Duke of Devonshire, Chatsworth / Bridgeman Images

Figs. 30, 33; plate 34; pp. 112–13: The National Galleries of Scotland

Fig. 31: MiBACT—Galleria Borghese / Photo: Luciano Romano

Fig. 32: Stamp.Barb.N.XIII.200, courtesy Biblioteca Apostolica Vaticana © 2020 Biblioteca Apostolica Vaticana. All rights reserved

Fig. 34: © RMN-Grand Palais / Art Resource, NY. Photo: Jean-Gilles Berizzi

Plate 1; pp. xiv–1: © Photographic Archive Museo Nacional del Prado

Plate 3; p. 4: su concessione del Ministero per i Beni e le Attivà Culturali e per il Turismo—Museo Archeologico Nazionale di Napoli. Photo: Giorgio Albano

Plate 5: Fondation Jan Krugier, Lausanne, Switzerland

Plate 8; p. i: © RMN-Grand Palais / Art Resource, NY. Photo: Thierry Ollivier

Plate 9: Photo: bpk Bildagentur / Gemäldegalerie Alte Meister, Staatliche Kunstsammlungen, Dresden, Germany / Elke Estel / Hans-Peter Klut / Art Resource, NY

Plate 14: © RMN-Grand Palais / Art Resource, NY

Plate 15; pp. ii–iii: © The National Gallery, London. Bought with a contribution from the Art Fund, 1945

Plate 16; front cover (J. Paul Getty Museum edition): MASP, Museu de Arte de São Paulo Assis Chateaubriand. Photo: Alexandre Leão

Plate 17; pp. 50–51: © The National Gallery, London. Bought with contributions from the National Heritage Memorial Fund and the Art Fund, 1982

Plate 18; p. 58: Image courtesy of The Nelson-Atkins Museum of Art, Media Services / Photo: John Lamberton

Plate 33; pp. 102–3; front cover (The National Gallery, London, edition): Wallace Collection, London, UK / Bridgeman Images

INDEX

Page numbers in *italics* refer to illustrations. Art institutions or collections are indexed by location. All works are by Nicolas Poussin unless otherwise indicated.

Aaron, 35
The Abduction of Rinaldo, 107
The Abduction of the Sabine Women (Louvre, plate 31), 79–82, 86–89, 90n8, 90n10, 91n41, *99*, 118
The Abduction of the Sabine Women (Metropolitan Museum, plate 30), xiii, 79–89, 90n4, 90n7, 90n11, *98*, 118
Accademia di San Luca, xii, xiii
Adonis, 8–9, 10, 11, 15n38, 15n40
The Adoration of the Golden Calf (plate 15), xiii, 35–37, 41n30, *48*, 117
The Adoration of the Magi, xiii
Aeneid (Virgil), 79, 90nn2–3
Agasias of Ephesus, 56
Ajax, 8–9, 11, 15n38
Alberti, Cherubino, *83*
Alberti, Leon Battista, 90n31
Aldobrandini, Pietro, Cardinal, 14n25
Alfonso I d'Este, Duke of Ferrara, 14n25
altarpieces, xii, 111n3
Amphitrite, 62, *77*
Anguillara, Giovanni Andrea dell', 14n24, 15n41
Antaeus, 79, *80*, 82
Antinous, engraving after Poussin (fig. 9), 29–30, *30*
Apis, 37
Apollo, 9, 10, 51, 59, 103–6, *105*, *106*, 110, 111n11
The Arcadian Shepherds, xiii, 91n34, 104, 111n3
Ariadne, 2–3, *18*, *19*
Arikha, Avigdor, 90n19
Art of Love (Ovid), 90n2
Atalanta, 40
Aurora (Dawn), 103–5
Avice, Henry, 111n3

Bacchanal (Bayonne, fig. 17), 52–53, *52*
Bacchanal (Bayonne, fig. 18), 52–53, *54*
Bacchanal (Metropolitan Museum, plate 21), 53, *74*, 117
Bacchanal and Studies for a Group Approaching a Sleeping Silenus (fig. 19), 53, *54*
Bacchanal around a Herm (plate 14), 8, 33–35, *47*, 117
Bacchanal before a Temple (lost), 11–13, *12*, 15n61, 65n61
A Bacchanalian Revel before a Term (plate 13), 32–33, 35, 36, 40, *46*, 104, 117
Bacchanal of Putti, 41n11, 41n16
Bacchanal with a Guitar Player (plate 8), 6–7, *23*, 116
Bacchus
    Annibale Carracci's depiction of, 6, *6*
    and Egyptian god Apis, 37

    Poussin's depictions of, in triumphal parade, 51, 57–59, *69*
    Poussin's depictions of, with Ariadne, 2–3, 6–7, *18*, *19*
    and theater, 51
    See also Dionysus
Bacchus and Ariadne (plate 1), 1–3, 6, 14n6, 14n9, *18*, 116
ballet
    and battle or violence, 1, 79–80, 86, 89, 90n4
    Poussin's collectors as dancers or patrons of, 1, 14n4, 62, 86
    and Poussin's wax models, 53
    Poussin's work as balletic, 13, 14n2, 63, 102
    in Rospigliosi's operas, 106–7
Ballet de la marine (Paris, 1635), 62
Ballet des bacchanales (Paris, 1623), 86
Ballet des volleurs (Paris, 1624), 86
Barberini, Francesco, Cardinal, xii, 2, 14n9, 15n46
Barberini family, 14n9, 103, 109, 111n26. *See also* Palazzo Barberini, Rome
Bayonne, Musée Bonnat
    Bacchanal (figs. 17, 18), 52–53, *52*, *54*
    Bacchanal and Studies for a Group Approaching a Sleeping Silenus (fig. 19), 53, *54*
Beauchamps, Pierre, 14n4
Bellini, Giovanni, 14n25, 15n29
Bellori, Giovanni Pietro
    on Poussin and the Sacchetti family, 14n9
    on Poussin's *Abduction of the Sabine Women*, 81
    on Poussin's paintings for Richelieu, 55, 60, 62
    on Poussin's paintings for Rospigliosi, 104
    on Poussin's study of Titian's bacchanals, 6, 7
Belvedere Antinous, now known as *Hermes* (Roman statue), 29–30, *30*, 41n6
Berlin, Gemäldegalerie, 107
Bernini, Gian Lorenzo
    admiration for Poussin, 63
    Apollo and Daphne (fig. 31), 105, *105*
Bernstock, Judith, 90n17
The Birth of Venus, also known as *The Triumph of Neptune and Amphitrite* (plate 25), 62–63, *77*, 117
Blunt, Anthony, 14n17, 15n61, 51–52, 53, 63, 90n6
Borghese, Scipione, Cardinal, 29
Borghese Dancers relief (Roman, plate 11), 1, 29, 31–32, 36, 39, 40, 41n1, 41n12, *44*, 104–5, 116
Borghese Gladiator by Agasias of Ephesus (Hellenistic statue, fig. 21), 55, *56*
Borghese Sacrifice relief (Roman, fig. 15), 39, *39*
Borghese Vase (neo-Attic, plate 23), 1, 3, 14nn15–16, 36, 60, *75*, 117
Brigstocke, Hugh, 64n38, 65n60, 90n4
Bruni, Antonio, 15n37
Buen Retiro Palace, Madrid, xiii, 38, 41nn35–37, 41n45, 61, 64n44

Camassei, Andrea, *106*
Cambridge, Fitzwilliam Museum, xiii
Cameo of a Dancing Satyr (Roman, fig. 2), 3–5, *5*, 14n20
Camillus and the Schoolmaster of Falerii, 107
Caravaggio, Michelangelo Merisi da, 2, 86
Carnival entertainments, 86, 106
Carracci, Annibale, *The Triumph of Bacchus* (fig. 4), 6, *6*, 57, 64n22
Carracci family, 2
Cartari, Vincenzo, 38
Cassiano dal Pozzo. *See* Pozzo, Cassiano dal
Castel-Rodrigo, Manuel de Moura y Corte Real, 2nd Marquis of, 41n35
centaurs, 3, 51, 53, 57–59, 61
Cesari, Giuseppe (Cavaliere d'Arpino), 107–8
Chantelou, Paul Fréart de, 15n61, 31, 107
Chantilly, Musée Condé
    fragment of a cartoon for *The Triumph of David*, 15n33
    Study for Bacchanal before a Temple (fig. 8), 11–13, *12*
Chatsworth, Collection of the Duke of Devonshire, *Study for the Abduction of the Sabine Women* (plate 29), 8, 79, 81, 84, 86–87, 90n9, *97*, 118
chiaroscuro, 104
Clayton, Martin, 15n40, 15n63
Clement IX, Pope. *See* Rospigliosi, Giulio
Clytie, 8, 9–10, 15n38
Codazzi, Viviano, and Domenico Gargiulo
    Constantine's Triumphal Entry into Rome, 41n37
    Vespasian's Triumphal Entry into Rome, 41n37
Colbert, Jean-Baptiste, 89
Cortona, Pietro da
    The Abduction of the Sabine Women (fig. 25), 82, *83*
    The Gathering of Manna, 41n30
    as Poussin's rival or foil, 2
Costa, Lorenzo di Ottavio, 60, 64n31
Créquy, Charles I de, duc de Lesdiguières and Maréchal de France
    art collection, 86, 88–89, 91n35
    as ballet dancer, 14n4, 86, 90n27
    and Poussin's *Abduction of the Sabine Women*, xiii, 81–82, 85, 86, 88–89, 90n7, 90n11
Créquy, Charles III de Blanchefort, duc de, 14n4
Crocus, 8, 10, 15nn38–39
The Crossing of the Red Sea, xiii, 41n30

Dal Pozzo, Cassiano. *See* Pozzo, Cassiano dal
dance, depictions of
    in *The Adoration of the Golden Calf*, 35–37
    in ancient sculpture, 3–6, 14n14, 29–32, 33, 36, 39, 60, 104–5
    chains or rings of dancers, 8–9, 31–32, 35, 36–38, 41n11, 103–5, 110